Hartley, William

Osceola, the unconquered Indian

DATE			
MAY 25 1980			
OCT 30 1981			
MAR 17 1985			
NOV 9 1986			
DEC 21 1988			
APR 11 1991			
JAN 7 1995			

OSCEOLA

THE

UNCONQUERED INDIAN

Other Books by William and Ellen Hartley:
Your Important Years
A Woman Set Apart
Young Living

Other Books by William Hartley:
The Cruel Tower

Other Books by Ellen Hartley:
The Ellen Knauff Story

OSCEOLA
THE UNCONQUERED INDIAN

by William and Ellen Hartley

HAWTHORN BOOKS, INC.
PUBLISHERS / *New York*

OSCEOLA: THE UNCONQUERED INDIAN

 Library of Congress Catalog Card Number: 73-341.

1 2 3 4 5 6 7 8 9 10

CONTENTS

ACKNOWLEDGMENTS

Many persons have been most helpful in our attempts to reconstruct the life of Osceola and the troubled days when the Seminole nation fought for its survival. We are particularly grateful to Charles Heckelmann for his invaluable advice and inspiration.

Among those who have given us help or encouragement are the following: Dr. Elaine C. Everly, National Archives, Washington, D.C.; Monroe H. Fabian, associate curator of the National Portrait Gallery, Washington, D.C.; Catherine F. Harris, National Anthropological Archives, Washington, D.C.; Jack F. Marquardt, chief, General Reference, Information Services, Smithsonian Institution Libraries, Washington, D.C.; Peggo Cromer, Miami, Florida.

Colonel Phillip H. Stevens, chief, Public Information Division, Department of the Army, Washington, D.C.; Louise Walker, the St. Louis (Missouri) Art Museum; Colonel and Mrs. John K. Eney, Arlington, Virginia; Roy L. Struble, Miami, Florida.

Kathleen M. Leathen, Florida Collection librarian, Miami Public Library, Miami, Florida; Evelyn Doll, Florida Collection librarian, Miami Public Library, Miami, Florida; Charles A. Gauld, Ph.D., associate professor of history, Miami-Dade Community College.

And Joe Dan Osceola, past president of the Seminole Tribe of Florida, Inc., and the United Southeastern Tribes, Inc.

OSCEOLA

THE

UNCONQUERED INDIAN

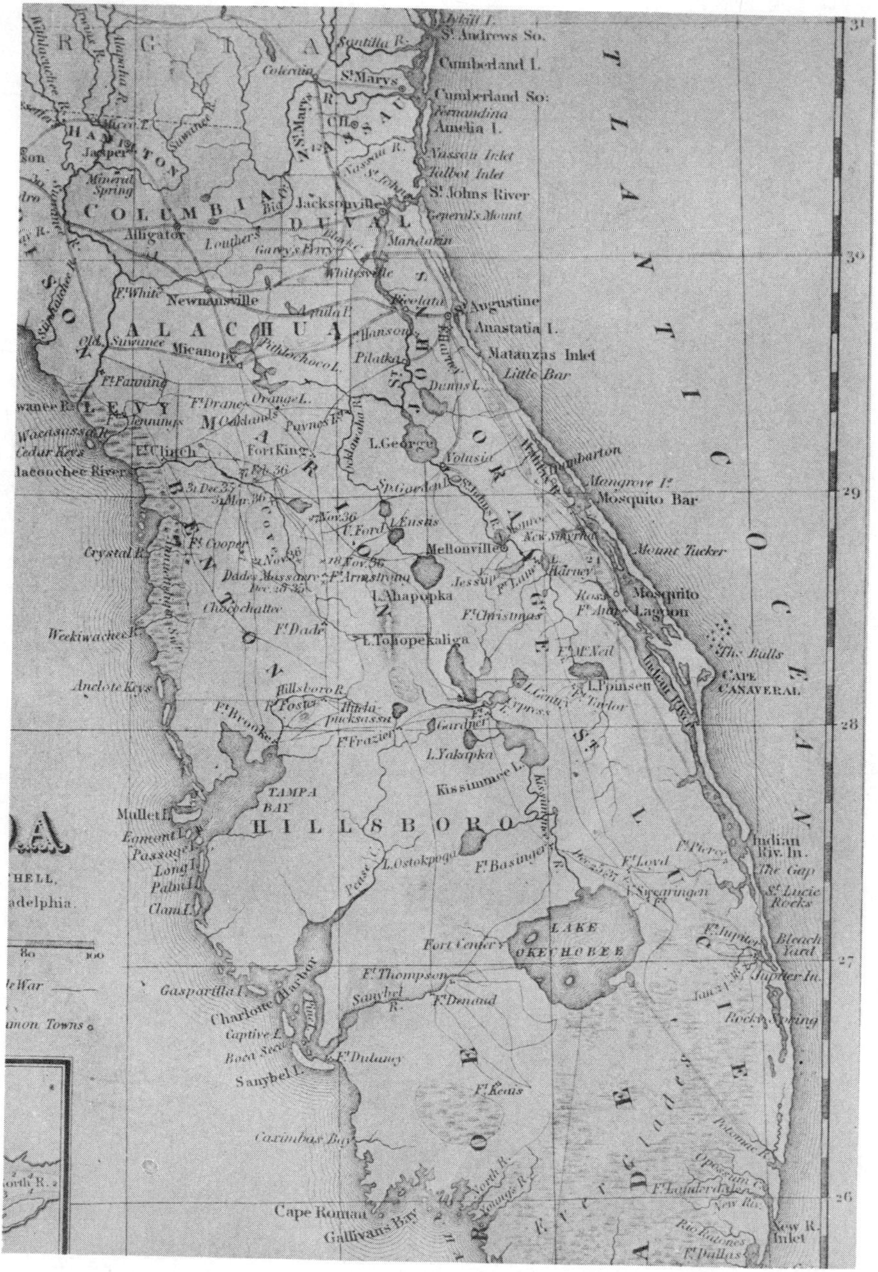

St. Andrews So.
Cumberland I.
St. Marys
Cumberland So:
Fernandina
Amelia I.
Nassau Inlet
Talbot Inlet
St. Johns River
General's Mount
Jacksonville
DUVAL
COLUMBIA
HAMILTON
NASSAU
Jasper
Mineral Spring
Alligator
Mandarin
Whitesville
Newnansville
ALACHUA
St. Augustine
Anastatia I.
Matanzas Inlet
Little Bar
Micanopy
Pilatka
LEVY
MARION
Fort King
L. George
Volusia
Mosquito Bar
Mount Tucker
Mellonville
Mosquito Lagoon
L. Ahapopka
L. Tohopekaliga
The Bulls
CAPE CANAVERAL
L. Poinsett
Hillsboro R.
TAMPA BAY
HILLSBORO
Kissimmee L.
Indian Riv. In.
The Gap
St. Lucie Rocks
LAKE OKEECHOBEE
Fort Center
Jupiter In.
Charlotte Harbor
Gasparilla I.
Sanybel I.
Carimbas Bay
Cape Roman
Gallivans Bay
New R. Inlet
ATLANTIC OCEAN

Introduction

On May 28, 1830, President Andrew Jackson signed the Removal Bill, a law aimed at driving the southeastern Indians into Indian Territory west of the Mississippi. Jackson, who had conducted punitive expeditions against the Indians during the Creek War (1813–1814) and the First Seminole War (1817–1818), had wanted the law for a long time. It advanced his expansionist desires, and it gave the dignity and force of federal law to national policies of Indian removal.

Many northern congressmen opposed the Removal Bill not because of respect for Indian rights but because it tended to invite increased white settlement in the slave-holding South. A few may have remembered the words of Thomas Jefferson who, in 1786, had written hopefully:

> It may be regarded as certain that not a foot of land will ever be taken from the Indians without their consent. The sacredness of their rights is felt by all thinking persons in America as much as in Europe.[1]

But Jefferson's views had generally been disregarded long before Jackson turned the Removal Bill into law. By armed force, by threats, bribery, corruption of Indian chiefs, by deceitful persuasion, treaties of questionable integrity, discriminatory state laws, outright annexation of Indian lands, even starvation, the southeastern Indians were gradually being forced into cession of their territories and eventual removal from their homeland. The Removal Bill was simply a final blow in a series of actions designed to get the Indians out of the Southeast.

One of the groups subject to the removal policy was the Seminole Indian amalgam in Florida. Their position was particularly tragic because, in a real sense, many were actually exiles. A large portion had drifted south into Spanish Florida as fugitives from tribal conflicts or white harassment. Sometimes they had been joined by runaway slaves, a source of bitter annoyance to slaveholders outside the Florida peninsula.

The Seminoles owned slaves themselves. Of these Negroes who lived among the Indians, the historian Charles H. Coe says:

> These people formed two distinct classes: the Maroons, and the more recent fugitive slaves. The former had been living with the Seminoles for so long a period that, although they had once been runaway slaves from Georgia and Alabama, or were descended from such, their identity had now become completely lost. The title, "Maroons," a Spanish word of West Indian origin, signifying "free Negroes," had been appropriately applied to them by the Spanish settlers in Florida. . . . The Maroons were thoroughly established among the Seminoles, had in a few cases intermarried with them, and were regarded more as brethren and allies. Most of them, however, were still held by the Indians in a mild form of servitude. Their happy and contented condition formed a striking contrast to the hard life of unrequited toil which was the usual lot of slaves under white overseers.[2]

Some of the Seminoles had purchased slaves. Whatever the case, historians agree that the relationship between the Indian and the Negro maroon or slave was largely paternalistic and of mutual benefit. James Pierce, a contemporary writer, noted in 1825 that the slaves "are well treated, being rarely required to do much labor, except in pressing seasons of tillage, having acquired the erect independent bearing and manners of the aborigines, and are faithful."[3]

Coe also mentions the comment of a staff officer of General Edmund P. Gaines on the Indian slave: "His life among the Indians is one, compared to that of Negroes under overseers, of luxury and ease; the demands on him are very trifling. . . . The Indian loves his Negro as much as one of his own children." [4]

The slaves knew English; most of the Seminoles did not. Thus Negroes could interpret for Seminoles and whites alike. Moreover, the Negroes (the term "black" was not used extensively until modern times) had agricultural experience and at least limited knowledge of the use of tools. Indian agriculture, at its best, was primitive and haphazard. Although Negroes did not change Indian subsistence farming to any appreciable extent, they made it a trifle better in some Seminole villages.

The Seminoles, who had emerged slowly as an identifiable group after 1710, were a mixture of the Alachua or Lower Creeks from central Georgia who had separated from the Creek Confederation; Mikasukis and Tallahassees, also Lower Creeks from Georgia; Upper Creeks mostly from Alabama, including Red Stick fugitives from the Creek War of 1813–1814; Apalachees absorbed by Lower Creeks; Yamassees from South Carolina and Georgia; various dissident segments of other southeastern tribes; and the scanty remnants of Florida's original Indians.

The last group is important. Until recent years, many authorities held to the belief that the Seminoles had no aboriginal roots in Florida. This was the position of the United States government during the early 1950s when it began to fight the Seminoles' claim to compensation for the Florida land taken from them in the 1800s. The government contended that the Seminoles were not possessed of aboriginal title to Florida because their progenitors were not aboriginal occupants.

But attorneys for the modern Seminoles refuted the government arguments by carefully documented research in which they proved, to the satisfaction of the Claims Commission, that prior to 1600 more than twenty-five separate aboriginal tribes existed in Florida, and that enough of these people had intermarried with the later Creek migrants to give the Seminoles aboriginal title.[5] (The Seminole compensation claim was approved in May, 1964, but is still unpaid at this writing.)

Most of the Lower Creek migrants who had drifted into Florida before and after the Revolutionary War spoke Hitchiti and fused into the Mikasuki branch of the Seminole nation. Upper Creeks usually spoke a different tongue, Muskogee, but all became designated as Seminoles, a word generally accepted as meaning "wild people." (The two modern Florida branches are still known as Mikasukis, of hunting and fishing tradition, and Muskogees, primarily an agricultural people. All, however, are called Seminoles.)

The Seminoles of the removal period had never seriously questioned their ancestral ties to Florida. In 1822 they said of themselves, "An hundred summers have seen the Seminole warrior reposing undisturbed under the shade of his live oak, and the suns of an hundred winters have risen on his ardent pursuit of the buck and the bear, with none to question his bounds, or dispute his range." [6]

The language is a white man's flowery translation, but the sense of the statement is generally valid. The words that might be questioned are "Seminole warrior," and "ardent pursuit." "Warrior" was a white man's description of any adult male Indian. Until the whites provided a blueprint, the Indians were not often warlike.

Coe says emphatically:

> . . . consider that the Seminoles were far from being naturally a cruel and war-like people; that they had lived for many years on terms of peace with the white race, under both Spanish, English and American rule, and all they desired . . . were the simple rights which our Constitution guarantees to all men.[7]

R. S. Cotterill, a modern authority on Indian history and culture, sums up the southern Indian's nature in these words:

> There is much to suggest that previous to their contact with white men the Southern Indians were ardent neither for hunting nor for war. The frantic mourning in an Indian town over the death of a warrior reveals their high regard for human life and suggests that they would not lightly risk in a war what they so highly valued. There were few occasions for intertribal quarrels: boundaries were matters of indifference when hunting grounds were so wide, game so plentiful, and hunters so few; there were no conflicting economic interests because there were no economic interests to conflict; there was no struggle for power because there was no use to which power could be put; and the Southern Indians no more considered war a sport than they considered hunting a pastime.[8]

Hunting, as Cotterill puts it, was a "species of work"; and it is probable that the Seminoles' "ardent pursuit of the buck and the bear" was more ardent in the physical demands of pursuit than it was in any burning desire to hunt. The Seminole preferred to repose "undisturbed under the shade of his live oak."

When Spain ceded Florida in 1819, the United States recognized the rights of inhabitants. Article 6 of the treaty with Spain read:

> The inhabitants of the territories which His Catholic Majesty cedes to the United States, by this treaty, shall be incorporated in the Union of the United States, as soon as may be consistent with the principles of the Federal Constitution, and admitted to the enjoyment of all privileges, rights, and immunities of the citizens of the United States.[9]

Nothing in the treaty says, "except Indians." The United States met its commitment of extending to Florida's inhabitants "all privileges, rights, and immunities of the citizens" by first talking the Seminoles into the 1823 Treaty of Moultrie Creek, the creek being a meeting place near St. Augustine. This treaty, obtained by threats and bribery, forced the Indians to cede 28,040,991 acres and move into a Florida reservation consisting of 4,032,940 acres of poor land. The treaty was to have a lifetime of twenty years.

In 1832, however, before the Moultrie Creek treaty ran out, the Seminoles were again persuaded by force and trickery to sign a new agreement at Payne's Landing on the Oklawaha River near Silver Springs, Florida. This document, a flagrant violation of the earlier Moultrie Creek treaty, implemented Jackson's 1830 Removal Bill by forcing the Indians to remove west of the Mississippi into what then was called Arkansas Territory. The top chiefs may or may not have signed; there was considerable question later about their marks on the Payne's Landing Treaty.

Whatever the case, a delegation of seven Seminole chiefs and a Negro named Abraham journeyed to the Arkansas Territory in 1833, inspected the land, and signed another document known as the Treaty of Fort Gibson. This said in effect that the western land was satisfactory, and that the Seminoles "shall commence the removal to their new home as soon as the Government will make arrangements for their emigration satisfactory to the Seminole nation." In addition to having no authority to make such an agreement for the Seminoles, the members of the inspection team were tricked into signing the Fort Gibson treaty.

Details of these treaties, and the fraudulent means by which they were obtained, will be discussed in detail later. For the present, it is sufficient to point out that treachery compounded treachery during this shameful period of negotiations. Even many whites of the period were aware of the frauds.

If the Indians of Florida had been truly hostile in the period following the First Seminole War, there might have been a justification of sorts for the treatment they received from the United States. However, although there were isolated episodes, mostly involving theft of cattle by individual Indians, the Seminoles were not particularly dangerous to white settlers. When the inevitable explosion came, it was the result of long and often vicious badgering of an essentially peaceful people.

The explosion took the form of the Second Seminole War, a tragic conflict lasting from 1835 to 1842. The Seminoles, numbering some five thousand men, women, and children, undertook to fight for their homeland against a nation with a population of some thirteen million.

The war cost the United States between thirty and forty million dollars, a huge sum for the times, and resulted in more than fifteen hundred deaths among white combatants. A total of some forty thousand white soldiers were involved at one time or another, while the entire Indian force never exceeded fifteen hundred warriors. The number of Seminole deaths is not known, but the percentage in terms of warriors engaged is believed to have been much lower.

Of this war, Theodore Roosevelt wrote:

> Our troops generally fought with great bravery; but there is very little else in the struggle, either as regards its origin or the manner in which it was carried on, to which an American can look back with any satisfaction.[10]

There is a curious and chilling modern parallel to the Second Seminole War. In talking to civilian and military authorities in Washington, D.C., the writers of this book were repeatedly reminded that the war with the Seminoles was a microcosm of the war in Vietnam. Both were wars of frustration for the United States. In each, vast power was checkmated by lesser force. Moreover, as one high-ranking officer put it, "Both wars may be regarded as fundamentally immoral. History will find that neither casts much credit on United States policy."

The Second Seminole War was the costliest ever fought against the American Indian. The United States won in the sense that the conflict finally limped to an end. In another sense, however, it was the only war the United States ever lost, if Vietnam is disregarded. It failed in its basic purpose of removing all Seminoles from Florida. Although more than three thousand Seminoles were eventually forced to relocate within Indian Territory, small bands refused to surrender and found refuge in the Everglades of South Florida.

As a unit of people, the Seminoles never signed a peace treaty with the United States. Thus they are the only unconquered American Indians. During World War II, they expressed their independence by declaring war on the Axis as a separate nation. Until about thirty-five years ago, it was almost impossible for the United States government to strike any kind of bargain with the Mikasuki branch of the Florida Seminoles. Almost all men of this group deeply but quietly disliked whites, even refusing to enter a white man's building.[11]

This independence, however archaic, is the direct heritage of Osceola, a warrior who was the inspired leader of the Seminoles during the early years of the Second Seminole War. More than any other native American leader, Osceola personifies the spirit of Indian resistance to white domination. He was both the Patrick Henry and the George Washington of the Seminoles. An accomplished fighter, he was also the tragic victim of almost incredible white treachery. Today, from a distance of more than one hundred thirty years, most Americans have difficulty remembering the names of the white leaders who directed troops during the Second Seminole War; but the name of Osceola rings out clearly.

This book is about Osceola and the war in which he played so important a role. Most historians of his period say he spoke no English, but this is an illogical conclusion; he spent too much time with whites to be totally unfamiliar with English. Probably he refused on most occasions to speak the white man's language.

The Indians could not leave written records, so details of Osceola's life are drawn primarily from reports by whites who knew him or fought against him. Accounts of later historians have also been consulted, along with sources in the National Archives, the Smithsonian Institution, and various other repositories of historic records. When accounts conflict, as they sometimes do, the likeliest version has been used. The authors have also carefully reconstructed certain scenes of Indian life in which Osceola must have participated.

The authors have talked at length with modern Florida Seminoles, some of whom proudly bear the Osceola name. Research for the book started more than twelve years ago when the authors first met the late Harriet M. Bedell, Protestant Episcopal missionary to the Mikasuki Seminole Indians and a Seminole expert. Deaconess Bedell started them on the way to an understanding of the proud heritage of the Florida Seminoles.

All Americans can respect Osceola. His courage and independence represent the Indian spirit at its best.

1

"This Is the Only Way I Sign!"

Fort King, in the year 1835, was the American military installation least likely to be remembered. Perched on a grassy knoll near the present-day city of Ocala, Florida, the fort overlooked a thick hardwood forest and a small gleaming lake partially screened by giant oaks. Nearby stood the Seminole Indian Agency, a building quite as raw in appearance as the fort.

Approximately three miles away was a "translucent and placid spring, whereon was faithfully reflected the green foliage that thickened over and around it, and wherein might be clearly discerned the tiniest fish, and each minutest object that sported at the bottom, all clothed in the blent hues of the o'erarching sky—the impending shrubbery and the transparent waters." This was Silver Springs, a favorite Seminole Indian meeting place. The description comes from civilian David Levy, who saw the Springs in 1834.[1]

The little fort, squeezed into an area no more than 152 by 162 feet, or about the dimensions of a modern suburban residential lot, had been built in 1827. Palisades some twenty feet high around the perimeter had been made of upended logs. A crude firing platform ran along the inside of this barricade. Crammed within the enclosure were barracks, officers' quarters, kitchens, mess halls, and ammunition huts. There was a blockhouse at one angle of the stockade; another was planned but never completed.

These buildings had been erected by soldiers. It was hard work, and the officer in charge of the building, a Captain James M. Glassell, had written the quartermaster general: "I have used every exertion to curtail, as much as possible, expence [*sic* *] to the United States, by sawing lumber. . . ." Glassell was unhappy. His superiors had pinched on window glass, bricks, and various other essentials, and had told him that "chimnies can be readily built of logs and clay."[2]

About one hundred thirty soldiers could occupy the fort. Contemporary records as well as logic suggest that some had to live outside in tents, and that such facilities as washrooms and the bakeshop were beyond the stockade. A council house had been planned for the nearby Seminole agency, but the government had characteristically trimmed the building budget from five thousand to two thousand dollars. The council house was never built, so meetings with the Indians were held outdoors on raised platforms. The whites apparently did not share the Indians' indifference to snakes, chiggers, and other insects.

The Indians were the reason for Fort King. The little fort was closed down during the relatively quiet months of 1829, then opened again on July 18, 1832, when it became evident that the Seminoles might resist attempts to move them into a reservation west of the Mississippi in Arkansas Territory.

Fort King was near a number of major Indian settlements and thus was a convenient location for meetings. From the Army viewpoint, it was advantageous to meet with the Seminoles where a show of force could be made. Troops were often paraded to impress the Indians. The Seminoles originally believed that these displays were arranged to honor their presence at a conference, but by 1835 they knew better. Soldiers were

* All misspellings in quoted material have been retained throughout this book.

no honor guard. They were a token of overwhelming white force, and a visible argument at any meeting.

One such meeting was convened near Fort King on April 23, 1835. Records of the exact setting are sketchy, but we know from one account that a pavilion covered with tree branches had been erected for the Indian and white dignitaries. Since a platform had collapsed during an earlier meeting, dumping Seminoles and whites into a howling pile, the open pavilion was a safer structure.[3]

Conferences with the Indians followed an established pattern, so it is possible to visualize the scene at the April 23 convocation. Such sessions usually started at 11:00 A.M. Chiefs and the higher subchiefs sat on one side, with white officials on the other. A colorful group of Indian men and modestly dressed women, often numbering in the hundreds, squatted or sat in the surrounding area. Naked babies rolled on the ground beneath the trees. Conspicuous somewhere within the area was a detachment of troops probably standing at ease: Speeches were painfully long and the sun was hot. Smoke from the fort and the nearby Indian camps drifted over the gathering, pleasantly fragrant on the light morning breezes.

There was always a table at such meetings—a kind of altar to the white love for paperwork. This held treaties and related documents; and it was also convenient for the fist pounding that the whites sometimes used to emphasize their views.

Of the white officials present on this pleasant April morning, the most important was Brevet Brigadier General Duncan Lamont Clinch, commander of all troops in Florida. Clinch, who weighed about two hundred and fifty pounds and spoke in a voice between a croak and a whisper, was a kindly and thoughtful man of religious leanings who had been ordered by the War Department to manage "the peaceful and harmonious removal of the Indians, according to their treaty with the U. States." This treaty was the composite Payne's Landing and

Fort Gibson agreement between the Seminoles and the government for Indian removal from Florida in 1835.

Clinch had no illusions about an easy performance of his job. In January, he had written the adjutant general:

> The more I see of this tribe of Indians, the more fully am I convinced that they have not the least intention of fulfilling their treaty stipulations, unless compelled to do so by a stronger force than mere words.

General Clinch, on April 23, was worried about his family in Mobile. He knew that his son, Duncan, had suffered an attack of scarlet fever in March. What he could not have known was that his pretty wife, Eliza, had died of the same illness on April 15.[4]

The second most important white official was Indian agent Wiley Thompson, a man of powerful appearance and periodic temper outbursts. Thompson was usually addressed as "general" because of his service as a major general of Georgia militia between 1817 and 1824.[5]

Like Clinch, Thompson was not a bad man; rather, he was the instrument of bad policies and bad laws. Although he believed in removal and could hardly think otherwise as a government representative, Thompson was in the wrong place at the right time, for a salary of fifteen hundred dollars a year.

A large number of Seminole chiefs had assembled for the meeting. One authority says fifteen hundred Indians were in camp near the fort, but the number was probably lower. Whatever the case, the Seminoles were bitter, defiant, and deeply depressed. Most of them did not wish to leave Florida and regarded earlier treaties of agreement as not valid and not representative of the desires of the Seminole nation. As we will see later, this was very close to the truth.

Moreover, the Indians had gone through a brutally bad time. Drought had killed crops, or crops had not been planted because of the menace of the impending removal from Florida. To make matters worse, the past winter had been a cruel one; on February 7, temperatures in north Florida had dropped almost to zero.[6] Game had also been scarce ever since the Seminoles occupied their Florida reservation around 1824.

A meeting held the day before had been a fiasco. Thompson had made a long, pontifical speech reviewing the United States' position and referring to the questionable Payne's Landing and Fort Gibson documents in which, according to the government, the Seminoles had agreed to move west. Would they keep their word?[7]

Jumper (Otee Emathla), the "sense-maker," or spokesman, for top chief Micanopy, had said they would not move from their homeland. M. M. Cohen, a contemporary officer and historian, describes Jumper in these words:

> The crafty and designing Ote-mathla, is tall and well made, his face narrow but long, forehead contracted, eyes small but keen, nose prominent, countenance repulsive, and its expression indicative of sinister feelings. He is an orator, and what is better, a man of sense, and brave warrior.[8]

After Jumper had indicated the Seminoles would not move, Thompson had lashed out at them and Clinch, losing his temper, had croaked that he had been sent to enforce the treaties, had warriors enough to do it, and had every intention of performing this duty. The chiefs, he said, could think about it during the night.[9] Then they would be asked to sign a paper agreeing to the removal.

This was the situation when the Indians and white officials gathered on the morning of April 23. Whites as well as Indians were still angry and frustrated. To make matters worse, Chief Micanopy (Sint-Chakkee) was absent. Jumper said he was ill.

While Jumper talked in a pleasing, musical voice, repeating the Indian protest against removal, Agent Wiley Thompson glanced from time to time at one of the Seminoles who stood a little apart from the others. To General Clinch, he whispered, "Watch that man. He has great influence."

The Indian was Osceola, then about thirty-one years of age. Probably no American Indian of any period presented a more striking appearance. George Catlin's portrait, painted a few years later, show a remarkably handsome man with compelling eyes, a long straight nose, and a gentle, somewhat sensuous mouth. John T. Sprague, a contemporary white officer and later a historian, says, "In stature, he was about five feet eight inches, with a manly, frank, and open countenance." [10]

Cohen has this to say about Osceola:

> . . . his eye calm, serious, fixed—his attitude manly, graceful, erect—his rather thin and close pressed lips, indicative of the "mind made up" of which he speaks—his firm, easy, yet restrained tread—free from all stride or swagger—his dignified and composed attitude—his perfect and solemn silence . . . the head thrown backward, the arms folded on the protruding chest—all, all instantaneously changed, as by an electric touch, whenever the agent stated a proposition from which he . . . dissented.[11]

Osceola was probably somewhat taller than Sprague suggests. Although George Catlin's famous painting portrays a man with a huge chest and a disproportionately small head, writers of the period emphasize that he was slender and remarkably well built. His physical strength was that of a Hercules or Samson; indeed, he was so powerful that almost all contemporary writers comment on this characteristic. He had the tigerish walk of a hunter accustomed from youth to stalk game in the wilderness.[12]

The Catlin portrait shows a man whose face reflects great sadness and emotional depth. There is a spiritual quality about the eyes and gentle mouth, and one looks in vain for signs of the warrior whose shrill scream of rage could terrify experienced soldiers. But beneath the calm appearance was a fierce, passionate spirit not always controlled by a warrior whose very glance could be withering. Osceola had a violent temper that boiled over when he became aware of deception on the part of the white men.[13]

Despite his occasional outbursts, many whites admired him and saw in his straight nose, slightly flared nostrils, and strong chin a resemblance to the sculptured heroes of early Greece. This is particularly noticeable in the Catlin portrait. Osceola was also known, on most occasions, for his courteous, pleasant manner of speech; for his sense of humor; and, above all, for a beguiling smile.[14]

He was certainly aware of his effect on others; and even those who disliked him or feared his influence were impressed by his personality. An Army surgeon of the time, objective as a trained observer, was one of those who grudgingly noted Osceola's superior appearance, called him an indomitable warrior, and said he was a most remarkable man.[15] Almost all contemporary writers spoke of his high intelligence. Without question, he was a genius among the Indians he influenced.

Even Wiley Thompson, watching Osceola in the glare of the April sunlight, would have agreed that he was a superior individual. He had already described Osceola to the War Department as "a bold, manly and determined young chief." [16]

Jumper's long discourse finally came to an end. (Seminoles liked to talk, and Jumper was no exception.) There was silence broken only by the cries of birds. Agent Thompson picked up a document from the conference table and began to read it with pauses for the translator, a Negro named Cudjo. This paper acknowledged the validity of the Payne's Landing Treaty and the additional Treaty of Fort Gibson in which, according to the government's position, the Seminoles had agreed to go west. It read as follows:

> We, the undersigned chiefs and sub-chiefs of the Seminole tribe of Indians, do hereby, for ourselves and for our people, voluntarily acknowledge the validity of the treaty between the United States and the Seminole nation of

> Indians, made and concluded at Payne's Landing, on the Ocklawaha [sic] river, on the 9th of May, 1832, and the treaty between the United States and the Seminole nation of Indians, made and concluded at Fort Gibson on the 28th day of March, 1833, by Montford Stokes, H. L. Ellsworth, and J. F. Schermerhorn, commissioners on the part of the United States, and the delegates of the said nation of Seminole Indians on the part of the said nation; and we, the said chiefs and sub-chiefs, do, for ourselves and for our people, freely and fully assent to the above-recited treaties in all their provisions and stipulations.
>
> Done in the council at the Seminole agency, this 23rd day of April, 1835.[17]

At the end of the reading a long sigh rose from the Indians. Agent Thompson put the document on the table, glanced at General Clinch, then turned again to the Seminole chiefs. The agent, who was known for his "fatherly manner," was frowning.

"Who will sign?" he asked.

Several of the chiefs nodded reluctantly, but four shook their heads. These four, among the most important of the Seminole leaders, were Alligator (Halpatter-Tustenuggee), Arpeika (Sam Jones), Fuch-a-Lusti-Hadjo (Black Dirt), and the sense-bearer, Jumper (Otee Emathla). Micanopy, the head chief, was still not present; and the signature of this fat, aging, and somewhat lazy man was the most important of all.

Thompson pointed to the chiefs who had indicated their agreement to signing, and told them to come forward to make their marks. Eight complied. While this was going on, the agent looked at Osceola. The man stood like a rock with arms folded across his chest and his lips drawn into a tight, furious line.

Thompson now turned to Jumper and asked once more, "Where is Micanopy?"

"Sick," replied Alligator, who spoke a little English.

"I don't believe it!" Thompson exploded. "He's just shunning his responsibility. Jumper, you are his sense-bearer. Will you tell us whether or not Micanopy intends to honor the treaty?"

This was translated to Jumper, who began a lengthy, evasive reply. In all probability, Jumper was trying to avoid the responsibility of speaking for Micanopy, but Thompson would have none of it. He stopped the interpreter with a gesture.

"Ask the sense-bearer," he said grimly, "if Micanopy will honor the treaty. Nothing more. No more talk."

When the statement was translated, Jumper looked around defiantly. An angry mutter was beginning to rise from the people near the pavilion. Alligator, Black Dirt (Fuch-a-Lusti-Hadjo), and Arpeika stared back at Jumper and shook their heads slightly.

Osceola was still motionless. General Clinch, sweating in the hot sun, ran a finger under the collar of his dress uniform. This high-stocked garment was atrociously uncomfortable in Florida weather.

"He will not honor the treaty," Jumper said at last.

Thompson, red with anger, pushed the document aside and picked up another paper. This was the list of Seminole chiefs. Seizing a pen, he made five slashing deletions on the roll. Then he faced the Indians.

"I have removed five names from the roll of chiefs," he shouted. "These men no longer represent the Seminole nation. Their names are Micanopy, Jumper, Alligator, Black Dirt, and Arpeika."

The action was unprecedented, unwise, and certainly illegal. Thompson had made clear what the Indians already suspected —that the meeting was a sham, that the United States had no respect for Seminole leadership, that removal would be enforced whether or not the Indians agreed. Moreover, the action of deposing the chiefs was a deadly insult. As the contemporary historian John T. Sprague puts it:

> Their chiefs and counsellors derive their authority from inheritance, which is generally attained from valor in the field; and thus to be deprived of it in so summary a manner, setting

> at nought long-settled habits and customs, was destined . . . to arouse the most submissive of their warriors to retaliation.[18]

When Thompson's words had been translated, a roar of anger rose from the deposed chiefs. Arpeika screamed with rage, stamped his feet, and, reportedly, gnashed his teeth.[19] There were wild shrieks from warriors around the pavilion. Soldiers now stood at attention, and it appeared that the meeting might end in an open brawl.

Fortunately, the eight chiefs who had signed managed to restore order. Then they appealed for a delay in emigration until January 15, 1836, so summer crops could be gathered, cattle collected, and spring planting accomplished in the new western territory. Thompson and Clinch agreed to these demands, as did another of the white men present, First Lieutenant Joseph W. Harris. Harris was a disbursing agent in charge of funds for the removal.

Now it was time for other chiefs and subchiefs to sign the treaty adherence document. Eight more, not including the deposed chiefs, paraded unhappily to the table and made their marks. Osceola stood alone, arms still folded and his face unchanged. Finally his name was read by Thompson.

As if coming out of a deep sleep, he seemed to vibrate with sudden awareness of his surroundings. Then, moving in his graceful, catlike manner, he approached the table, gazed for a moment at Thompson, and said something softly. One historian believes he said, "This land is ours! We do not want an agent!"[20]

With a sweeping motion, he suddenly drew his hunting knife and stabbed down savagely at the table. The action was so abrupt that no one had time to recoil. His clear, piercing voice rang out in the instant of silence.

"This is the only way I sign!" he cried.[21]

Benches tumbled over as white officials and Seminoles leaped to their feet. Warriors in the surrounding area began to scream approval while others protested the dramatic action. In the confusion and uproar, Osceola yanked out his knife and calmly strode away.

Some romantics say that the Second Seminole War started with this gesture of defiance. It did not. That would come later. But Osceola had given a graphic illustration of his own convictions. The flash of his knife was also a clear hint of what was to come.

2

The First Seminole War

Osceola was not originally a Seminole Indian. He was born around 1804 in the region of present-day Macon County, Alabama, northeast of modern Montgomery. The exact location is unknown, but it must have been somewhere along the Tallapoosa River near Tallassee. In later years, he was called a Tallassee Creek—an Upper Creek of the Tallassee group. As such, his native language would have been Muskogee.[1]

There is no record of Osceola's "baby" name. As in the case of most American Indians, Creek (Muskogee) boys were named first for something seen or experienced by adults at the time of birth, i.e., Broken Arrow, Running Dog, Red Shirt, Rising Sun. The permanent or adult name was given sometime during young manhood, often for an act of valor and sometimes for an outstanding characteristic. Osceola's adult name would be derived from *Asi*, mean "Black Drink," and *Yaholo*, or "Singer." At one of the Indian rituals, men consumed a black drink while the server uttered a long, singing cry.

Mark F. Boyd, a modern authority on Florida history, mentions these variants of Osceola's name: Asseola, Assiola, Oceola, and Oseola. He also notes elisions of Usso Yaholo, Hassee Ola, As-sin Yaholo, Ossen Yaholah, Os-cin-ye-hola, As-see-a-hala,

Assyn-ya-hola, Yose-ya-hola, and As-se-se-he-ho-lar. Coe believed Osceola meant "Rising Sun," but Boyd offers excellent evidence that Asi-Yaholo ("Black Drink Singer") is correct. Whites anglicized it to Oceola or Osceola.[2]

But the name would come much later in Osceola's life. In youth, he was identified as Billy Powell, a circumstance that has created considerable historical controversy. "Billy Powell" was the son of William Powell, a white trader in the Tallassee area, and an Indian woman named Polly Copinger.

Osceola, however, later renounced the name Powell and declared emphatically, "No foreign blood runs in my veins; I am a pure-blood Muskogee."[3] To get around the contradiction between Osceola's own statement of lineage and the many references to "Billy Powell," some historians have decided "Powell" was a nickname.[4] Others have resolved the question too neatly by suggesting that white trader William Powell was a stepfather rather than Osceola's real father who, they assume, was an Indian.[5]

The account carrying the most credibility comes from Thomas S. Woodward, a contemporary white soldier and historian who knew more about the Creeks than any man of his time. He traced the Osceola lineage back to a Scot, James McQueen, who lived with the Creeks from 1716 until his death in 1811 at the incredible age of a hundred and twenty-eight. McQueen married a Tallassee woman. Two of their children were Peter McQueen (Talmuches Hadjo) and a daughter, Ann, who married a white or half-breed named Copinger. Ann's daughter was Polly Copinger who married William Powell, the white trader. Billy, later Osceola, was their son.[6]

Why, then did Osceola claim he was a full-blooded Creek (Muskogee) Indian? Did he lie? Not on the basis of Muskogee beliefs.

Almost all historians have apparently forgotten that Creek and Seminole tribal structure was matrilineal, with descent and inheritance following the mother's side. The contemporary his-st a later date.[10] In the Creek family structure, would have had little or no influence on his son. portant men in a Creek boy's life were the males r's side—uncles, or in Osceola's case, his granduncle, en.

s were grouped in small villages or towns where simple cabins similar to those of whites. The men cared for cattle, horses, and hogs, while women and ded the fields. Crops included corn, beans, sweet mpkins and squash, tobacco, and sometimes rice. and fruit were part of the diet.

nd every other Creek boy hated the "women's work" ls. Although the Creeks certainly were not child s, this field labor had a subtle effect in emphasizing nce of men. Osceola, grubbing at the beans and corn other, could glance across the fields and envy the when they prepared for a hunt or simply drowsed e.

esirable to be a man. Men did the proud work with cattle. Men hunted when they wanted to hunt, slept wanted to sleep, ate when they wanted to eat. Even as 1880, Creek-Seminole eating habits were informal. Cauley, an ethnologist who studied the Seminoles in noted:

> eminole . . . though observing meal times with some rity, eats just as his appetite invites. If it happens that a side of venison roasting before the fire, he will cut it at any time during the day and, with a piece of in one hand and a bit of Koonti or of different bread other, satisfy his appetite. Not seldom, too, he rises the night and breaks his sleep by eating a piece of asting meat.[11]

out the way the men in Osceola's time ate. They also terminably about the affairs of the Creek nation, never

torian M. M. Cohen rec
dians consider themselve
side." [7] The brilliant m
notes that, "Among both
was a member of his n
where the women of this
there was no evidence tha
would not have been sign

Osceola's mother probab
in words somewhat like t
am Muskogee. My mothe
who married the old white
gee. Your blood is Musko
leaves on a great tree."

By the same token, Osceo
McQueen, derived Muskoge
and thought of himself as a
lowing their own rules of l
for Creeks and Seminoles of
Indians whose native names v
less profoundly influenced by
blood with a Creek mother co

Osceola's convictions of M
powerful source. Among Cre
the Seminoles, women were v
of children. Osceola's world du
was centered around his mot
though these women dressed v
women in long gowns of trade
gee and adhered strictly to M
even disciplined solely by his n
custom, scratched him with a s
obedience.

The father, William Powell, w
Powell seems to have disappe

sources sugg
however, he
The most im
on the mothe
Peter McQue

The Creek
they lived in
hunted and
children ten
potatoes, pu
Wild berries

Osceola a
in the field
psychologist
the importa
with his m
village men
in the shad

It was d
horses and
when they
as recently
Clay Mac
that year,

The S
regula
he ha
from
meat
in the
durin
the r

This is a
talked in

interrupting each other and weighing their words carefully. To interrupt a speaker was the worst of bad manners.

Most important of all, men had the great responsibility of defending their honor and the honor of the clan. In times of war, a man could become a *hadjo* *—a "great warrior." Down through the years there had been many raids and petty wars. War had originally been a kind of game for men; but since the coming of whites war had become deadly serious. Men now talked of larger wars. It was not good to be a mere boy in the fields while the men spoke fiercely of honorable deeds.

However Osceola may have envied the men, he was not always obliged to work with the women. The education of a Creek boy came primarily from observation, imitation, and trial-and-error. Osceola learned to hunt by hunting with bow and arrow, killing squirrels and other small game, joining young boys in their moonlight hunts after opossums and raccoons. He learned by observation how to skin animals. Every Indian boy developed stealth in the woods, for bows had limited range and it was necessary to move quietly toward game. The trick of keeping hidden was training for a boy's later function as a hunter and warrior.

Osceola also learned caution. When he approached his own village after hunting, he would flatten himself behind a tree to inspect the place carefully before entering. Just as chattering birds and squirrels gave warnings in the woods, so the behavior of dogs and horses told a story of what was happening in the village. This caution among Indian boys appears to have been instinctive; for all southern Indians were notoriously careless about keeping sentries around their villages or camp. They de-

* A paricularly courageous warrior earned the title *hadjo*. The head of each town was a *mico* or chief, who was usually elected from a matrilineal hereditary strain. A lower title of leadership was *hinijas* or *enehas*. The leader of a band was called *emathla, amathla, emathlar,* or other spelling variations depending on how whites heard and wrote the word. *Micos* could appoint a *tustenuggee,* or war chief. The head of a number of war chiefs was called a *tustenuggee thlacko*. All of these titles are spelled in many ways.[12]

pended on hordes of dogs to detect intruders, a precaution that often worked poorly.

Osceola was excellent at wrestling and running. Every game played by Creek boys was a preparation for manhood and the days when strength and agility might be important in the hunt or in war. Boys wrestled as they might later wrestle in desperate conflict; they raced as they might pursue a future enemy. No one really knows how much of this conditioning was calculated; amusement was probably quite as important as the training involved in physical competition.

One game, for example, illustrates the combination of fun and training. It also merits brief attention because it shows that the stolid, unemotional Indians were neither stolid nor unemotional. When not confronted by whites, they were a people who liked jokes and tricks.

For this game, the small boys were masked with pieces of bark in which holes had been cut for the eyes. They then cavorted around a fire in imitation of a war dance. Presently, adult warriors, also masked, joined the boys in a whooping, screaming riot of dancing.

But menace lurked in the shadows. Suddenly a warrior in a frightening costume rushed among the dancers, leaped through the flames, and attempted to catch one of the boys. All of this was accompanied by an uproar from the warriors who screamed in mock terror. When the "enemy" caught a boy, the youth was tickled until his mask fell off. Then the assailant leaped back through the fire to conceal himself again. The boys continued their dance with the wariness of youngsters playing a combination of tag and musical chairs.

The prankster or ghost figure kept up his sudden forays until most of the boys had been eliminated. The dance was then taken over by the warriors who carried on a ritual of leaping and posturing until dawn.[13]

Osceola also enjoyed a ball game similar to modern lacrosse.

This sport, played by adults with a violence that often led to bloodshed, appealed to Indian boys much as baseball attracts modern youngsters. The difference, as Mahon points out, is that it was a substitute for war.[14] Adults played it with deadly seriousness. In modern analogy, rivalry between individuals was somewhat greater than the intense competition found in present-day South American soccer.

It appears that there were two versions of this ball game. Although the games described are relatively modern, it is certain one or both were played in Osceola's time. Indian traditions are slow to change.

In one delightful version, teams of boys and girls played each other during the annual Green Corn Dance. The object was to hit a pole with a thrown deerskin ball stuffed with deer hair. The girls could use their hands, but the boys had to catch or pick up the ball with a pair of rackets made of green laurel.

Teams took their positions on each side of the target pole, the boys playing the girls. One player began the competition by throwing the ball at the pole. The usual result was a miss, so a player on the other team would catch the ball and also attempt to hit the target, or perhaps pass the ball to a team member who was in a better position to score. The ball would fly back and forth until the pole was hit and a score registered for the successful team. Lively battles took place between the two teams, boys and girls feinting, blocking, and wrestling in their efforts to control the ball.[15]

Mahon suggests that this game had ritualistic significance.[16] In another version, as reported by two Indians writing for a school publication in 1916, the game was played on a ball ground about 150 yards long and 50 wide. The writers, B. McKenzie and R. Fish, said that at each end of the field were goal posts much like modern football goals but with an opening of only about three feet. The goalposts, topped by a cross pole, were about 12 feet high. Each player used two rackets somewhat larger than tennis rackets. The object of the game was to drive a ball slightly larger than a walnut between the goalposts.

Often as many as seventy-five Indians took part in a game. On the morning of the event, women would sing and dance to inspire the men and boys. Just before the game, the men would strip, paint their faces, and place eagle feathers in their hair. They would then march to the ball ground while women beat drums and shook rattles.

Games were fierce and noisy. McKenzie and Fish, describing a game certainly played by Osceola a hundred years earlier, said:

> It sometimes happens that the two sides playing get into a fight which makes it impossible to finish the game that day. . . . After the game, players go back to camp to discuss the game and to see how badly they were bruised by their opponents.[17]

As a very young boy, Osceola probably played another game enjoyed by Creek and Seminole children. This consisted of putting sharp sticks through small grass tubers called "deer-food." These homemade tops were then set spinning on a dried deerskin. The idea was to keep a dozen or more going at once.[18]

Although we know relatively little about Osceola's boyhood, there is abundant evidence that he was superlatively competent at all Muskogee sports. Those who knew him in later years invariably mention his skill as a wrestler, runner, ball player, jumper, and all-around Indian athlete.

Despite the fact that all historians mention these accomplishments, surprisingly few have recognized their significance in Osceola's later emergence as an Indian leader. Both Creeks and Seminoles deeply admired men whose physical skills were outstanding. Through hereditary lines, leadership sometimes passed to men of limited physical accomplishments; but the truly great leader possessed attributes of bodily strength as well as wisdom, remarkable endurance as well as an agile mind. Above all, the leader was courageous. A warrior could be a fool in battle providing his folly was heroic.

By 1813, when Osceola was nine, he was aware of the spreading troubles within the Creek nation. The Creeks were divided into the Upper Creeks, located mostly in Alabama, and the Lower Creeks, to be found mainly in Georgia. As noted earlier, Florida Seminoles derived in part from eighteenth-century Creek migrations. A confused linguistic dichotomy prevailed among both Creeks and Seminoles. Most but not all Lower Creeks and Mikasuki Seminoles spoke an Hitchiti dialect; most but not all Upper Creeks and non-Mikasukis spoke Muskogee. The two languages were not mutually intelligible.

No love was lost between Upper and Lower Creeks and their Seminole brothers. In 1796, the Creeks had signed the Treaty of Colerain, in which they agreed to surrender all runaway slaves in the Creek nation. They conceived of the Creek nation as including the Florida Seminoles, an idea that outraged the Seminoles who not only sympathized with Negro fugitives among them but also owned slaves and sheltered maroons—free Negroes.

The Creek War is recounted here only as it directly affected Osceola and his people. (One of the best semicontemporary accounts is found in James Parton's *Life of Andrew Jackson,* published in 1861. Parton, although favoring his hero, wrote with wit and almost a modern style.) [19]

Briefly, there was a growing schism in 1813 among the Upper Creeks. One faction, known as White Sticks, supported the Creek national council at Tuckabatchee which, in turn, was strongly influenced by the U.S. government agent Benjamin Hawkins. His policy was to try to "civilize" the Creeks by imposing upon them at least a superficial white culture.

Opposed to the action of the national council and the Hawkins' influence were the Red Sticks, among them Peter McQueen and the aged top Tallassee chief, Opothle Mico. These men were furious at white Americans for their steady encroachment on Creek lands; they were also angry about the encroachment of white culture on Creek thought and customs.

Lower Creeks in Georgia aligned themselves somewhat apathetically with the established White Stick Creek government. The Red Sticks (Osceola's people) had the sympathy if not the active support of the British who, at the time, were engaged in the War of 1812 and appreciated any Indian disturbance that could divert American attention from the main war.

The Creek War started as a civil war among Indians, then flared into a United States war against the Red Stick Upper Creeks. Osceola's role might be dismissed as that of a boy spectator and refugeee, except that he underwent a hardening process that led to his dislike of whites and pro-white Creeks.

The war came close to him. On a cool night late in 1813, with a yellow moon lifting above the cornstalks in the Tallassee fields, the boy was wakened by his mother.

"Come," Polly said, pointing toward the east. "White warriors. Messenger says very many."

A Georgia militia force, weakly assisted by some Lower Creeks, was moving west from the Chattahoochee River where they had stopped to build Fort Mitchell near the present city of Columbus, Georgia. Their aim was to attack Autossee, Red Stick headquarters, and Tallassee.

With a few belongings, probably no more than a sack of cornmeal, some cooking utensils, and Osceola's light hunting bow. the boy and Polly joined other refugees from the village. A logical hiding place would have been somewhere between the Tallapoosa and Coosa rivers. When the sun rose two mornings later, they could see smoke rising from the ruins of Tallassee.

During the following months, the Red Sticks fought bravely, often armed only with bows and arrows. But Andrew Jackson was now in the field with an army from Tennessee. On March 27, 1814, Jackson attacked a large Red Stick force near Tohopeka at the Horseshoe Bend in the upper Tallapoosa River. A thousand warriors were killed and the Creek War was over.

Jackson then built a fort and, on August 9, 1814, forced the Creeks to cede twenty million acres of territory. It bothered Jackson not in the least that part of the ceded land belonged to Creeks who had aided him in the fight against the Red Sticks.[20]

There is no clear record of young Osceola's movements during this period. He and his mother drifted with other refugees—ragged, impoverished, desperate—from one hiding place to another. The boy's bow must have provided a little meat—a squirrel roasted in its skin in the ashes of a lonely fire, perhaps a clubbed opossum or raccoon. Hoarded corn may have been found in some of the deserted villages. There was certainly theft when anything was available to steal.

The only avenue of escape was south to the Spanish lands of Florida. Word reached Polly that her uncle, Peter McQueen, planned to move south with many other Red Stick survivors. About a thousand Red Sticks were involved in the migration, a movement made in small bands.[21]

Osceola and his mother naturally joined McQueen's band. From later events, it appears that the aged grandmother Ann Copinger was also in the party. We know little of their early travels, but the situation must have been a grim one. An agricultural people, they suffered from a shortage of food and had to exist on hunting, fishing, and whatever could be scraped together in the way of berries and roots. There may have been a little ground corn for the *sofkee* or corn porridge favored as a staple by southern Indians, but food for a band of a hundred or more fugitives could not easily have been provided simply by hunting, fishing, and living off land where crops had not been planted because of the war.

The spiritual privation must have been as great. Southeastern Indians regarded land as a possession of God—the Great Spirit or the "Breathmaker" of the Seminoles. (God is *Sa-kee tom-mas-*

see. Sa-kee means "breath," *tom* means "everyone," *mas-see* or *mee-see* means "make it." A rough translation would be "Makes everyone breathe." In Mikasuki, God is *Fee-sa kee-kee o-meek-chee.* The meaning is the same. Creeks and Seminoles believed in one God for everyone, whites included. They also believed in *Este-fas-ta*, the giving person, who was intermediary between God and man and corresponds in some respects to the white Christ. *Este-fas-ta* gave the Indian everything but corn, the latter being a gift from *Fas-te-chee. Fas-te-chee* was a messenger for *Este-fas-ta.*[22] The Christian religion has no direct parallel for *Fas-te-chee,* but in many respects the Creek and Seminole religion and white beliefs have much in common. It is curious to note that a Trinity appears in Indian, Jewish, and Christian religions. The Indian believed in one God, his intermediary, and a lesser messenger. The Christian believes in God, Christ, and the Holy Spirit; the Jew believes in God, a Messiah, and Moses as the revealed messenger or lawgiver.)

There is, however, a pronounced difference between one aspect of Indian religion and white belief. The Creeks and Seminoles believed (and many still do) that God allowed the Indian to use the land, but it could not be owned in the white man's sense of personal ownership.[23] (When Indians used the expression, "This is our land," the wording was either borrowed from the white man's inadequate language or, more accurately, it meant, "This is land God has allowed us to use.")

The devout Indian could not sell, cede, or give away property belonging to God. Land, being sacred in its source, was viewed with something akin to worship.[24] So the Red Stick migrants from the Creek War suffered spiritual anguish as a result of leaving the land. Anger at their brothers who had signed away the land was based in part on religious doctrine.

McQueen hoped to receive help from the British who were still fighting the United States as he had done during the Creek War. Sometime in late 1814 or early 1815, his party, including Osceola, Polly, and grandmother Ann, arrived at the Yellow

Water River above Pensacola, Florida. The British may still have been at Pensacola, a Spanish town they had occupied in late August, 1814, but McQueen's plan of joining them was disrupted when his old enemy, Andrew Jackson, seized the town on November 8, 1814.

After a series of minor adventures including an unproductive contact with the British, McQueen moved his band to the Wakulla River, south of modern Tallahassee and near the Spanish town of St. Marks, and began to establish a relationship with Seminoles at Fowl Town and around Mikasuki. Chief Neamathla dominated the Mikasuki Seminoles at Fowl Town just inside the Georgia border; Bowlegs (a corruption of Bowlek) was chief of the Alachua bands far to the east along the Suwannee River.

Neamathla was a remarkable man. In later years, Governor William P. Duval of Florida would describe him to the Secretary of War in these words:

> This chief you will find, perhaps, the greatest man you have ever seen among the Indians. He can, if he chooses to do so, control his warriors with as much ease as a colonel could a regiment of regular soldiers: they love and fear him. . . . This chief should be seen by you, and then you can judge of the force and energy of his mind and character.[25]

McQueen found the Mikasukis friendly. Young Osceola, doubtless impressed by their welcome, would later identify himself strongly with this group of Seminoles. For McQueen and his band, there was even hope of a peaceful life among the Seminoles. The Creek War was over, although never entirely to be forgotten, and the Treaty of Ghent, on February 27, 1815, had ended the so-called War of 1812.

Unfortunately, a series of border incidents were heaping up fuel for the First Seminole War. This war would very nearly doom the southeastern Indians by eventually helping to make

Andrew Jackson President; it would also influence the cession of Florida by Spain, and it would thus lead almost inevitably to the Second Seminole War.

The spark (a considerable understatement) flashed at a place called Negro Fort. During the final months of the War of 1812, the British had built a strong fort at Prospect Bluff some fifteen miles up Florida's Apalachicola River. This, of course, was in Spanish territory, but neither the British nor the Americans had ever hesitated to intrude on Spanish Florida soil.

During the summer of 1815, the British commander left the heavily armed fort to Seminole Indians and a large number of runaway Negroes. The fort controlled the water supply route up the Apalachicola and thence along the Flint River and the Chattahoochee deep into Georgia and Alabama. The fort not only menaced river transportation but its considerable runaway slave population was also an affront to southern slaveholders. Their anguished screams led to what one writer called, "the first slave-catching expedition undertaken by the Federal Government." [26] In a horrible fashion, it did not work out quite that way. "Slave-killing" would be a more accurate description.

During the spring of 1816 Major General Andrew Jackson ordered Brigadier General Edmund P. Gaines to build Fort Scott upriver in Georgia on the Flint River fork of the Apalachicola. This was supposed to be a defensive installation for the American southern district, but it was really established to meet the annoying problem of Negro Fort.

General Jackson ordered a two-pronged attack on Negro Fort in July. An American naval force from the Gulf of Mexico worked its way upstream, while a land force under Lieutenant Colonel Duncan Clinch headed downstream from Fort Scott. (This was the same Duncan Clinch who would later play an important role in the Second Seminole War. Clinch had 116 regulars with him and about 150 friendly Coweta Creeks under a half-breed named William McIntosh [White Warrior].)

On the morning of July 27, Clinch attacked from land while

the naval vessels fired from their anchorage on the river. The ships—two supply boats and two gunboats—were under the command of Sailing Master Jarius Loomis, but it appears that Sailing Master Basset in Gunboat 154 had the bright idea of heating a cannonball cherry-red and firing it with a heavy charge.

It landed on the Negro Fort powder magazine. Some of the livelier writers of the time say the result was the biggest bang in American history to that date. The results were frightful. At least 270 men, women, and children, most of them Negroes, were killed instantly. More than 30 died later. Joshua R. Giddings, a writer who published his accounts in 1858, said 30 Seminoles were among those who perished in the fort.[27]

If this angered the Seminoles, another development enraged them even more. Colonel Clinch paid off his Creek Indian allies by giving them much of what remained in the fort—2,500 muskets, almost 1,000 pistols, 500 swords, and a large quantity of powder that had escaped destruction.

The Seminoles were angry enough to start a war party in the direction of the fort. Clinch with the Creeks moved out to meet it, but the Seminole warriors must have heard about the tremendous surviving store of arms. Thus warned, they slipped away. Clinch called them "cowardly wretches," [28] but apparently changed his mind in later years when he knew them better.

During subsequent months, there were a number of border incidents involving Seminoles and Georgians. It is interesting to note that David B. Mitchell, first serving as governor of Georgia and then as Creek Indian agent, later told an investigating committee, "Truth compels me to say, that before the attack on Fowltown [*sic*] aggressions . . . were as frequent on the part of the whites as on the part of the Indians, the evidence of which can be furnished from files of the executive of Georgia." [29]

Fowl Town, to which Mitchell referred, was Neamathla's village some fourteen miles east of Fort Scott. Plagued by white intrusions, Neamathla sent a message to Fort Scott during

November, 1817, in which he said, "I warn you not to cross, nor to cut a stick of wood on the east side of the Flint. That land is mine. I am directed by the powers above and the powers below to protect and defend it. I shall do so." [30] (This brave chief's reference to "powers above and below" was not mere Indian oratory. He undoubtedly meant that the Great Spirit had given him his orders.)

General Gaines, commanding at Fort Scott, was so enraged that he ordered a force of two hundred fifty men under Major David E. Twiggs to arrest Neamathla. Twiggs attacked Fowl Town, killed four warriors and a woman, drove the defenders out of the town, and burned the place. It may very well be that McQueen and the boy Osceola were among the fugitives. As we shall see, some circumstantial evidence places McQueen at a retaliatory event nine days later. This was an attack on Lieutenant R. W. Scott and a party of forty soldiers, seven soldiers' wives, and four children en route to Fort Scott on the Apalachicola.

The whites were in a large boat close to shore. Suddenly, according to historian James Parton:

> a heavy volley of musketry, from the thickets within a few yards of the boat, was fired into the closely compacted company. Lieutenant Scott and nearly every man in the boat were killed or badly wounded at the first fire. Other volleys succeeded. The Indians soon rose from their ambush and rushed upon the boat with a fearfull yell. Men, women and children were involved in one horrible massacre, or spared for more horrible torture. The children were taken by their heels and their brains dashed out against the sides of the boat. The men and women were scalped, all but one woman, who was not wounded by the previous fire. Four men escaped. . . . Laden with plunder, the savages reentered the wilderness, taking with them the woman they had spared.[31]

She seems to have been a Mrs. Stuart. Joshua Giddings, whose accounts are not always reliable because of strong pro-Seminole bias, says she was taken to Suwannee Town far to the east and "treated with great kindness." [32] But she was definitely a prisoner with Peter McQueen's band in April, 1818.

The United States was now at war with the Seminoles, and Andrew Jackson was back on the scene. He arrived at Fort Scott on March 9, 1818, with a force of thirty-five hundred, including two thousand Creek warriors, rebuilt Negro Fort and named it Fort Gadsden, then launched his attack on the Seminoles. His route took him first through the Mikasuki towns near modern Tallahassee, next down to Spanish St. Marks where some of the Indians had fled in the hope of protection by the Spanish. Jackson took possession of the St. Marks fort on April 7.

He then set out on April 9, 1818, to attack Suwannee Town 107 miles to the east where Bowlegs was holed up with a large body of Indians and Negroes. The whites were in the advance party while the Creek Indians, under Major William McIntosh and Major Thomas Woodward (the historian of later years), brought up the rear.

The route lay through flat, wet country dotted with cypress, pine, wiregrass, palmetto, and cabbage palm. Swamps were encountered frequently.

On the night of April 11, sentinels in the main or forward force heard the barking of dogs and the lowing of cattle. A message went back to McIntosh and Woodward ordering them to scout the area with their Indians. Spies must have been operating, for McIntosh said later, "I heard of Peter McQueen being near the road we were traveling."

On the following morning, McIntosh and Woodward learned that a large enemy force was encamped in a swamp near the Econfina River. The brief accounts of what happened come from white sources, but one can imagine the other side of the story without distorting the truth.[33]

McQueen's party, consisting of about 150 warriors and at least 100 women and children was, indeed, camped in the swamp. With them they had some seven hundred head of cattle, a large number of hogs, a few horses, and a supply of corn. Because of the animals, it was an unwieldy force.

Osceola, now fourteen and still not a warrior, had helped guard the stock during the night. Shortly after dawn, he joined Polly and his grandmother, Ann, to eat a little *sofkee*. There was no hint of an attack. If McQueen knew about Jackson's movements, which is doubtful, he must have believed the entire force had already passed him on the way east.

Suddenly there was a rattle of shots from the edge of the swamp. At the same moment, the attacking warriors began to utter their war cries. Women screamed, McQueen's Seminoles and Red Stick Creeks fired back, terrified cattle and hogs smashed crazily through the underbrush. Sprawled in the mire and armed only with his useless bow, young Osceola could not even see the attackers.

An uneven battle raged for an hour. Smoke drifted over the swamp, and from time to time a cry rang out as one of McQueen's warriors was wounded or killed. The women either huddled together with their children or attempted to flee deeper into the swamp. Since their men were beginning to retreat, this only exposed them to the sporadic fire from their own warriors.

Presently the confusion became hopeless. The attackers, firing from behind trees, began to infiltrate the swamp. Realizing that his granduncle's warriors were retreating, Osceola tried to join them, but he was seized and hurled to the ground. Some of the attacking warriors began to round up the women and children while others pursued McQueen and his fleeing men.

Considering distances involved—a pursuit of three miles from which McQueen and a number of his warriors escaped—the battle lasted more than three hours. Then Osceola found himself being marched to the camp of General Jackson some six miles away. With him were his mother and his grandmother, Ann. All told, thirty-seven of McQueen's warriors had been killed. Ninety-eight women and children and six men were captives. If the various records can be believed, McQueen's scattered force still numbered a hundred warriors.

Mrs. Stuart, the white woman who had been spared during the attack on Lieutenant Scott months earlier, was among the prisoners. Incredibly, her husband and father were with Jackson, so reunion with her family was immediate.[34]

The other prisoners, Osceola among them, were a nuisance. Jackson wanted to press on to Bowlegs' Suwannee Town with his entire force; thus it would be unwise to detach a guard for ninety-eight women and children. The problem was resolved by Osceola's aged grandmother, Ann Copinger, who apparently had inherited the shrewdness of her father, the Scotsman James McQueen.

She pleaded with Jackson for the release of the women and children, but she also hinted that McQueen might somehow be delivered into the hands of the whites. Jackson may not have known who she was, which is unlikely, or he may have had the naïve, arrogant belief that an Indian woman of Creek tradition would actually betray her own brother. For all his vaunted understanding of Indians, Jackson constantly revealed throughout his life almost total ignorance of Indian thinking.

His proposition to the old woman reflected his low assessment of Indian honor and the strong clan ties among Creeks: If she could manage to have McQueen captured and taken to St. Marks, she and the other captives would be returned to Upper Creek lands in Alabama. Here Jackson compounded his error by not understanding the animosity between Red Stick Creeks and the Creek loyalists who had remained in Alabama after signing the treaty at the end of the Creek War. Throughout his career, Jackson would view all Indians as one group with unimportant minor differences that could easily be resolved.

Ann agreed to Jackson's proposal and was given a letter to the garrison commander at St. Marks. With this confirmation of the deal, she and the other women and children were released to wander off and presumably corrupt McQueen's warriors into turning him over to the Americans.

The old woman simply led her band into the swamp, waited for Jackson and his army to move away, then turned north and east to join Mikasukis who had fled to the southern borders of the Okefenokee swamp. (Old maps indicate that the swamp was then supposed to extend deeply into Florida, much farther to the west and south than it does today.)

Jackson fought several engagements on his way to Bowlegs' town on the Suwannee River, found it deserted, burned the village, and headed back to St. Marks where he had one British agent hanged and another shot. He then went on to capture Pensacola on May 26, 1818, thus annoying his government, which was negotiating delicately with Spain for cession of Florida.

However, Jackson's romp through Spanish territory revealed to Spain her hopeless position in Florida. On February 22, 1819, she ceded Florida to the United States. (The United States ratified the treaty two years later, on February 22, 1821.) The First Seminole War ended with Jackson's departure from Florida. Most of the Mikasukis stayed, at least temporarily, in the central portion of northern Florida. The Alachuas moved into the center of the state north of present-day Orlando.

As for the fugitive Red Sticks, the largest number drifted into the region around Tampa Bay, or as far from hostile Alabama and Georgia as they could reasonably go. Peter McQueen settled here on Peas Creek to stare gloomily at the sunset over the Gulf of Mexico and wonder what had gone wrong. Old and broken in spirit, he was only a few years from his death. (No one knows exactly when he died.)

Osceola, his mother, and his grandmother lived for a while with the Mikasukis in north-central Florida. Then they heard about McQueen's village on the east side of Tampa Bay and started the long trek south. Circumstantial evidence suggests that Polly and Osceola joined McQueen early in 1819 after a journey of some three hundred miles. There is no further record of the indomitable Ann.

Osceola, now fifteen and almost a man, found many old and new friends at Tampa Bay. In 1822, John R. Bell, acting agent for the Indians in Florida, listed the Indian settlements for Thomas Metcalfe, a United States representative from Kentucky. Thirty-five towns are named, among them in Bell's account:

> *Tate-ta-la-hoats-ka,* or Water Melon Town on the sea coast west side Tampa Bay, the greatest part of all these fled from the Upper Creeks when peace was given to that nation.
>
> *Low-Walla* Village, composed of those who fled from the Coosa & followed McQueen & Francis their prophets.*
>
> Peter McQueen's Village East side Tampa Bay.

Bell went on to say:

> The foregoing exhibit, is respectfully communicated, to show the dispersed state of the Indians in Florida; requiring some immediate steps to be taken on the part of the government, authorizing the collecting or concentrating these scattered bands at some place suitable for them to become cultivators and to extinguish their title to so much of their country as may not be required for themselves as cultivators of the soil, if it should be found, they possess the title. . . .[35]

Poverty was widespread among most of the Florida Indians, but the Tampa settlements could not have starved. Fish and

* The "prophets" had emerged during the Creek War as a result of the influence of Seekabo and probably Tecumseh whose younger brother Laulewasika (Tenskwatawa) had founded the movement. They believed they had supernatural powers including the ability to turn away bullets. From an original creed of abstinence, they developed a strong antiwhite doctrine. Josiah Francis was their leader. He was captured, tried, and put to death in 1818. He probably was with McQueen part of the time during the flight from Alabama, although it is known that the British entertained him briefly in England. The writers can find no evidence that McQueen was also a member of the prophets, although he was certainly sympathetic to the movement.

shellfish, at least, were abundant, although this diet was unfamiliar to agrarian Indians. Hunting, at which Osceola began to excel, was conducted far inland along the myriad rivers and creeks entering the Tampa Bay region.

Much of Osceola's boyhood had been spent as a helpless fugitive in strange forests. He had learned to mistrust the whites, but most of his anger was directed at Upper Creeks who had signed Jackson's treaty in 1814, and the Lower Creeks who had helped the whites in the recent war. Creek warriors had been with Clinch in the attack on Negro Fort, they had been with Jackson's force when Peter McQueen's party was attacked. Osceola had been captured by Creeks.

During the months of flight, the boy had gradually come to think of himself as a Florida Indian. He would always be an Upper Creek with a heritage as a Red Stick, but his place was now with the Seminoles. Since most of the customs and much of the language were similar to what he knew, the transition was not difficult. Osceola began to see that the only difference between Seminoles and fugitive Creeks was that the Seminoles had come to Florida earlier. All were refugees from the same enemy.

He would have a few years of relative peace in which to earn his adult name, Asi-Yaholo, gain respect for his strength and endurance, and establish himself as a young man with qualities of leadership among Seminoles. But these quiet days would be changed in 1823 by the Treaty of Moultrie Creek.

3

The Treaty of Moultrie Creek

On a cool evening in March, 1820, a young Indian hunter might have been observed encamped beneath a huge live oak on the bank of a creek entering the Hillsborough River northeast of Tampa Bay. The youth squatted beside a small fire he had built Indian-fashion with logs radiating out from the low central blaze. Later he would spread the ashes and scorch the moss to kill chiggers, then sleep on the warm ground.

He had wrapped some venison in moist leaves and was cooking it in the coals. A haunch of deer meat lay nearby on two bloody deerskins. Within reach was a powerful bow, a small bundle of three-foot arrows with fire-hardened tips, a trade hatchet much like the white man's flat-sided shingle hatchet but smaller, and a length of bright cloth for the turban the youth had removed.

The hunter was Osceola, then only sixteen but already lithe and powerful. He wore a cotton hunting shirt with a belt, long leather stockings, and moccasins.[1] A sheathed hunting knife was attached to his belt. He had smeared the exposed parts of his body with bear grease to ward off mosquitoes.

Huge purple clouds, tinged at the edges with the pink of the setting sun, darkened the western sky. In the shadows beneath the tree, firelight gleamed on long cascades of Spanish moss. Occasionally a bird cried sleepily or a fish plopped in the dark creek. A faint, sweet odor of wild flowers mingled with the smell of woodsmoke and cooking meat.

Osceola, motionless as the oak tree, reflected that he would like to own a rifle. The bow was fine for hunting—better, perhaps, than a gun—but a man should have a rifle. Spanish traders from Cuba had good rifles, and so did the scattering of American traders, but the trade was high. The value of a deerskin was only twenty-five cents per pound. Raccoon skins were worth twelve and a half cents each. Good otter skins were tremendously valuable; they represented a trade value of three dollars, but wildcat or tiger (panther) skins counted for only twenty-five cents each. To trade for a rifle, even a white man's muzzle-loading musket, required a great many skins. For a young man without cattle—worth up to ten dollars—shoulder arms were not easy to obtain.[2]

The warning scream of a jay interrupted Osceola's thoughts. There were no enemies to fear in the forest, but Osceola had been trained in caution during the period following the Creek War. Sweeping up his bow, arrows, and hatchet, he slipped into the shadows. Without the stench of rancid bear grease on his face, he could easily have smelled the presence of another man.

The visitor was cautious, too. No twig snapped, no leaf rustled. The stranger, although betrayed by the jay, was carefully inspecting the camp site and evaluating the situation. He knew perfectly well that the man who had built the fire was somewhere nearby, watching and waiting. As the intruder, he would have to make the first move.

After a few moments, the stranger stepped to the edge of the circle of firelight. He was a tall Seminole, about two years older than Osceola and dressed in approximately the same costume. He carried a fine Cuban gun, which he placed carefully on the ground. After this gesture of goodwill, he squatted by the fire to wait for Osceola. Egret plumes were tucked in his turban.

Osceola waited a moment, then stamped, spat noisily, and walked to the fire. After placing his weapons on the ground, he sat cross-legged some five feet from the tall newcomer. This was a gesture of friendship, for a sitting man cannot move as quickly as one who is squatting. For several minutes, neither Indian spoke. At last, Osceola established himself as host.

"Brother," he asked, "is it well with your mother and sisters?"

"It is well, brother," the Seminole replied. "And with you?"

"It is well with my people."

Osceola pushed one of the logs a few inches into the fire. Then he asked, "Have you come far?"

"Almost from the big water," the Seminole said, pointing toward the east.

"I have not seen it. But I will." Suddenly smiling, Osceola asked, "Is it true that the white man has a great camp there?"

"It is true. At the place called St. Augustine. This was the place of the Spanish white man. Now it is the place of the American. Many moons."

"As many as six."

"As you say, brother," the Seminole said politely.

Though the treaty of amity, settlements, and limits by which Spain had ceded Florida to the United States was still a year away from actual ratification by the government in Washington, the Florida Indians were well aware that, with the protection of Spain removed, they were now at the mercy of the United States. With this shift of government, they feared for themselves, the maroons or free Negroes among them, and their black slaves.

At the same time, they hoped for the best from the United States. Acting Agent John Bell, writing to Metcalfe in 1822, noted:

> At present there is no white settlements in East Florida within the Indian boundary, and they will not permit any

> to be made, until they are brought under the protection of the U. States—which they look to with great solicitation, for that justice & liberality which the govt has extended to other Indian nations.[3]

The Indians were almost literally between the devil and the deep blue sea. Some had even decided the sea provided a safe refuge; Coe states that on September 29, 1819, a party of twenty-eight Seminoles arrived at Nassau, Bahamas, in a wrecking vessel. "The exiles were entirely destitute, and said they had been robbed and driven from their homes."[4]

All of which was undoubtedly true. With Spain out of the Florida picture, whites from Georgia and Alabama constantly harassed the Indians. Many were renegades who had no intention of settling in Florida and found the region excellent for lawless activities that would have been punished promptly if conducted in a more civilized part of the nation.[5] It was relatively easy to steal slaves from Indians who could not testify in court, to lure Indians into selling slaves for almost nothing, to steal Indian cattle, or simply appropriate Indian property.[6]

Osceola and his guest shared the roasting venison, eating chunks chopped off with their hunting knives. While the moon painted a silver filigree on the moss and the fire burned low, they talked of the Indian problems—deliberately and with long pauses for thought and the choice of exact words.

"The white man will drive us away, brother," the Seminole said quietly. "He is very many. We are few. We can hope only for the protection of the great father of the white man."

"The warriors of the great father drove me from my home," Osceola said. "I was a prisoner of the white man. I do not like him. But I can live with the white man if he leaves me alone. Perhaps that is the best way to believe. Now we will sleep, brother."

The foregoing episode is, of course, fictitious, but firmly grounded on probability. There are almost no known details of

Osceola's life during this period, but certain deductions are possible; and there were events in the life of a Creek-Seminole youth that must have played an important part in shaping Osceola's personality. We know he must have attended certain ceremonies, and we can be sure that he was aware of Seminole thinking of the time. Thus it is possible to reconstruct various scenes without distorting the truth. What a man says or does is usually a reflection of what he said or did in youth. If we can say with Milton, "The childhood shows the man," we can also say, reasonably, "The man predictably mirrors his youth."

Not that Osceola's youth was entirely obscure. There is no indication of what happened to Polly or Grandmother Ann, and there is no way of telling with whom Osceola lived between 1819 and the years of his emergence as a leader. An accomplished hunter, he probably provided meat for women to whom he was somehow related.

We know, however, that he identified himself strongly with the Seminoles. They were a remarkable people. A great many contemporary writers described them in glowing terms, but perhaps the best description comes from Clay MacCauley who studied them in 1880 when they were not significantly changed in characteristics or customs from the 1820–1842 period. MacCauley wrote:

> Physically both men and women are remarkable. The men, as a rule, attract attention by their height, fullness and symmetry of development, and the regularity and agreeableness of their features. In muscular power and constitutional ability to endure they excel. . . . I noticed that under a large forehead are deep set, bright, black eyes, small, but expressive of inquiry and vigilance; the nose is slightly aquiline and sensitively formed about the nostrils; the lips are mobile, sensuous, and not very full, disclosing, when they smile, beautiful regular teeth; and the whole face is expressive of the man's sense of having extraordinary ability to endure and to achieve. . . . There are, as I have said, exceptions to this rule of unusual physical size and strength,

> but these are few; so few that, disregarding them, we may pronounce the Seminole men handsome and exceptionally powerful.[7]

This is the type of man who would be *dominated* by Osceola! As for the women, MacCauley sounds almost like a spectator at a beauty contest:

> The women to a large extent share the qualities of the men. . . . Large or small, they possess regular and agreeable features, shapely and well developed bodies, and they show themselves capable of long continued and severe physical exertion. Indeed, the only Indian women I have seen with attractive features and forms are among the Seminole. I would even venture to select from among these Indians three persons whom I could, without much fear of contradiction, present as types respectively of a handsome, a pretty, and a comely woman. Among American Indians, I am confident that the Seminole women are of the first rank.[8]

If this suggests exaggeration, consider the account of Comte de Castelnau who saw the Seminoles around 1837. Of the women, he wrote:

> The Seminole women . . . are physically more attractive than most other Indian women. Some chief's daughters owning slaves, and spending their lives lying carelessly on mats, may even be considered pretty. They are marriagable at twelve or thirteen, and at twenty-five may be considered as in the decline of life.[9]

The latter may or may not have been true. Some white women of the period considered themselves aged at twenty-five or thirty. Although many modern Seminole women live almost as their ancestors lived, the writers have not observed premature aging among them.

Some light may be cast on the question of aging among Seminole women by the observation of Major General O. O. Howard, U.S.A., who saw them some years before the Civil War. He mentions a military expedition to Lake Okeechobee during which a Seminole woman "prisoner" accompanied the troops as interpreter. He said she was in "miserable condition," poorly clad, wrapped in an Army blanket, and looking as if beyond middle age. Her daughter, about five, was with her.

Howard wrote: ". . . On arriving at Lake Okeechobee a wonderful transformation took place in our Seminole woman. . . ." She bathed herself and her child, repaired their clothing, combed tangles out of matted hair. She then dug roots containing saponine, powdered them, and washed her hair in the lather until it was smooth and glossy. With her toilet completed, she was transformed into a good-looking woman no more than twenty-five years of age.[10]

Osceola fitted in easily with these remarkable Indians who were, after all, his hereditary brothers and sisters. They were truthful and frank—deceit was almost unknown among them during the 1820s. MacCauley, writing about them in later years, noted this characteristic. He also observed: "Parental affection is characteristic of their home life," and said, ". . . they are affectionate to one another, and, so far as I saw, amiable in their domestic and social intercourse."[11]

Osceola found that living conditions among the Seminoles were quite similar to those of his boyhood. They lived in log or palmetto houses—the thatch-covered *chickee* would be a later development—and their food was much like that of the Creeks. Under good circumstances, corn, peas, beans, pumpkins, melons, and carrots were part of the diet. Meat was usually venison or wild turkey, sometimes the tail meat of alligators. The Koonti root provided a kind of flour.

As noted earlier, the Red Stick fugitives and the Seminoles near Tampa Bay could not have starved. They may have been short of corn and other agricultural products, but meat and seafood were abundant. When Robert Hackley, a Florida pioneer, arrived at Tampa Bay in 1823, the Indians presented him with "a young fat doe they had just killed and four wild turkeys." [12] This could not have been the act of a starving people. There are numerous records of abundant oysters as well as mullet, redfish, flounder, sole, and other seafood.

Indians in other parts of Florida were close to starvation, however, and Osceola certainly must have been aware of that circumstance. This was partly due to the fact that a great many Seminoles had been driven from their cleared and planted lands. Others had failed to plant because of uncertainty about their status under the United States. Still others, riddled by doubts, had sold their stock for ridiculously low prices before concealing themselves in the wilderness.

It is doubtful that Osceola, as a youth, was particularly concerned about the plight of the Seminoles. We can assume that he was comfortable. He could hunt in the great forests. There is excellent evidence that he was admired by his peers. Coe says:

> As a youth, many testify to the fact that Osceola was a great favorite with his tribe, being uncommonly bright, accomplished and energetic. "Cudjoe" [Cudjo], who was interpreter to our army for several years, and who had known Osceola from his childhood, said he was a very active youth, excelling in the chase, in running, leaping, ball-playing, and other Indian exercises.[13]

These skills are noted repeatedly by other contemporary writers.

It would seem, in fact, that Osceola in his youth was an uncomplicated individual with a tendency toward action rather than reflection. He was an unlettered primitive, although not a "savage" in the white man's sense of the term. Seminoles and Creeks were not "savages" when the meaning is "fierce or ferocious"; they were not even "uncivilized." They had attained a high level of primitive culture, in some respects far superior to that of many unlettered whites who scorned them, feared them, or preyed on them. Family life was exceptionally advanced; children were loved and protected. White settlers might beat their children; but such practices were unbelievable to the Indian. Women, although expected to work unless slaves were available, were respected and, it would seem, regarded with real affection.

Morality was high. Men were permitted to have two wives provided they could support them, but a woman could have only one husband. Adultery was punished by cropping the ears and nose. The Seminole view of crime was far more advanced than the attitude of the white man. A criminal was sick—crazy—because he had broken laws made for the good of all. To perform such an act was a clear indication of aberration. He could either rehabilitate himself with the help of the medicine man, or he was simply ruled out of Indian society. If he could not or would not reform, he would be killed for the protection of all. The Seminole believed that the insanity of crime against the common good might be contagious. Crime was a disease.

We can assume reasonably that Osceola's leadership among other young Indians was primarily in sports, hunting, and the simple ceremonies or rituals. His thinking would come later; although he probably would have agreed strongly with some lines written by Acting Governor William Worthington in a letter of December 4, 1821, to John C. Calhoun, Secretary of War. Worthington wrote that the Indians "never will consent to go up amongst the Creeks—They will assume no hostile attitude, against the United States, no matter, what Course they may adopt respecting them—But if they are ordered up amongst the Creeks, they will take to the bushes—." [14]

Andrew Jackson, who had arrived to take over the governorship of Florida on July 17, 1821, had believed naïvely that the Seminoles would willingly rejoin the Creeks. He might have tried to force this union, but he resigned in October to be replaced by two acting governors, Worthington and George Walton. They, in turn, were replaced by William Pope DuVal in April, 1822. Some weeks later, Colonel Gad Humphreys was named Indian agent.

This period, as it affected the lives of Osceola and the Seminoles, is best reflected in some of the official white correspondence of the time. The letters and documents also show the confusion of the government.

Sometime in July, 1822 (the exact date is not given), DuVal sent the following dispatch to the Secretary of War, John C. Calhoun. He noted first that two chiefs had told him:

> The Indians were becoming restless, with the uncertainty of their Situation, That General Jackson in his talk with them in September . . . promised that in a few months the place or land intended for the Florida Indians should be marked out for them, that they have waited a long time, and yet nothing has been done, that they wish to know when their Father the President would determine where they were to live—That White men were settling in and near their towns which they did not like. . . .

Duval reported his reply made to the Indians on July 28. In part, he said:

> Brothers, I am glad to see you, But I am sorry your Great Father has not yet directed me where you are to live —I look every day now when the President will send me his orders and then I will send you word.

He then mentions the recent murder of two whites and says:

> [The killers] must be delivered to the commanding officer at the post of St. Marks—this is what your Great Father the President will expect, and if it is not done his warriors will soon raise the hatchet. If a white man murders a red man the white man must suffer death, so all shall be fair and strait—bad men white or red must be punished so is the rule or law of all nations. . . .[15]

On the following day, DuVal issued a proclamation in which he prohibited the purchase from Indians of cattle, hogs, horses, or slaves without a special license. He also prohibited the sale of liquor to the Indians, and concluded with these words, "The Citizens of the United States and all other persons are hereby forbid to settle in or near any Indian Town or village, as they will be liable to be removed by Military force." [16]

DuVal believed the Seminoles were occupying the best land in Florida, a section roughly east of the Suwannee River in the north-central part of the peninsula, and that there was no good land remaining elsewhere in the territory. Plantation areas along the east coast were occupied; land in the west was unsuitable for agriculture. (To understand the error in DuVal's thinking, one must remember no one of this period saw any promise in the central Florida highlands, rich citrus-growing country of later years. Moreover, south Florida with its potential for cattle raising and vegetable production was virtually unexplored.)

At any rate, DuVal told Washington authorities that the Indians should not be permitted to stay on the land he considered valuable near the Suwannee. Nothing of importance would be left in Florida except a few seaports. He also argued that no matter what land the Seminoles occupied in the territory, they would always endanger communications between Pensacola far to the west and St. Augustine on the Atlantic. The best procedure, he concluded, would be to get the Seminoles out of Florida completely: They should be sent to join the Creeks in Georgia (the old fallacy of reunion with the battered Creek Confederacy) or moved west of the Mississippi.

And, whatever the case, no treaty should be made with them until the country they were occupying was properly explored.[17] DuVal could evaluate it only from hearsay; he was almost three hundred fifty miles away on the outskirts of Pensacola. For DuVal and other authorities, the territory was huge and generally unknown; Key West was about eight hundred miles from Pensacola depending on sailing conditions.

DuVal's views were a virtual blueprint for the future of Osceola and the Seminoles. Paradoxically, he also knew that, good land or poor, many of the Seminoles were so close to starvation that they were living on Koonti flour (also known as briar root) and whatever meat they could shoot. There had been floods to plague the bands in west Florida; moreover, the Indians were still not planting as a result of the government's indecision about the land they should occupy.

Presumably, Osceola was more concerned at this time about personal matters. He probably received his name in 1822, although we have no direct record of the date when he was first called Asi-Yaholo. It may even have been earlier, but it is certainly reasonable to believe that the event took place during an annual Green Corn Dance when adult names could be given.

Osceola had been attending these busks since boyhood. As a "black drink singer," he would have been at least eighteen years of age, so the arbitrary selection of a date may be close to correct. Boyd gives some support to this idea when he writes:

> In view of its implication it is evident that the title *Asi-yaholo* was conferred after the attainment of manhood, as was also the later mentioned "Talcy" or Tallassee Tustenuggee, his probable ceremonial name. In view of his youth when brought to Florida, it is certain that these titles were bestowed subsequent to arrival. The former is indicative that he discharged the duty corresponding in the annual feast of the busk or green corn festival.[18]

The Green Corn Dance was (and is) the most important ritual of the Seminole Indians. In some respects, it has had for these people the significance of the Christian Easter. More aptly, it is somewhat like the Jewish Yom Kippur. Louis Capron has noted in a brilliant ethnological study that:

> The Medicine Bundle is to the Seminole what the Ark of the Covenant was to the Jewish Nation. The Medicine was given to him directly by God, and the Bundle contains everything necessary for the Indian's well-being. When new conditions arise and something is needed to control them for the Indian's benefit, es-te fas-ta reaches down sometime during the last night of the Green Corn Dance and places in the deerskin that holds the Medicine a new kind to meet the new need.[19]

It is possible to re-create Osceola's Green Corn Dance experience with accuracy, using Capron's account.[20] Capron points out that little has changed in Seminole culture; rituals performed today are nearly identical with those known in Osceola's time.

Thus, in 1822, Osceola attended the Green Corn Dance at the time of the new moon in late June or early July. The ceremonies would last for five days, with ritual dancing, feasting, fasting, and the drinking of the "black drink." Location of the dance would be in a remote clearing in the forest far from any villages.

Some days before the event, Osceola arrived at the dance site to assist in the preparation. He was a medicine man's helper; everything is consistent with this deduction. As helper, he and another young man would keep order, find herbs for the black drinks, and perform the ritual serving. Older men would be the medicine man's assistants, a higher rank at the ceremonies and one involving different functions.

Upon his arrival, Osceola found a clearing of several acres screened on every side by towering pines. This was an old dance site, so most of the preliminary work consisted of clearing away underbrush, grass, and weeds, and repairing the *tchoc-ko thloc-go* ("warriors' clubhouse"). This crude building was west of the dance circle, an area about forty feet in diameter with a dance track approximately ten feet wide. In the center of this circle would be the dance fire.

Osceola spent a good part of the early days gathering herbs for the black drink. Among them were *pa-sa* (button snakeroot, *Eryngium synchaetum*), the inner bark of willow, and such ingredients as St.-John's-wort, red bay, various wild grapes, and other roots or shrubs. These were stored carefully for the black drink preparation.

Every evening at about sunset the boys and girls played the ball game described in an earlier chapter. Osceola watched from the *tchoc-ko thloc-ko* where he sat talking with the men. His duties and age prevented participation in the game. In addition to ritual functions, he was one of the two "policemen" at the Green Corn Dance, a tribute to his strength and leadership. (Later we will see an extension of this "police" duty on Osceola's part. If his early life is a jigsaw puzzle, some of the pieces fit together neatly.)

After the ball game each evening, Osceola and the second helper swept the dance circle with bundles of palmetto fronds. Then the dance fire was lighted and the dance master began his instructions. A dance leader—not the master—started the men in a counterclockwise direction around the circle, intoning the chant, which was picked up by his companions. Presently women joined in, turtleshell rattles attached to their legs. Each man carried a palmetto fan in his left hand between the fire and his face.

Dances lasted until midnight or a trifle later. One of Osceola's tasks was to keep the dance fire burning brightly and also to stop any disorder. To him, of course, the scene was normal and familiar; only a white man would have found anything barbaric or bizarre in the chanting, yipping, and rattle cadence of the dancers as they circled the fire. And no white man saw the Green Corn Dance until relatively recent years. It was private and sacred.

Osceola had little to do except eat on the feasting day, the third in the ceremonies. The medicine man provided venison, which he cut up and distributed to the surrounding camps with the assistance of his two helpers. Women cooked the food, then brought it to the edge of the dance ground where the men picked it up. Except when dancing, women were not allowed on the dance ground, never in the *tchoc-ko thloc-ko.*

On the fourth day, court day, Osceola began his important participation in the ritual. While the medicine man and his assistants bathed and sang in a nearby creek, Osceola and the second helper began to prepare the first black drink from chopped *pa-sa* tubers. With this job completed shortly after sunrise, they prepared the second black drink from the inner bark of willow. Both of these drinks were served cold. Meanwhile, the medicine man had gone to a secret place in the forest where he had concealed the sacred medicine bundle.

When making the drinks, and at all times during rituals, Osceola remembered always to turn only to the left. A great disaster might take place if he, the other helper, or the assistants ever turned toward the right.

And now the medicine man returned with the medicine bundle, which he placed east of the dance circle. He and an assistant inspected the sacred contents, then transferred them to another deerskin bundle that was then hung from a forked stick. Osceola, meanwhile, was placing the black drinks and drinking gourds just to the northeast of the dance circle.

Men could not eat on court day. Young boys, however, were permitted to eat after making their own black drinks from *pa-sa,* rubbing it on their bodies, and receiving a light ritual scratching with animal claws or snake fangs. Boy babies were scratched at the *tchoc-ko thloc-ko.*

Next, at about 9:00 A.M., the feather dance was performed. With this ritual dance out of the way, Osceola's main duty began. He served the black drinks, giving the long cry while the men gulped down the infusions. His voice, clear and somewhat shrill, could be heard at a great distance. He was Asi-Yaholo, the black drink singer, and he would be so identified in formal fashion later in the day when the medicine man addressed him by that name.

The black drinks were (and are) strong emetics. The ritual concept was to cleanse and purify the system prior to the more sacred events. Osceola joined in gulping down the emetics, of course, and in performing the ritual vomiting.

Court began at noon with all of the men and boys present. After crimes had been discussed and disposition agreed upon, talk returned to the problems of the Seminoles. Osceola spent most of this meeting listening to the views of the chiefs. One of them summed up the thinking of all.

"Brothers!" he said. "This is our land! Now the white man says we do not belong here. He would move us to land that he chooses! I say that we must not go to any land beyond our fields and hunting grounds! If we are the children of the Great Father in the country to the north, let him treat us as we treat our children. Do we drive them from their homes? Do we punish them for being our children? Are we slaves to be driven away by the white warriors? I say we must stay on the land the Breathmaker has let us use!"

"Ho!" the men roared in approval. The strong voice of Osceola could be heard above the others.

His duties were not yet completed. Following the afternoon dances, the fire of the medicine man was started and the sacred medicine bundle placed near it. Private medicines were placed near the medicine bundle to draw strength from it. Osceola, meanwhile, brought up ingredients for the third black drink, a strong combination of the first two plus a secret herb provided by the medicine man. This infusion would boil until midnight, when it would be taken four times to the accompaniment of Osceola's cry.

The important Green Corn Dance began at midnight. This dance was accompanied by a strange chant, the meaning of which had long since been forgotten. The principal sound in the song was "eeee" and "yo" or "o." While all of this was going on, the medicine in the sacred bundle was gathering power. To Osceola, to others engaged in the ceremony, Este fas-ta was now present in the flickering light, in the pools of black beneath the trees, in the dark sky above.

At dawn, the women departed to prepare the corn and meat. With the women busy at the camps, the ritual scratching began on the men's arms, legs, breasts, and backs. This was to purify the blood. After Osceola had been scratched, he began his job of rounding up all men and boys who had not gone through the ceremony. Some of the young boys feared the scratching, which could be quite deep, so Osceola and the other helper had their hands full.

"Come, little brother," Osceola would cry, grasping a boy's wrist with powerful fingers. "You are not afraid. It is good to let out the blood." And the youth would be pulled to the side of the dance fire.

While Osceola wrestled his captives to their blood baptism, the other men were taking sweat baths in a hut beyond the medicine man's fire. Meanwhile, the medicine man inspected the sacred bundle to see if any new medicine had been added during the night. Finally he took the bundle to a hiding place, where he would later recover it, and the eating of corn and meat concluded the ceremonies.

Osceola's participation in this and later Green Corn Dances undoubtedly played an important part in developing his position as a leader. For one thing, he was a figure of authority particularly among the younger Seminoles who would later follow him without question. He was also cast in the role of a major participant in the most important of all Seminole rituals. It seems clear that he performed his duties with reverence, firmness, and the diplomatic good humor that invited obedience. This good humor stood by him for more than a decade, repeatedly tempering the fury that would finally explode after 1834.

The events of 1823 swirled around nineteen-year-old Osceola like a hurricane. He lacked both age and hereditary rank to play a part in them, but inevitably they shaped his later life. If not a participant in what happened, he must certainly have been a spectator. Any strong, inquisitive young Indian man would have witnessed various of the scenes.

American policy toward the Seminoles was still seriously confused in early 1823. There was no question about concentrating them somewhere, and the official tendency was to settle them at least temporarily in Florida, but there was considerable doubt about the exact location. Many officials wanted them moved west of the Mississippi, but land was not yet available. Where in Florida could they be concentrated?

One plan was to place them south of "Charlotte's River," which must have been the modern Peace River entering Charlotte Harbor south of Tampa Bay. The area was unsurveyed and almost unknown at the time; even in the early years after the Seminole War, maps were remarkably incorrect. It may be said categorically that no one knew whether or not this land would support the Seminoles.

Gradually a concept grew for settling the Seminoles in the south-central part of peninsular Florida, away from the coasts and below the communications line between St. Augustine and Pensacola. To achieve this, on April 7, 1823, Secretary of War Calhoun commissioned James Gadsden, a former Army colonel, and Bernardo Segui to treat with the Indians. Gadsden, thirty-five, would later arrange the Gadsden Purchase of 1853 (Arizona) and be recalled as minister to Mexico in 1856 for exceeding his instructions.

On June 11, 1823, Gadsden wrote Calhoun his views on removing the Seminoles totally from Florida.

> It is possible that all the Florida Indians might be induced to remove and, if so, an object so vitally important in a national or territorial point of view would be gained. Florida, as a

> maritime district of the American Union, is peculiarly exposed; possessing more than 900 miles of sea coast, with Capacious bays or Estuaries easy for acess; and her good to inferior lands bearing but a small proportion, and the territory consequently unsusceptible of a dense population. . . . An Indian population under these circumstances, connected with another class of population which will inevitably predominate in Florida, must necessarily add to her natural weakness, and endanger the security of one of the most exposed but most important sections of the Union. It is useless to enlarge on the policy of removing the class of savages from where they may prove dangerous to where they would be comparatively harmless.[21]

By "another class of population," Gadsden meant Negroes. He was saying, not too delicately, that unless the Indians were driven out of Florida, slaves would join them. He also asked for a show of force when the Indians met "as to render them perfectly Subservient to the views of the Government." [22] Here, in blunt terms, was the key to Gadsden's views of persuasion. The Indians must be "subservient." They would be made to realize they had no choice other than obedience to the dictates of the United States government.

DuVal was appointed third commissioner on June 30. The Indians were ordered to meet at Moultrie Creek, a few miles south of St. Augustine, on September 5, 1823, where they would engage in a "Treaty of peace and friendship." To make certain those west of the Suwannee arrived, Indian Agent Gad Humphreys went out to lead them in. Micanopy and Jumper had already been persuaded to bring in their people. Many Indians remained in the forests, but more than four hundred arrived at a location about a mile and a half from the treaty site. Here they selected Neamathla as the top chief.

Osceola probably was present, having come in with bands controlled by Micanopy. If he was indeed present at the meeting, he certainly played no part in subsequent events. He was not a chief and not yet a *tustenuggee* ("war chief"). We can only assume that it would have been difficult for him to stay away from an event of this magnitude.

At first, the Seminoles must have been somewhat relieved and hopeful about the meeting. As noted earlier, some had almost begged DuVal for a decision as to where they would live. Privation had struck sharply at many of them; almost any reasonable decision would be better than the existing unsettled situation. Their attitude was as peaceful as it could be under the circumstances.

Someone had built a bark conference house at the treaty site. Twenty-five soldiers, in red leggings, and a number of officers arrived on the morning of Saturday, September 6, to provide the show of force Gadsden had so clearly desired. These were men of the Fourth Artillery who served as infantry according to the practice of the times.

There is an excellent description of the scene. A group of St. Augustine residents came visiting, as if to a Sunday school picnic, and among them was a clergyman, the Reverend Joshua Nichols Glenn, who kept the following record:

> Sat 6th the Treaty with the Floriday Indians [the good man could not spell, but had a great deal of company] commenced to day in the morning Capt Wm Levingston his wife and Daughter Mr & Mrs. Streeter and my Self went up to Moultry the place of holding the Treaty in a very comfortable Boat—accompanyed by many other gentlemen and Ladies in other Boats—a little after we landed the Indians came from their Camps to the Commissioners Camp to Salute the Commissioners & hold their first talk this was quite Novel—the Indians came in a body with a White Flag flying—beating a little thing Similar to a Drum and Singing a kind of a Song and at the very end of every appearant verse one of them gave a Shrill hoop—which was Succeeded by a loud and universal Scream from them all—in this way they marched up to the Commissioners—when two of them in their birth day Suit and painted all over white with white Sticks in their hands and feathers tied on them—came up to them [viz., the commissioners] and made many marks on

> them—then their King Nehlemathla came forward and Shook hands and after him all the chiefs in rotation—after which the King Smoked his pipe and then observed that he considered us gentlemen as Fathers and Brethern and the Ladies as Mothers and Sisters the Commissioners then conducted the chiefs into the bark Hous they had bilt to hold their talk in and after they had all Smoked together they held their first Talk—in the evening we returned to Town and as the Governor was unwell he came with us—[23]

Gadsden began the conference at 11:00 A.M. with typical bombast. Among other things, he told the Seminoles they could count on being restricted to one area. He also said:

> Four years ago, the same Redsticks, with the false prophets McQueen and Francis and bad men from across the water, poisoned the minds of some warriors. . . . Friends and brothers: the hatchet is buried; the muskets, the white men's arms, are stacked in peace. Do you wish them to remain so? Listen, then, to the talk of your father the President. He wishes the red stick eternally buried; he drinks with you the black drink; he exchanges with you the white feather; he unites with you in the feather dance and eagle tail song. He smokes with you the pipe of eternal peace. . . .[24]

There was nothing veiled about the threat. Behind the flowery language, Gadsden was simply saying that unless the Indians agreed to the government proposals, the white men's arms might be used again. Despite the views of apologists for Moultrie Creek, a threat was made in no uncertain terms.

The Seminoles thought it over for two days, probably while the governor was recovering from whatever ailed him. Gadsden's reference to the Red Sticks among them was troubling. He had said that the Red Sticks had poisoned the minds of some of the Seminole warriors. Was he trying to set the Indians apart, thus weakening their limited unity?

Neamathla spoke strongly about this question in his opening remarks. He told Gadsden the Red Sticks were now part of the

Seminole nation and must be viewed as such. Somewhat later, he begged the commissioners not to drive the Indians south "to a country where neither the hickory nut, the acorn, nor the persimmon grows." Mahon points out that "The allusion to the acorn and the hickory nut [were] not mere caprice. Like most savage peoples the Seminoles needed oils, and they derived them from nuts." [25]

From here on, the historical records become vague. Whether by oversight or for concealment of negotiations, Gadsden failed to keep minutes from September 12 to September 18. This may be interpreted only as an incredible act on the part of a United States negotiator—secret diplomacy at its worst.

We know, however, that Neamathla, John Blunt, Tuski Hadjo, Mulatto King, Emathlochee, and Econchatimico were strongly opposed to leaving their lands. These men were among the most powerful chiefs; their signatures were important on any treaty. Somehow they had to be persuaded to sign. Sprague says that they "for a long time obstinately and stubbornly refused to negotiate in any manner. It was feared the attempt to effect a treaty would be an entire failure." [26]

But they signed on the eighteenth along with twenty-six other chiefs. Some of the thirty-two who signed may not have had the authority to do so. Historian Mahon points out that Neamathla had submitted a list of thirty-seven towns and chiefs, only seventeen of whom marked the treaty. What happened to the other twenty chiefs? Did the fifteen signers on Neamathla's list actually represent bands within the Seminole nation? [27] Were these signatures fraudulent? Certainly there is suspicion that they were.

On September 19, an additional article was signed by Neamathla, Blont, Tuski Hadjo, Mulatto King, Emathlochee, and Econchatimico. "In consideration of their friendly disposition, and past services to the United States," they were given large private reservations just where they wanted them—*on the excel-*

lent land they had been occupying! In other words, they were bribed with land to sign the main treaty.

There is no escaping this concluson. Mahon says, "Using balder terms it would be possible to call this article a bribe." [28] The contemporary historian, Sprague, implies this when he writes, ". . . large concessions were made to these head men." [29] Joshua Giddings, another early historian, says of the six chiefs, "They were, however, prevailed upon to agree to the treaty, when it had been so modified as to give them each a reservation of fertile lands, to meet their own necessities." [30] The late Dr. Rembert W. Patrick, former president of the Southern Historical Association, has written bluntly: "In 1823 American commissioners . . . bribed and intimidated the Seminoles into the Treaty of Moultrie Creek." [31]

Gadsden himself told Calhoun, "It is not necessary to disguise the fact to you, that the treaty effected was in a degree a treaty of imposition." [32]

Finally, the Petitioners' Motion for Summary Judgment in the modern Seminole claim, decided in favor of the Seminoles on May 8, 1964, contains these damning words.

> Petitioners contest that six chiefs were bribed to sign the treaty of Fort Moultrie. Therefore the United States obtained said lands by duress, bribery, unconscionable consideration and by dealings that were not fair and honorable.

By approving the Seminole claim in 1964, the Claims Commission implied acceptance of the accusation.

The main Treaty of Moultrie Creek, signed by the thirty-two chiefs, is a lengthy document containing ten articles. In the first and second articles, the Seminoles agreed to cede and "relinquish all claim or title . . . to the whole territory of Florida, with the exception of such district of country as shall herein be allotted to them." They would hereafter "be concentrated and confined" to a reservation that eventually consisted of 4,032,940 acres. They had ceded 28,040,991 acres of land (if one uses the figure given in the modern petition before the Claims Commission).

The one point won by the Indians was to get the concentration area moved north. The reservation had a southern boundary ranging roughly from the latitude of Tampa Bay toward Vero Beach on the east, a northern boundary some miles above modern Ocala. The western boundary was no closer than fifteen miles to the Gulf of Mexico, the eastern boundary no nearer the Atlantic than twenty miles.

For Seminole agreement to this, the United States (Article 3) would give the Indians $6,000 in stock and farm implements. It would also pay the Seminoles $5,000 a year for twenty years. (Later the Indians contended that this treaty could not run out until 1843.) Unauthorized whites (Article 4) would not be permitted to hunt, settle, or intrude on the reservation.

The United States (Article 5) would give the Indians rations of corn, meat, and salt for twelve months beginning February 1, 1824. A sum of $4,500 would be distributed among Indians who had to abandon improvements made on land outside of the reservation. To transport Indians to the reservation, a sum not to exceed $2,000 was authorized.

An agent would be appointed (Article 6) and $1,000 a year for twenty years would be provided to establish a school on the reservation. Another $1,000 per year would be paid to support the services of a blacksmith and gunsmith for twenty years. The Indians (Article 7) would prevent runaway slaves from entering the reservation, and would attempt to capture any who came in.

Boundary lines (Article 8) would be surveyed in the presence of a chief or designated warrior. If land proved to be poor (Article 9), the northern boundary could be extended. Finally (Article 10), Colonel Gad Humphreys would receive a present of a square mile of land. (This was later disallowed.)

The treaty was a remarkably cynical document; even without

the bribery involved, it would have been unconscionable. Mahon points out that the total cash considerations added up to $221,-000, or a payment per acre of roughly three-fourths of a cent.[33] Even in 1823, this was a ridiculous price for an acre of land anywhere.

By agreeing to the treaty, the Florida Indians not only forfeited their independence but also placed every aspect of their future in the hands of the United States government. Presumably, not many of them realized that by agreeing to the restrictions of reservation boundaries they had placed an invisible fence around themselves. The United States could now control them by demanding their obedience to the terms of the treaty; if they disobeyed, the treaty would be interpreted as a sufficient instrument to justify their expulsion from Florida.[34]

If this was temporarily obscure to Osceola and his Seminole brothers, other implications of the treaty were immediately apparent. The Florida Indians were now cut off from the sea and its supply of food. They were also beyond the reach of traders from Cuba who had been a source of supply for generations. Some white Americans thought these traders actively encouraged the Seminoles to deal in runaway Negroes and stolen cattle.[35] This was probably untrue; but Cuba had, indeed, been an important source of rifles, ammunition, and such essential hard-goods as knives and hatchets.

Neamathla and five chiefs had been given grants of their own good, developed land; the reservation, as Gadsden told Calhoun, was wet in spring and summer and could only be penetrated in winter "with comfort & without sacrifices of health." [36] This is the clearest evidence that the commissioners at Moultrie Creek knew full well they were concentrating the Indians on poor land.

Most injurious of all, the defection of Neamathla and his acceptance of a bribe injured whatever unity existed among the Seminoles. Osceola and many others among the Indians certainly recognized that they had been sold out by their own chosen chief. What had happened to the defiant Neamathla of the early days? Clearly, he had been bought by the white man. His integrity had been lost when he signed the additional article at Moultrie Creek.

Osceola asked himself what a man should do when boxed in on all sides. He was now nineteen, and quite capable of thinking calmly in new dimensions. Fighting was out of the question; the Seminoles wished only to be left in peace and to have a chance at reconstructing their lives. Food was more important than fighting.

The treaty, good or bad, had been signed by Seminole leaders, good or bad. Simple logic suggested that the Seminoles should try to abide by its provisions. Any idea that the white man would violate it was incomprehensible. Important white men, including the governor of Florida, had signed the terms for the white President. Such men could not possibly lie, could not deceive, could not break their promises. Even Neamathla had not lied; he had simply struck a bargain.

There was, at least, hope for a peaceful future. Osceola decided to cooperate with the white man. There really was no other choice.

4

The Treaty of Payne's Landing

Osceola's cooperation with the white took the form of serving as a guide, and, probably, as a surrogate in the surveying of reservation boundary lines and the new roads the whites so desperately needed in Florida. Article 8 of the Moultrie Creek treaty had called for a party with a surveyor to mark the reservation boundary, blazing the trees along the line. A Seminole warrior, selected in council, would be present to represent Indian rights. He would receive three dollars a day, a large sum for the times.

The deduction of Osceola's employment is logical. There is no record that he was ever seriously impoverished, so he must have had some source of white income. Up to 1834 there is considerable evidence of his friendship with whites. Thomas L. McKenny, Indian Superintendent, had ambivalent views of Osceola; he thought he was a dissembler. He says in his great work, *The Indian Tribes of North America,* "The mind of Asseola was active rather than strong, and his conduct that of a cunning and ambitious man, who was determined to rise by his own exertions." [1]

The general brilliance of McKenney's account seems to be colored by the preconceptions of his times. McKenney had originally been director of the government factories or trading posts until he was appointed to head the Office of Indian Affairs within the War Department in 1824. He could not have been wholly objective, and it is unlikely that Osceola, in the 1820s, was a dissembler. Even McKenney says,

> His habits were active and enterprising, evincing an entire freedom from that indolence of mind which degrades the great mass of this race into mere sensual beings, who are only roused into action to indulge the appetites of hunger or revenge, and sink into apathy when those passions have been satiated.[2]

History proved McKenney wrong about the Seminoles; history also proved him right, to some extent, about Osceola. The key words are "active and enterprising."

To say he was "active" is an understatement. One warm morning, probably in 1825, he arrived at Tampa Bay to guide a party of horsemen. Although he could ride, he was on foot; Florida Indians rarely used horses. Except where crude roads cut through the forests, it was far easier to walk or run.

The party started off at a slow pace, the riders walking their horses. Osceola strolled ahead for some moments, then turned to ask the interpreter why the party was so slow.

"Because of you. You're not riding."

"Tell them not to be slow for me," Osceola said, smiling. "I can stay with them."

Grinning when this was explained to them, the horsemen increased their speed to a trot and sometimes a gallop. To their amazement, Osceola not only kept the pace on foot but even laughed at their surprise. When the riders slowed to rest their horses, they saw that Osceola was not even breathing heavily. He regarded his challenge as an excellent joke.

This kept up all day. The narrator of the story later wrote, ". . . nor did he exhibit the slightest symptoms of fatigue at the close of the day, but arrived at the point proposed as early as the mounted body." [3]

Although few Seminole men could approach Osceola in endurance, notable stamina was not unusual among the Florida Indians. It was still sufficiently impressive to cause comment in later years. Clay MacCauley, writing in the 1880s, told of seeing a slight Seminole boy of ten leave camp in the morning to hunt with a heavy Kentucky rifle. He was back at sunset with fifty pounds of venison he had carried for many miles along with his rifle. The same boy astonished MacCauley by covering forty miles in a day just to visit his home.[4] As recently as 1930, Seminoles in the Everglades would hike from their villages to Miami or Everglades City, making a round trip of as much as sixty miles between dawn and dark.

During the early 1820s, however, Osceola was a truly outstanding specimen of a young Seminole. When he was not working as a guide or reservation line runner, he hunted skillfully, ranging as far east as Euchee Billy's village above modern Orlando and probably to the village of King Philip near Kissimmee. He surely went north to Big Swamp near present-day Ocala. These wanderings advanced his intimate understanding of the incredibly wild Florida terrain, and he also learned quickly that the reservation land was shockingly poor. Part of Big Swamp was fine, a condition Osceola noted carefully, but Big Swamp was off limits in 1824.

Travel through the wilderness also brought Osceola into contact with numerous Seminole chiefs and warriors, all of whom were pleased to welcome the young hunter, share food with him, hear his hunting exploits, and inevitably talk about Moultrie Creek and the white man. A popular visitor, he pleased the young men by racing and wrestling with them. Of great importance in later years, he became well known to the Seminole people, and they to him.

He also observed white ways in the 1820s. Although historian Cohen is the only contemporary writer who suggests Osceola could speak a little English, it is unreasonable to agree with most authorities that he was totally unfamiliar with the white man's language. Until the outbreak of the Second Seminole War, he was frequently in contact with whites; no Indian in Osceola's situation could have avoided knowing some English. As we will see later, he even made friends with white soldiers.

The year 1824 was the first in a series of cruelly bad years for the Florida Indians. It began with the arrival on January 22 of Brevet Colonel George M. Brooke at Tampa Bay. Brooke had four companies of the Fourth Infantry with him. His job was to establish a cantonment or fort.

Brooke, essentially a fine man and an outstanding officer, also appears to have been quite as arrogant as most military men of his times. For his cantonment, he selected a site already developed by the pioneer, Robert J. Hackley. Hackley had put up superior buildings and carved out a good plantation before sailing off for a vacation in Pensacola.

Knowing a good thing when he saw one, Brooke simply built his cantonment on Hackley's development. No one truly knows how all of this happened. There was a lawsuit many years later, but the results are obscure and Fort Brooke was already firmly established. We know, at least, that the site was beautiful; huge live oaks were festooned with Spanish moss and there was a sweet odor of jessamine (jasmine) at night. Fort Brooke, the parent of modern Tampa, would be tremendously important during the Second Seminole War; in a sense, Osceola's future was tied up with this installation.

Colonel Brooke was jumpy. On April 6, 1824, he wrote Major General Jacob Brown, commander in chief, Washington:

> The Indians appear to me, to be more & more displeased at the Treaty, and still more so, at the running of the line, and I am not unapprehensive of some difficulty. They have an idea, that the nation, is about to go to war with Great Britain, and was it to be the case, they would most certainly join our enemy. [This may have been a distorted reaction to

> the Monroe Doctrine.] In Consequence of its having been reported to me that a large number of Indians, were seen near the Camp, after tattoo, who appeared to have an intention of taking us by surprise, the Troops were put under arms, and Continued so during the night . . . but no Indian was discovered. . . .[5]

Brooke was also worried about evidence of pirates in the neighborhood; incredibly, pirates were still so active in 1824 throughout Gulf of Mexico and Caribbean waters that a joint British-American expedition against them was planned for the following year.

Probably Osceola was not with Brooke's real or imaginary party of Indians. Brooke was seeing menacing Indians behind every tree, an illusion from which he would rapidly recover. Later, he was remarkably friendly toward the Indians; but in 1824 he was disturbed about not having field artillery at Tampa Bay. In his letter to Washington, he begged for two six-pounders with an adequate supply of ammunition.

Brooke was not entirely unwise in his jumpiness. During July, 1824, Governor DuVal was bombarded with reports that Neamathla's warriors were showing signs of hostility. Cattle and hogs belonging to whites were killed, several settlers were ordered by Indians to leave the territory, and some of the warriors even threatened to make war on the governor and drive all whites from Florida.[6]

DuVal was a tough individual whose early exploits as a frontiersman had attracted the attention of writer Washington Irving. DuVal had no intention of hearing threats from anyone. With more bravura than common sense, he hurried to Neamathla's town, confronted the chief and three hundred warriors, and ordered them to meet him at St. Marks on the twenty-sixth. In Washington Irving's dramatized account of the event (*The Conspiracy of Neamathla*), DuVal physically attacked the chief. He grabbed him by the throat.

However unlikely that may be, DuVal met with Neamathla

and six hundred warriors on the twenty-sixth and deposed Neamathla as chief, an act that was, of course, illegal. He then appointed John Hicks (Tuckose Emathla) in Neamathla's place. The disgraced Neamathla eventually left to join the Creeks, a decision that must have been extremely painful, but this did not happen for many months.

Osceola could not have cared less. Hicks, a Mikasuki, was far to the west of the Suwannee River and had limited influence over the peninsula Indians. He had signed the Treaty of Moultrie Creek (his name appears as Tokose Mathla), and he was well liked by the whites, the probable reason for his appointment by DuVal.

Osceola was quite aware, however, that all Seminoles were growing hungry despite the issue of rations at Hambly's store on the St. Johns River south of modern Palatka, and at Tampa Bay. One reason for privation was that the number of Indians entitled to rations had been seriously underestimated. Moreover, many refused to travel to Tampa Bay, the result being that stores at Hambly's were quickly exhausted.

Incredibly enough, the official response to the shortage was to reduce the rations even more. It is extremely difficult to assess the reason for this, but several explanations have been advanced by historians who have studied the period. The government may have felt that reduced support would inspire the Indians to clear land and start planting. Or officials may simply have wished to save money.[7] The panic of 1819 had not been forgotten and the national economy was still shaky.

Some of the correspondence between officials of the period suggests indirectly that a policy of starvation may even have been given consideration. But it appears more likely that Washington simply did not understand the Seminoles' need, despite a bombardment of communications from officials in Florida. Moreover, many white citizens in and out of government regarded Indians as a species of subhuman; they were more of a nuisance to these white men than a national responsibility. With a few exceptions, sympathy for the American Indian was rare until well into the twentieth century. (It is still more phenomenal than common.)

Drought struck the reservation area in 1825. From the agency he was establishing near modern Ocala, Gad Humphreys called desperately for additional rations. With DuVal temporarily out of the territory, Acting Governor George Walton wrote a revealing letter to Thomas McKenney, Superintendent of Indian Affairs, on October 6. Much of it merits repeating:

> Many of these Indians, resident in the Reserve East of the Suwannee River, have recently abandoned their country; and I have received information . . . that most, if not all, of those who formerly resided between the Rivers Suwannee & Appalachicola are on their return hither. They state to me as a reason for their return, that they have always been furnished with a scanty supply of provisions only & which has sometime since ceased altogether; that they have no means of subsistence within themselves; that there is no game in their country; that it is moreover exceedingly unhealthy, exposing them to sickness and inevitable death, and in fine, that no part of the country alloted to them for a residence is of such a description as to afford them comfortable settlements; or of such a quality as will enable them either to have stocks or raise corn. I have myself never been in that part of Florida, but from information that I rely upon, I am inclined to believe that all that the Indians represent respecting its unhealthiness & want of fertility of soil is strictly correct. . . .[8]

On October 10, 1825, the issue of rations to the Indians, as called for in the Treaty of Moultrie Creek, came to an end. During the next two months, most of the Seminoles experienced hunger so severe that some actually died of starvation. The living were often obliged to exist on the roots of the sweetbriar as a substitute for bread. Fearing the situation would result in attacks on the white settlements, and for purely humane reasons,

Colonel Brooke literally pleaded with Washington for additional rations.[9]

From about this point on, Congress began making appropriations to aid the Seminoles, but never enough to prevent serious want. The situation at the beginning of 1826 was so bad that DuVal decided to inspect the reservation. He seems to have started from the agency near modern Ocala, although he sometimes mixed up right and left as he moved down the military road toward Tampa Bay. Maps were so poor, however, that this confusion is understandable.

He saw Big Swamp, which lay to the southwest of the agency, although he fails to mention it until the end of his report. The Indians had long wanted Big Swamp, which had fertile ground and would later be Osceola's home. Although DuVal for some reason did not know it, Big Swamp had already been granted to the Seminoles on December 26, 1825, for *temporary* use.

At any rate, DuVal visited Long Swamp, south of the agency, and found it "entirely too wet for cultivation." He then went on to Okahumpki (Okihumky), which is marked on at least one old map as "swampy." DuVal thought little of it. Still farther south, he visited Pelacklakaha (many spelling variations), which he described as a town occupied by the Indian Negroes. Abraham, the interpreter, lived here, as did Micanopy. DuVal said that in the rainy season the best of it was under water.

He then went west to Chicuchatty (Checuchatty) in the Big Hammock region, an area already given to the Indians and touted as fertile. It seems that Fuch-a-Lusti-Hadjo had settled here. DuVal was disgusted. No decent drinking water was available and the fertility was illusory. The governor noticed abundant stands of timber, a condition erroneously suggesting good soil. When he dug down, a practice he followed in numerous areas, he found that a few inches of topsoil covered a base of white sand. If plowed for any length of time, the sand would become dominant and the mixture useless for agriculture.

DuVal was plagued by heat, mosquitoes, swarms of horseflies, and some strains on his own conscience. Travel must have been atrocious to bother an experienced woodsman. From Chicuchatty, he headed straight south toward Tampa Bay, observing he had not seen a more wretched tract of country. He wrote: "The best of the Indian lands are worth but little:—nineteen twentieths of their whole country within the present boundary is by far the poorest and most miserable region I ever beheld." He concluded by suggesting that Big Swamp be given to the Indians." [10]

At the time of DuVal's inspection tour, Osceola had already moved, at least on a temporary basis, to Big Swamp where he joined Holata Mico (Blue King), a Mikasuki leader. With him were some warriors—Woodburne Potter, author of an account published in 1836, says they were seven in number, but Cohen puts them at thirty or forty by 1832. The number doubtless increased rapidly.

Even if we accept Potter's small number of Osceola's followers in the period prior to the war, Potter himself confirms what Cohen says: that Osceola had risen to the position of *tustenuggee*, or war chief. McKenney explains the process, although he says Osceloa's first followers were only two men.

> The term [tustenuggee] sub-chief, which we use, is not descriptive of any actual office or formal appointment, but merely designates those individuals who, by their talents or popular qualities, obtain followers, and become leaders or persons of influence. Those who are expert in war or hunting are followed by the young braves, who desire to learn under them, at first, perhaps, only by their own relatives who depend on them; but as their reputation increases, the train swells in number: and there are, therefore, leaders of every grade, from those who head a few men, up to him who controls his hundred warriors, vies with the chief in influence and authority, and at last supplants him, or supersedes him in every particular except in name.[11]

McKenney then elaborates on Osceola's growth to power with sharp criticism, a progression that will be described later.

In 1826, however, we can place Osceola in or about Big Swamp. By the time the building of Fort King started in 1827, he had a camp or village some three miles southwest of the fort. The site of Osceola's camp was close to modern Interstate Highway 75, wild, beautiful country in 1826. Some ten years ago, the writers of this book hunted wild boars on perhaps the same land where Osceola lived and hunted. The country has almost a mystical quality, with great live oaks and almost impenetrable jungles flanking the black creeks. So dense are these thickets even today that a skilled woodsman can be lost, at least temporarily, in a matter of seconds.

Osceola was now close to the center of Florida Indian affairs. In February, DuVal ordered the Seminoles to surrender all runaway slaves that were among them. Many complied, but DuVal was annoyed by what he called "left-handed justice." The whites refused to surrender slaves they had stolen from the Seminoles.

In May, an Indian delegation under Hicks (Tuckose Emathla) and including Holata Mico, Osceola's nominal chief, went to Washington for a conference. Here, on May 10, they heard a talk by the new Secretary of War, James Barbour, successor to Calhoun in the Adams administration. They replied to this speech on May 17. (The Negro Abraham had gone along as interpreter.)

Upon his return, Holata Mico told Osceola what had happened. The young *tustenuggee* was now worthy of attention; his qualities of leadership were unmistakable and his influence was beginning to grow.

"The white man asked us to give up all runaway slaves," Holata Mico reported. "He then said the agent would return any of our slaves from the whites. He also said our young men go to the settlements and steal from the whites. That must be stopped. The young men must be kept within our boundaries."

There was a pause long enough for Osceola to speak without interrupting Holata Mico. Presently the young man said, "This is true. Perhaps I can keep the young men from going to the settlements. Many will obey me."

"It is good. The whites also wanted to establish a white man's school. There was much talk about this."

"That is not good," Osceola said sharply. "We want no school."

"They were told that. They also want us to visit a country far to the west. If we want to live there, they will give us part of it."

"And what was said?" Osceola asked.

"We said first that we wanted to have the Big Swamp as our property forever, not just for moving again. We said our present land was poor. As for the country beyond the Big River toward the setting sun, we said we would not go there. It is not our place. Tuckose Emathla told them that here our navel strings were cut, and the blood from them sunk into the earth and made the country dear to us. We would not leave our home."

"It is good," Osceola said. "There has been enough moving."

"We said we would not prevent whites from coming into our country and taking their runaway slaves, but we wanted our slaves held by whites returned to us. We also said we would not let the young men go among the whites, that it was not our wish to disturb our white neighbors but to live with them in friendship. And finally we said we did not wish a school. If the Great Spirit had intended we should read and write, he would have given us the knowledge as early as he gave it to the white man." [12]

"I believe I can control many of our young men," Osceola repeated thoughtfully. "They are angry and many are hungry. In all of this, great brother, there are three cores to the fruit. The problem of the slaves will answer itself. If the white man is honorable, he cannot expect us to return slaves when he refuses to make the white man give back those taken from our people. The school is not of much matter. You cannot force the bird to be a bear; you cannot force the Indian to learn the white reading. It will pass.

"But there are three things of importance. The hunger must be stopped. The young men must not harm the whites or steal the white man's property. That will simply bring the white man's warriors upon us. Most of all, there must be no talk of moving beyond the Big River. Why should we move if we give no harm? As for me, I have moved enough!"

Others who heard Holata Mico's account of the Washington trip included Hitchiti Mico, Catsha Tustenuggee, Char Char Tusnusk, and Cheti Haiola, all of whom had decided to live in Big Swamp or Ouithlocko. Nearby or within a distance of about forty miles were Micanopy, Abraham, Jumper at Wahoo Swamp, Yaha Hadjo and Arpeika at Okahumpki, Coa Hadjo at Negro Town, and Fuch-a-Lusti-Hadjo at Big Hammock.

Osceola and his small band of followers began their police duties around mid-June. His experience as a helper during the Green Corn rituals was useful to him; and he was also a persuasive speaker. In most instances of border violation, he was able to talk the offenders into obedience. A modern parallel would be the star athlete who can exert a powerful influence over delinquents because of prestige in sports.

In July, the police duty became formal for a few days. Agent Gad Humphreys had persuaded the Seminoles to elect a top chief. (Hicks [Tuckose Emathla] had been appointed by DuVal, not "elected" by his people.) Clearly, the government was less concerned about a democratic election than it was about having one leader with whom to deal.

The contestants were Hicks, the tall, handsome Mikasuki, and Micanopy, dark, fat, but a chief through hereditary right. Feelings ran high among the Indians, and Humphreys, fearing an outburst, called upon Colonel Brooke for two companies of troops. Osceola, meanwhile, busied himself with attempts to keep order at least among the Mikasukis. Presumably Jumper (Otee Emathla) was performing a similar function among Micanopy's followers, with help from Alligator (Halpatter-Tustenuggee), the chief warrior in Micanopy's band. Jumper was Micanopy's brother-in-law.

It could not have been an easy job. Lieutenant G. A. McCall later stated that three thousand Indians attended the conference.[13] But everything went off smoothly. Hicks won the election, after which a hundred warriors took part in the rattlesnake dance. Hicks was then inducted as supreme chief. His acceptance speech lasted for three hours.

However dramatic this show may have been, Hicks's election did little to calm the Seminoles. Many were very nearly starved, raids on the cattle of whites became numerous, there were even several murders. White settlers kept loaded guns handy at all times and called desperately on DuVal for protection.

There was another side to the coin, however. During this period, whites repeatedly entered the Indian reserve on slave-catching expeditions. One chief was forced to give up twenty of his slaves, others were robbed in a similar manner. The Indian, John Blunt, was beaten and robbed of several hundred dollars.

Cattle thieves also preyed on the Indians, often turning them against their neighbors. These white men, who based their operations in rum shops bordering the reservation, would watch for likely prospects among Seminoles who strayed over the boundaries. A good candidate was an Indian who drank and wanted more. (Providing liquor for Indians was not an American innovation; the English and Spanish had poured freely when it suited their purposes.)

The cattle thief would propose to his selected Indian that he drive the cattle of a neighboring Seminole to a chosen spot outside or inside the boundary line. There the Indian would be paid with a quart or two of rum. Seminoles were also induced to steal stock from whites for similar payments in liquor.[14]

They were also accused of stealing stock for their own use. To these charges, they often protested that cattle they were said to take were the same cattle whites had stolen from *them.* In the words of one writer of the period, the Seminoles were "mild and forbearing . . . under the most trying circumstances." If they were attacked by renegade whites, they could not resist without inviting severe punishment. To make matters worse, the Indians had no recourse to white law—however bad it might be. The evidence of an Indian could not be accepted in court, but the oath of an illiterate, drunken white could doom the Seminole to eventual death in a jail or the dungeons of St. Augustine.[15]

Osceola, of course, knew the scales of justice were weighted in favor of the white. Thus, much of his police duty consisted of preventing trouble that could only doom the Indian troublemaker—even when the trouble was justified from the Indian viewpoint and, in fact, from any reasonable consideration.

Late in 1826, an event of great personal significance took place in Osceola's life. The year has been chosen arbitrarily because the time fits quite well into subsequent events.

Osceola was twenty-two years of age. One day, while visiting a village near the Seminole agency, he paused to refresh himself with a gourd of water. Glancing up, he saw a young, remarkably beautiful girl of Creek ancestry. Cohen called her "particularly pretty." [16] Sprague says her name was Che-cho-ter (Morning Dew).[17] No record of her clan exists, as nearly as the writers can determine. She was probably about fifteen years of age at the time, slim and possessed of the magnificent figure of the Seminole-Creek young woman.

Osceola was literally overwhelmed by this girl. (Che-cho-ter was certainly delighted by the obvious interest on the part of the famous athlete.) Neither said anything; that would have been improper. But Osceola promptly set in motion the procedures that would lead to marriage.

We do not know exactly how this was handled in Osceola's case, because we have no record of his relatives at the time. Under normal circumstances, he would have told relatives of his choice. They, in turn, would have contacted Che-cho-ter's family who would have discussed the suit with the girl. If the girl was willing, gifts would have been exchanged. Then, on the marriage night, Osceola would have gone to the girl's home to be received by his bride. On the following day, they would be considered husband and wife.

After living with the wife's family for a while, the couple would establish their own home—anywhere except among the husband's relatives.[18] However casual this marriage ceremony may have been, the family life of married couples was a warm one. There is every reason to believe that Osceola and Che-cho-ter loved each other deeply; she even joined him in prison years later. At that unhappy time, Osceola asked for his family—the act of a deeply affectionate man.

Of more than parenthetical interest, the Seminole wife was a remarkably "liberated" woman. Some writers of the period saw her only as a drudge, subject to her husband's whims, but they confused work with domestic slavery. The average white woman of the time worked quite as hard, but was less visible because she was usually indoors. Moreover, she had fewer rights.

Che-cho-ter could have refused her suitor, a right not extended to many white girls whose parents really chose the husband. All of her own property, and indeed the household possessions, belonged to the Indian wife. In-law problems were unknown to her; she was even forbidden to live with the husband's family. As mentioned earlier, heredity followed the female line. If a marriage failed, the partners simply separated, children being retained by the wife and her family.

Women were isolated during childbirth and menstruation, and were surrounded by other taboos. Although permitted to listen to tribal councils, they could not participate in decisions. Widows were obliged to mourn for years, but eventually they could marry again. There is some indication that infanticide was permitted during the first month after birth, although this was probably a means of disposing of weak or deformed infants who could not survive in the wilderness. Seminole women deeply loved their children but never pampered them.

It is unfortunate that so little is known about the family of Che-cho-ter, for Osceola certainly lived with them during the early months of marriage. They must have been of some importance, and the reported beautiful appearance of the girl suggests that they were reasonably comfortable—probably of superior hereditary level. The authors of this book think Che-choter may have been a member of a Mikasuki family. As nearly as they can determine, the name is closer in sound to Hitchiti than to Muskogee. And there is some additional evidence stemming from Osceola's close affiliation in later years with Mikasuki bands. Although all Seminoles rallied around Osceola when he became a Seminole leader, the Mikasuki affiliation was the strongest.

The year 1827 brought no improvements over earlier years. In January, the legislative council of the Territory passed a singularly vicious law that said if any Indian ventured to roam or "ramble" beyond the reservation boundaries, a citizen could arrest him and take him before a justice of the peace who was *required* to punish the offender with up to thirty-nine lashes, and take away his gun.

Unhappily, Agent Gad Humphreys is not adequately portrayed by writers of his time. From the available evidence, he was a tough, clear-minded man of high intelligence and unusual sympathy for the Seminoles he was supposed to guide. He also had a fine temper. When he heard about the lashing law, he wrote a furious letter to Indian Affairs Superintendent McKenney in which he said:

> Carry this law into effect and war in reality may be expected sooner or later to follow as a consequence: indeed, if I may take the word of a member of the council, such consequence was calculated upon by that body, when the bill was under consideration. "For," said he . . . "it is found

> impossible to bring them to negotiate for a removal from the territory, and the only course, therefore, which remains for us to rid ourselves of them, is to adopt such a mode of treatment towards them, as will induce them to acts that will justify their expulsion by force."

To which the furious Humphreys added bitterly, "This, sir, is the benevolent language of an *enlightened* American legislator." [19]

Osceola certainly heard of this remarkable law. To Holata Mico, he must have said, "Any white who tries to whip me will never again see the rising sun!" Humphreys knew this clearly; so did McKenney, who was shocked to the bones. He wrote DuVal, who said the law would not be enforced. This may not have been entirely true; in his letter Humphreys had told McKenney that an Indian had been whipped to death. A citizen had done this—something McKenney feared.

Humphreys was even angrier by March 6, when he wrote DuVal:

> . . . the condition of the Indians of this nation is one of great suffering from hunger. There is not at this moment . . . in the whole nation a bushel of corn, or any adequate substitute for it. The coutee and briar root [Koonti] . . . are entirely consumed. For nearly a year past they have been compelled to rely mainly upon these, and the cabbage tree [the cabbage palm, which has an edible core], for sustenance of the vegetable kind. . . .
>
> On an occasion when a party was sent to collect stragglers, it gathered a number, among whom was a female far advanced in pregnancy. When a return march to headquarters took place, this helpless and unpitied woman was forced onward with such precipitancy as to produce a premature delivery, which was near terminating her life.

With bitter scorn and fury that summed up the entire treatment of the Seminoles, Humphreys added, "Truly, this is the most extraordinary lesson in humanity for a civilized nation to place before a people whose barbarism we so loudly and freely condemn." [20]

Humphreys was by now so angry and shocked that he no longer addressed his superiors politely, an oversight that would eventually contribute to his dismissal. He saw clearly that the white man could match or even exceed persons of other races in brutality, a characteristic frightfully demonstrated in later years at Custer's Washita massacre (1868), at Wounded Knee Creek (1890), and in the Vietnam of recent years.

Colonel Duncan L. Clinch had been given command of all military forces in Florida on January 4, 1827. (He was promoted to brigadier general in 1829.) He promptly ordered Fort King to be built near the Seminole agency, and sent Captain Glassell (see Chapter 1) to perform this task. As indicated earlier, the fort was closed on July 3, 1829, then reopened in July, 1832.

During the period when the fort was open, Osceola was a frequent visitor. He also spent a great deal of time at the agency where he became friendly with the troubled Gad Humphreys.

One morning, while Osceola was at the agency, a messenger arrived with news that three Indians had violated a boundary on the eastern side of the reservation. They had also killed some stock belonging to a white settler. When Humphreys explained what had happened, Osceola nodded and said briefly, "We can take care of this."

Hurrying to the village of Holata Mico, he asked for the services of eight warriors. The chief agreed that the renegades should be captured and told Osceola to pick his own men. After the selection had been made, the party set off at a fast pace toward the east.

Beyond the Oklawaha River (later called by Sidney Lanier "the sweetest water-lane in the world"), they smelled woodsmoke and quickly approached the source. Three Mikasukis were camped in a small glen. Osceola divided his party and surrounded the Mikasukis, then walked into the camp alone. The surprised Indians grabbed for their guns.

"No, brothers," Osceola said calmly. He gave a curious, high-pitched cry that was immediately echoed from the north, east, and south. "Put down your guns. If you kill me, you will all die at once. Now sit on the ground with your guns pointed away."

When his order had been obeyed, he smiled and asked, "Brothers, did you kill cattle beyond our country?"

"It is true," one of the Mikasukis replied. "We hungered."

"That was not a good thing to do." Osceola seated himself in front of the men and addressed them as if speaking to children. "My warriors and I must take you to the agency where you will be punished. If you hungered, you could have gone to the western water to catch fish."

Gad Humphreys, desperate over the plight of his charges, had permitted fishing in the Gulf of Mexico beyond the reservation boundary. This was a violation of the treaty, but Humphreys and even DuVal were willing to bend the law in a time of serious privation. Small fishing parties were constantly leaving the reservation to camp on the shores of Vacassa (Waccasassa) Bay and Crystal Bay.

Osceola's men herded the renegades back to the agency where Humphreys met them more in sorrow than anger. How should they be punished? If their guns were taken away, they would surely starve. If turned over to white justice, they would be lashed and perhaps imprisoned at St. Augustine. Prison would be a virtual death sentence.

"They say they hungered," Osceola told the agent. "A man who hungers is sick. Let their chief punish them, good brother. Let the white man who suffered be paid from the Indian money. He lost three cows and this is not much. Let my white brothers be merciful."

Humphreys agreed. On numerous occasions, Osceola performed this task of capturing offenders—usually Mikasukis. Cohen wrote:

> By his boldness and energy, he always succeeded in bringing them in to receive punishment for offences committed—latterly he would beg them off. . . . The U.S. officers, as well as the Indians, all looked to Osceola to secure offenders—knowing his resolution and prowess. And for this purpose, as well as to restrain the Seminoles within their limits, he has taken more pains, and endured more fatigue, than any four of the Indians put together.[21]

The year 1828 was marked by the departure of Colonel Brooke from Florida, and the arrival at Tampa Bay of Colonel Clinch. During 1829, Gad Humphreys predictably fell out of favor with the authorities and the white settlers because of his constant defense of Indian rights. The hatchet descended in 1830 after Andrew Jackson became President. John Phagan, a man of dubious merit, took over Humphreys' job. McKenney was also removed as Superintendent of Indian Affairs in 1830, and was not replaced until 1832.

When news of the Removal Act of May 28, 1830, reached the Seminoles, they simply did not know what to make of it. There had been much talk of removal to the country beyond the Mississippi, but the Seminoles had never agreed to the idea. The concept had always been represented as a matter of choice—a decision to be made by the Indians themselves. Now they were being compelled to agree to the government's wishes. To make matters worse, the White Father in Washington was the same Andrew Jackson against whom many of the Seminoles had fought.

"Is it not true," Osceola asked the new agent, Phagan, "that the treaty at Moultrie Creek was to last for twenty years? Only seven of those years have passed."

"I was not there," Phagan replied.

"But is it not true?"

Phagan shrugged, spat, and turned away. How was it possible to explain to a mere Indian that the great United States government could change its mind, could make or break treaties at will? Phagan, moreover, agreed that all Indians should be removed from Florida. He was entirely lacking in compassion or ability; Sprague said of him:

> Though totally unqualified, both by education and morals, as an example and an adviser, he nevertheless bore an important part in the measures adopted during his period of office to expel the Indians. . . . Complaints had been frequently made by the chiefs of his brutal treatment of their people, and his total disregard to their demands for justice and protection.[22]

Osceola certainly believed, during 1831, that the white man could not conceivably go back on his word. Even his old enemy, Andrew Jackson, would never break a solemn treaty made between the great white government and the Seminoles. The sun did not rise in the west; agreements were not broken casually.

Osceola had sound reasons for not wishing even to consider the idea of moving. He was fairly comfortable at his home in the fertile portion of Big Swamp. He could find game where others failed, he could raise a few vegetables. The whites liked him; his beautiful wife literally adored him. Most important of all, he now had a lovely little daughter, the first of four children. This child was Osceola's delight. It would be unthinkable to take the mother and child to a strange and perhaps hostile country.

But more trouble was in the making. On January 30, 1832, James Gadsden was ordered to treat with the Seminoles with respect to moving them west of the Mississippi. Gadsden had negotiated and signed the Moultrie Creek treaty; now he would be the white man's representative in violating it. There is no indication that this ever bothered him. He was probably even pleased that he would receive the large per diem pay of eight dollars. In addition, he would get eight dollars for every twenty miles of travel, a well-paid secretary, and travel pay for this assistant. Forty cents a mile for travel! It paid to be Andrew

Jackson's friend, and it is little wonder that Gadsden rushed toward his Indian conference at the pace of a turtle. The meeting did not take place until early May.

The conference site was Payne's Landing on the Oklawaha River northeast of Fort King. We know that Osceola attended at the head of thirty or forty warriors—admirers who had performed police service with him. He was present as a *tustenuggee*, not a chief, and his duty was to keep order. Cohen said Osceola and his warriors were posted "nearer to the Colonel's position than the other Indians" and reported Osceola as saying he was more like the white man than they.[23] Was this a reference to his white blood? Perhaps. But it seems more likely that he was referring to his record of cooperation with the whites.

The conference was a mess. At Moultrie Creek, Gadsden had kept at least some minutes of the discussion, but at Payne's Landing he kept no minutes at all. One wonders what the secretary, a mysterious Douglas Vass, was up to—at five dollars per diem. His name appears on the treaty, but that seems to have been his sole contribution. He could easily have kept a record of the discussions: Three interpreters were present, a Stephen Richards who had been at Moultrie Creek, and the two Negroes, Abraham and Cudjo. Oddly enough, the agency sutler, Erastus Rogers, was along as a witness. Rogers' main claim to historical fame is that he was murdered some years later. Someone named B. Joscan was also present; he is even more obscure than Rogers.

John Phagan was also at Payne's Landing, but this was certainly a curious delegation to negotiate or witness an important treaty: James Gadsden, the "totally unqualified" Phagan, an obscure secretary, a wilderness storekeeper, Richards—about whom little is known, and Joscan—who is a mystery man.

There is not even a clear record of the names of all chiefs and subchiefs who were present. Fifteen chiefs signed the treaty and we know that Osceola was at least present, if not qualified to sign, but many important names are missing. Just on the basis of Potter's list of Seminole chiefs and subchiefs, twenty-one top Seminoles did not sign.[24] Moreover, Potter's list is far from complete.

The important part of the treaty appeared at the very beginning. The key sentence is long and indigestible, but the sense was this: The Seminole Indians agreed to send a party of chiefs to examine the country assigned to the Creeks west of the Mississippi, and should "they" be satisfied with the country the subsequent articles for removal would be binding. The trick word was "they." Who were "they," the nation or the investigating chiefs? Either this was a slip in wording or an attempt to fix all responsibility for agreement on the Indians chosen for the delegation. The former is probably true; Gadsden knew perfectly well that no delegation could make a decision for the entire Seminole nation.

The articles themselves were clear enough. Osceola listened with growing anger as they were interpreted. The first stated that the Seminoles would relinquish all claim to the land they occupied, would emigrate to the land assigned to the Creeks west of the Mississippi, and would become part of the Creek nation. To Osceola, indeed to most of the Seminoles, nothing could have been more shocking. They were being asked to give up their identity and rejoin a people against whom they had fought!

For this (Article 2), they would receive $15,400 for their Florida reservation and any improvements they had made on it. Like a carrot dangling in front of the horse's nose, the money would be paid on their arrival in the west. Abraham and Cudjo would get handouts of $200 each.

When they reached Creek territory (Article 3), each Seminole would be given a blanket and a homespun frock. In addition to annuities described in the Moultrie Creek treaty, the nation would receive $3,000 a year for fifteen years. But these sums would be added to the Creek annuities, the whole amount to be divided between Creeks and Seminoles *as members of the Creek Confederation.*

Article 5 stated that Seminole cattle would be paid for "at the valuation of some discreet person." Claims against the Seminoles (Article 6) for slaves and property allegedly stolen by them would be liquidated up to the amount of $7,000. Finally (Article 7), they would remove within three years, starting in 1833. The first group to be removed would be the Seminoles occupying the Big Swamp.

This was the amazing document signed by the fifteen chiefs and subchiefs. Micanopy later said he never made his mark on the treaty; Charley Emathla said the signers were "forced." Some of the signers may have pretended they were the persons designated on the treaty, although this is unlikely.

Ethan Allen Hitchcock, an Army officer, later stated that Abraham had been bribed to misinterpret the first article.[25] Hitchcock had good evidence, and the special payments to Abraham and Cudjo are truly mysterious. Gadsden himself later said the Indians were *induced* to sign the treaty. We do not know how, but everything about this document has a fishy aspect. It is inconceivable, as almost every historian has pointed out, that the chiefs would agree to an arrangement under which the Seminoles joined the Creeks. If coercion was used, it must have been verbal. We know Gadsden made some threats, but because of the lack of records there is no clear account of what he said.

The delegation chosen to inspect the land west of the Mississippi consisted of Jumper (Otee Emathla), Fuch-a-Lusti-Hadjo (Black Dirt), Charley Emathla, Coa Hadjo, Holata Emathla, Yaha Hadjo, and Arpeika (Sam Jones). They would be accompanied by Abraham, the interpreter, and John Phagan. (Arpeika was later replaced by John Hicks, Fuch-a-Lusti-Hadjo by Nehathoclo.) Their experiences will be described in Chapter 5.

Osceola left Payne's Landing in silence and alone. Everything about this tentative treaty was foul. To move among the Creeks—impossible! He seethed with rage when he thought of the white government's magnanimous gift—a blanket and a frock! He now knew enough about the white man's money to realize that $15,400 was no price for more than four million acres, however poor. To make matters worse, he and the others in Big Swamp would be removed first.

Why the urgency for removing the Big Swamp Indians? Osceola could not have known the reason, but it appears clearly in a letter written in 1835 by John H. Eaton to Lewis Cass, then Secretary of War. Eaton had placed DuVal as governor of Florida. On March 8, he wrote in part: ". . . the Big Swamp, which in the treaty is declared to be the first of their country to be vacated . . . is that on which the eyes of speculators are fixed. . . ." [26]

The passage offers damning evidence of what was really going on. If Gadsden phrased the treaty himself, he must have known about the speculators' intended land grab. And if the government had given Gadsden a prepared script for the treaty, as many authorities believe, then the United States was guilty of playing into the hands of the speculators. Neither alternative is a pleasant one.

As he walked home from Payne's Landing, Osceola considered another troubling thought. He owned no slaves, but he was deeply sympathetic toward all Negroes among the Seminoles. Any Seminole slaves, free Negroes, or runaways stood in danger of being seized during removal. Osceola was no abolitionist and would not have understood clearly the meaning of the word, but he knew the value of freedom. Abraham was a friend, so were Cudjo and many others. Emigration would doom them to enslavement by the whites.

He stopped at a creek to refresh himself and consider his own future. The heart of the matter rested on what the delegation found during its visit to the territory west of the Mississippi. The conditional aspect of the treaty had not escaped him; the

Seminole nation would only act after hearing the delegation's report. The nation would have to be satisfied with the description of the country. If not, there could be no removal.

Meanwhile, it would be reasonable to remain on good footing with the whites. Nothing would be gained by angering them. If a time came for fighting, then there would be fighting. But until then, cooperation was still the best policy.

5

Osceola Declares War for the Seminoles

During the early summer of 1832, Fort King, closed since 1829, was reoccupied by Company D, Fourth Infantry. When the soldiers moved in, they found the place a shambles. Chimneys had collapsed, some of the wood had rotted, rats were camped under floors, and the general condition was so bad that the officer in charge of repairs estimated that repairs would involve two months' work for thirty soldiers. A soldier could earn fifteen cents a day at this extra duty.

Osceola would sometimes rise before dawn to slip through the woods and watch the day begin at Fort King. On these dark mornings, with the last of the moonlight spilling on the trail, the forest was pungent with the cool, wet odor of leaf mold. Dew dripped from the leaves to settle heavily on the underbrush. The wolves, gaunt with hunger, had stopped their nightly howling, but sometimes a rare fox barked sharply or an alligator bellowed from a swamp.

As dawn whitened the eastern sky, a single bird would scream shrilly to be answered in moments by others. Squirrels began to chatter in the pines. From behind the store of Erastus Rogers, a rooster crowed bravely, paused to scratch the wet dirt, crowed again. Dogs at the fort, the agency, or the sutler's store howled and barked, then shrieked when someone beat them into silence.

Osceola's only weapon on these early morning visits was his knife, for there was no game near the fort and thus no reason for a rifle. He carried tobacco and pipe in a neckerchief; flint, steel, and tinder in the twist of another. But the usual way to obtain a light was to take coal from an existing fire. He had seen the magic English fire stick, invented five years earlier; this convenience, however, was still rare. Flint, steel, and a pinch of gunpowder on tinder served adequately when a fire was not available.

As a Seminole of increasing importance, Osceola dressed carefully for these visits to Fort King. His knee-length dress-frock bore an intricate floral design and was caught at the waist with a sash. Ornamented garters held up his leggings, and he often wore plumes in his turban. The Seminole Indian, dressed for a visit or a meeting, was an imposing figure; and Osceola, perhaps the most handsome of all, was no exception. (It is true, however, that Seminoles seen on their permitted visits to towns were sometimes ragged, beggarly, and filthy. But as portraits of the period indicate clearly, slovenly appearance was not characteristic of the Indian. Seminoles delighted in sweat baths; moreover, their pleasure in ornamentation and the neat moustaches of many of the men—rare among American Indians—suggest their pride in personal appearance. White settlers, who sometimes knew water only when drenched by rain, were far more offensive.)

Osceola, watching the dawn slowly outline Fort King, was aware of its distinctive smell. Soldiers were obliged to bathe with some regularity and wash their clothing; many, in fact, enjoyed swimming when an opportunity presented itself. But there was always an odor of too many men packed into limited space. This was mixed with the smell of woodsmoke, horses, stale cooking, and sometimes the baking of bread. The latter was pleasant, for the white man's bread (*tuggilaggi* or *toklike*) was vastly better than Koonti bread, or *sofkee.*

Osceola knew that the white warriors always did everything according to signals or commands. Although he did not clearly understand the fat gold watches so frequently consulted by white officers, he realized they played some mysterious part in starting the day, rousing the cooks, getting the bugle blown or a drum rattling.

The soldiers rose together, dressed alike, ate when ordered to do so. As the day progressed, they drilled obediently or labored in the sun with hammers, mallets, saws, and double-bitted axes until permitted to rest. At last tattoo sounded and all but the sentries slept. With few variations, the routine was followed day after day.

To an Indian, this was strange behavior, but Osceola began to appreciate its merits. Men who worked as a unit finished jobs. When they fought on command, something Osceola had not yet seen, it was reasonable to assume that their strength would be greater. If Seminoles were ever to fight the white man, they would first have to learn obedience.

Why did white warriors obey their leaders? Part of it was fear, of course. A disobedient white warrior would be punished severely—confined in a hot pen or even made to straddle a log for hours in the burning sun. Insects would swarm over him until blood ran from the red bites and he screamed to have his hands freed from the bonds beneath the log. Osceola had once poured water over a soldier who was riding the log, the man's eyes had thanked him, and no one had interfered.

But why did the soldiers suffer such debasing punishment, why did they even submit without protest to the monotonous daily routine? There were more soldiers than officers who gave commands. Ten soldiers, twenty soldiers, could easily overpower the few officers. What kept them from doing it? Did the officers have some rare medicine, some mysterious power not given to their soldiers? Osceola believed in the spirit power of medicine; you gave yourself good medicine by believing that it entered you, or it passed to you through the mysterious words of the medicine man.

The medicine of strength and power came to some but not to others. Osceola knew he had been given the gift, and perhaps this was also true of the white officers. But was there more? Perhaps their power to command came from the fact that they knew more about fighting than their men. They had been taught what to do and the men, knowing this, obeyed their leaders. Leaders were obliged to think of results and how to achieve them; the white warrior's job was simply to obey. You became a leader by watching and learning.

Some of the actions of the white soldiers seemed senseless, of course. Osceola, drawn closer every day to the life of Fort King, began to ask questions. The officers, who liked him for his smile, good manners, and obvious intelligence, tried to provide sensible answers.

"Why do you sometimes walk all together?" Osceola once asked Lieutenant Joseph W. Harris while the troops were drilling.

When this was translated, Harris replied, "To keep the men together."

"But this wouldn't be good in the forest," Osceola protested. Laughing, he imitated a marching soldier and the barking commands of the drillmaster. The performance, ending with an about-face and a perfect salute, was excellent mimicry.

"We wouldn't do that in the forest," Harris said, grinning.

"Then why do it at all?"

"We really only do it for parading in front of people."

"But why is that important?"

The questions were numerous and the answers often difficult to understand. Osceola wanted to know why soldiers sometimes stood in lines to move their weapons into senseless positions. No warrior in battle would ever go through such meaningless motions.

"To teach them to shoot together," Harris explained.

"At the sky?" Osceola asked, smiling.

"Well, no." In the time-honored explanation of the manual of arms, Harris added, "To make them familiar with their weapons."

"Strange! Don't they understand their muskets? I know my rifle."

"It's difficult to explain," Harris said patiently. "Listen, my friend, they say you're a mighty wrestler. We have an Irishman who's good, too. Will you wrestle him for sport?"

Osceola's expressive dark eyes brightened. "Gladly, brother. But what's an Irishman?"

"A man from beyond the Great Water. An Englishman who speaks a different kind of English. White men talk in many different ways."

"Do they also have interpreters?"

"Some of them do."

"Ho! Then they are like the Indian!"

The match with the Irishman took place on a warm evening after the soldiers had finished mess. Such bouts were common in the civilian world as well as the Army; at about the time Osceola was wrestling at Fort King, a tall, rawboned young man named Abraham Lincoln was struggling with Jack Armstrong in the frontier town of New Salem, Illinois. The style of wrestling among whites and Indians throughout America was based primarily on strength and a "no-holds-barred" technique.

Soldiers from Fort King formed a crude circle in the open area beyond the entrance gates. Seminole men joined the group, and as Osceola stripped to the waist the soldiers and Indians wagered knives, trinkets, and money on the two contestants. There was no referee except the crowd itself; victory in such matches was established by the reaction of the audience.

Osceola's opponent was a powerful individual with a mat of red hair on his chest, and arms that looked as thick as an average man's thighs. He towered over Osceola, who looked frail by comparison. But some of the officers and several of the soldiers, seeing the trim, muscular development of the Seminole contestant, began placing their bets at excellent odds.

"Get the sun to your back, Red!" someone yelled to the Irishman. "He cain't move fast lookin' at the sun!"

Osceola was also aware of the sun glare above the trees. He circled cautiously, moving almost like a dancer while his opponent plodded toward him. Trick holds were almost unknown in this frontier wrestling; tripping was common and various throat holds were used, but balance and strength were more important than holds. Thus Osceola and the soldier gripped each other at arms' length, tested strength, broke apart, gripped again.

Suddenly their hands locked. Each man now tried to force the other off balance. The soldier's huge arm muscles bulged like ropes as he grunted and tried to force Osceola's arms down to waist level, but the Indian stood like a rock. Sweat began to gleam on the faces of both men.

When Osceola took a backward step, the soldier, encouraged, thrust forward abruptly with all his weight. Moving like a cat, Osceola slipped beneath his opponent's arm and seized him from in back. There was a sudden frenzy of twisting before the two men crashed to the ground, Osceola on top.

He leaped away quickly, preferring to use his agility in a crouching position. The soldier, rising, lunged for Osceola's legs, but the Indian jumped away. Again, the wrestlers circled and gripped for a hold. Once again, they locked hands and tried for leverage.

Minutes passed before Osceola fell back abruptly, drawing the soldier down in the same motion. Before the big man knew what had happened, he was twisted over on his back and pinned. Osceola held him for a moment, then jumped free. A few minutes later, he won a second fall and the bout was over.

Lieutenant Harris, who had bet on the soldier, wondered how

a man weighing no more than 185 pounds could win at wrestling an opponent of at least 220 pounds. No unusual tricks had been used but Osceola had won the second fall easily. When an interpreter asked the lieutenant's question, Osceola smiled and dropped to his knees. He pointed at the ground. Harris, bending down, saw an ant carrying a large beetle.

"He wants to win his prize," Osceola said simply. "So do I."

In the days to come, officers respected him so much that he was sometimes asked to capture the desperate, pitiful deserters who chose escape in the dreaded forests to the daily life of hard work, discipline, low pay, and a diet of stringy beef or rancid pork, bread, bitter coffee, wormy beans or potatoes, and very little more. Molasses for sweetening. A rum ration while the rum lasted. (Alcohol had not yet been disallowed, and was never successfully banned from frontier posts.) If an Army traveled on its stomach, Washington officials had not yet heard about it.

Osceola tracked deserters much as he hunted down Indian renegades.[1] He had no compunction about performing this service; the white runaways had broken their law and thus, by Indian standards, were subject to the justice of their own people. If the sickness of lawbreaking endangered the Indian, so it also endangered the total welfare of the white group. It was no matter who captured the white offender; the job had to be done. When an Indian could do it more effectively, so much the better. Moreover, the white officers, at least in the microcosm of Fort King, were good people—even fine friends.

The chiefs selected for the land inspection party to Arkansas Territory had not yet left their villages. Nothing had changed greatly and, whatever the case, the inspecting chiefs would never report that the Seminoles might be happier west of the Great River than in their Florida homeland. When they told the Seminole nation that the western reservation was unsatisfactory, that would be the end of the whole matter of removal. So it seemed to Osceola during 1832 while he observed the white soldiers, played at their games, won their sincere friendship.

The Seminole inspection party did not set out for Arkansas Territory until early October. No one today really knows why, but it must have had something to do with the gathering of the scanty summer crops or, more probably, government interest in other removal problems. Indians in the special Apalachicola reservations were to be moved, and some dealings with the Creeks required negotiations.

When the Seminole reservation delegates finally left, the seven Indians were accompanied by Agent John Phagan and the Negro interpreter Abraham, a remarkable man. He was of ordinary stature and somewhat slim, shrewd in appearance and soft-spoken.[2] Abraham was a diplomat as well as an interpreter, and there has always been a serious question about whose interests he served during this and earlier periods of Seminole negotiations. In the kindest evaluation, he was a manipulator who eventually fought with great competence on the Seminole side.

Whatever the case, the Seminole party examined the proposed reservation and, on March 28, 1833, signed an additional treaty at Fort Gibson, Arkansas Territory. This said that the delegates, on behalf of their nation, "hereby declare themselves well satisfied with the location provided for them . . . and agree that their nation shall commence the removal to their new home as soon as the government will make arrangements. . . ."

This document was amazing on several counts. First, the seven chiefs had no authority to speak for all Seminoles. Their job was to evaluate the new country, then report on it back in Florida. Secondly, three of them denied later that they actually had signed the Fort Gibson treaty.

Further, someone tampered with the wording of the Payne's Landing Treaty. This document had said, "and should *they* be satisfied with the character of that country," the word "they" being interpreted by the Indians to mean the Seminole nation.

In the Fort Gibson treaty, this passage was changed to read, "and should *this delegation* be satisfied with the character of the country." No one knows to this day who changed the wording except some historians are inclined to ascribe the action to Phagan.

Among the whites present, including three government commissioners, Phagan was the only one who stood to gain. The next to the last paragraph in the Fort Gibson treaty said the commissioners recommended Phagan as a suitable person to be employed in removing the Seminoles. On the face of it, this seems harmless enough; but Phagan would have access to the funds used during removal. He would later be dismissed as agent in Florida for juggling accounts to his own financial benefit. Historian Mahon's deduction is that Phagan fooled both the Seminoles and the government commissioners at Fort Gibson, and this is far too logical for any serious disagreement.[3]

The delegation returned to Florida in April. When it finally became known that the members had signed the Fort Gibson treaty, they were derided and scorned. They could not very well say they had not understood what they were doing; that would have made them appear even greater fools. So they found excuses that may or may not have been true accounts.

"I never signed," Jumper told Osceola. "Neither did Coa Hadjo or Holata Emathla. I don't know how our marks got on the paper."

Charley Emathla, although agreeable to emigration, said the delegates had known perfectly well that they could not bind the entire Seminole nation. Jumper later made the curious statement that "the agents of the United States made us sign our hands to a paper." Contradictions of this sort were voiced repeatedly.

The remainder of 1833 was marked by three significant events. First, Agent John Phagan was dismissed as a result of accusations to the effect that he had altered Indian accounts in his favor. He was replaced by Wiley Thompson, who has been described in Chapter 1. Then, in November, John Hicks died. As a result of the Fort Gibson affair, he had already lost the respect of his people. Micanopy, who ranked highest on an hereditary basis, became the top chief.

Most important of all, the prestige of Osceola increased among the young men, almost all opposed to emigration, and even with the older chiefs and subchiefs. He began to exert a strong influence on Micanopy; in this he was joined by Abraham, Alligator (Halpatter-Tustenuggee), Jumper (Otee Emathla), Arpeika (Sam Jones), and a number of others whose names will appear as they become important.

At the same time, Osceola still maintained his friendly relationship with the whites. This is not as puzzling as it seems. The Seminole nation had not ratified the Fort Gibson treaty; thus Osceola considered it meaningless. Since in his view it was no more than a scrap of paper, it could not put into effect the provisional treaty drawn up at Payne's Landing. Even the white men in Washington had not said officially that it bound the Seminoles to any westward move. (The Fort Gibson treaty was not ratified until April, 1834.)

So Osceola continued his visits to Fort King, joked with the officers, sometimes even brought his pretty young daughter to be admired. There is evidence that later one of the officers gave her gifts.

With Phagan out of the picture, Captain William M. Graham became acting agent. He was a fine officer, but apparently not particularly active as Indian agent. When Wiley Thompson arrived on December 1, 1833, he was surprised to find the agency building occupied only by a handyman named Dunlap. (Thompson called him a "mechanic.") The lock to the office door was broken. Thompson pushed the door open and glanced at Phagan's files. Few records had been left behind by his predecessor, and Thompson was distressed by what he had learned on his way to the agency at the doors of Fort King. Liquor shops had proliferated around the borders of the reservation. These "trading stores" preyed on the Indians who were willing to sell almost anything for a bottle or two of rum[4]—the cheap trade rum that was cut with water and sometimes flavored with vinegar or even pine oil.

Thompson met Captain Graham, who promised to have a new lock put on the agency office door. Why the absence of a lock bothered Thompson is a mysterious footnote in history. The Indians could not read, Phagan was long gone, and no one in Florida could have been interested in dull official correspondence.

Lock or no lock, Graham was helpful in briefing the new agent. He told Thompson the Seminoles were on the verge of starvation, with the Mikasukis in particular distress. They were completely out of corn and beans.

"If we move them to Arkansas in 1834," he said, "we'd better get at it soon. They ought to be moved during winter or early spring, so they won't plant and gather another crop. But the government will have to supply them with rations if we are going to get the matter pushed along." [5]

John H. Eaton replaced DuVal as governor of Florida during April, 1834. In the same month, as noted earlier, both the Payne's Landing and Fort Gibson treaties were ratified and proclaimed by the President. When word of this action reached the Seminoles, they were literally dumbfounded. How could such a thing happen? *The Indian nation had not been consulted about moving!*

Osceola still maintained his friendly relations with the whites. But he met in secret with Alligator, Jumper, and various of the other leaders opposed to emigration. (There is abundant historical evidence of these meetings. Alligator even admitted to the planning conferences later.) [6]

Osceola was silent at the beginning of the first meeting. He stared at the ground, frowning slightly, and sometimes struck his right fist gently against the palm of his left hand. There was no sign of anger in his eyes; his expression, rather, was that of a man who has reached a troubling decision. Sometimes, as the others talked, he scratched aimlessly at the dust with a splinter of pine. At last, he jabbed it through a leaf and began to speak in a quiet, controlled voice.

"Brothers, all of the talk is good. But now we must prepare for the worst. First we must get all of our people to agree not to move. They must realize their blood may soak the earth. But we need to be joined as a people, just as the white soldiers come together under their leaders."

"Some of our chiefs are willing to emigrate," Alligator said. "Holata Emathla and his brother, Charley Emathla, believe in it. Fuch-a-Lusti-Hadjo said first he would not move. Now his mind is changing."

"We must try to persuade them. We must also persuade Micanopy to stand firm. Micanopy above all. Jumper can influence him."

"So can anyone," Jumper observed wryly. "We know of my kinsman's weakness. But Micanopy would rather die than move from his home. He will stand when others strengthen him."

"As we know, brother," Alligator agreed. "But words are not enough. Suppose the white warriors try to move us by force. Do we fight them?"

"If we must, we will fight," Osceola said. "And we should be ready to fight. Save all powder and lead, or as much as possible. When the annuities are paid in October, we must buy kegs of powder. I hope we don't have to fight the white man, but if it happens every one of our warriors will be ready. And our plans will be made."

On October 23, 1834, Agent Wiley Thompson convened a meeting at the agency. Of great historical consequence, this conference revealed how far Osceola had progressed in Seminole leadership. It was well reported, even to a secret meeting held by the Indians; the following account is a synthesis of the various stories.

The day was a Thursday. The Seminole chiefs gathered

within the agency building while lesser warriors crowded the porch or squeezed into the main room. Historian Cohen suggests that women were also on the porch; perhaps not, but at least they were close by and it is not difficult to imagine beautiful Che-cho-ter gazing solemnly toward the building where her husband had joined the chiefs. This day meant much to all Seminole women.

Among the whites present were Wiley Thompson, Captain Graham, and David Levy of St. Augustine, who aided history by taking some lively notes. Levy was later a territorial delegate in Congress. Captain J. B. F. Russell was also present as one who would assist in the projected removal.

Thompson began with a long speech, the tone of which suggested that he considered removal all but accomplished. He said first that the Creeks west of the Mississippi had invited the Seminoles "to settle promiscuously among them." (One wonders how Abraham, the interpreter, handled the word "promiscuously.") This drew groans and angry muttering from the Seminoles, a breach of Seminole etiquette so astonishing that Thompson later mentioned it in an official letter. The Indians deeply feared that the Creeks or white slave-catchers would claim their Negroes.

With unusual brevity for him, Thompson then outlined the proposition to be considered by the chiefs:

1. Will you accept the invitation of your brothers of the Western Creek nation?
2. Do you prefer cattle or money when you arrive at your new home, for the cattle which under the treaty you must give up here?
3. Will you petition to go by water, or do you prefer to go by land?
4. How will you have your next annuity paid to you, in money or in goods?

Thompson then said that if the chiefs wanted any further explanation, "I will attend you, give the desired explanation, and retire immediately, so as not to be an intruder on your private council. You are at liberty to retire."

Thompson had no need to "intrude" on a subsequent "private council," for he had arranged for a spy or spies to be present when the Indians met alone. The Seminoles left for their council grounds at Silver Springs. There, under the oaks and Spanish moss, they began their deliberations. Probably the women prepared whatever food was available, but this assembly was no occasion for feasting. The very life of the Seminole nation was at stake.

Shortly after 4:00 P.M., Osceola rose to address the people. Until now, he had chosen to remain behind the scenes, influencing others who did the talking. Moreover, Osceola was still only a subchief, or *tustenuggee,* so permission to speak must have been arranged with the approval of Micanopy. Dressed in full regalia, the plumes in his turban giving him additional height, Osceola was an impressive figure. Without doubt, he was aware of his commanding presence; we know from some of the old records that he thought enough of his appearance to own and use a looking glass—probably a scrap of mirror carefully protected by bark. Che-cho-ter was certainly present beyond the ring of warriors, and her dark eyes must have gleamed proudly as her man spoke to the nation.

"My brothers!" Osceola cried in his clear, strong voice. "The white people got some of our chiefs to sign a paper to give our lands to them; but our chiefs did not do as we told them to do. They did wrong; we must do right!

"The agent tells us we must go away from the lands which we live on, our homes, and the graves of our fathers, and go over the big river among bad Indians. When the agent tells me to go from my home. I hate him; because I love my home and will not go from it.

"My brothers! When the Great Spirit tells me to go with the white man, I go! But he tells me not to go! The white man says I shall go, and he will send people to make me go; but I have a rifle, and I have some powder and lead. I say we must not leave our homes and lands!

"If any of our people want to go west, we won't let them. I tell them they are our enemies, and we will treat them so, for the Great Spirit will protect us!"

Indians did not applaud speakers in the white manner. But as Osceola sat down, a low murmur like distant thunder began to run through the assembled warriors. It grew to a roar, then exploded in the sharp, barking "Ho!" that signified approval. A man had spoken what was in the minds of most of the people. There was a new voice among the Seminoles, a powerful voice that aroused their battered sense of pride. Were they not men? Then they would act like men!

Osceola's speech was that of a remarkably skilled politician. The chiefs had done wrong but "we must do right!" Osceola had spoken of leaving "the graves of our fathers," a compelling emotional argument calculated as such. He had brought in the religious aspect of obedience to the Great Spirit. Finally, he had made it clear that those who wished to emigrate would be stopped—as enemies.

Holata Emathla and Jumper protested the vigor of Osceola's speech, Jumper with secret reservations. He may have felt Osceola had gone too far, too openly. He may also have suspected the presence of spies who would carry every word back to Thompson.

But Arpeika, well past seventy years of age, slight, white-haired, and a prominent medicine man, concluded the meeting by saying angrily that he did not want to move and neither did the nation. That was what the agent must be told. Nothing else mattered.

The Indians assembled at Fort King the following day, October 24, 1834. Holata Mico (probably Blue King with whom Osceola was associated, although there was a second Holata Mico—Billy Bowlegs) offered a sort of invocation that was more touching than significant.

"We were all made by the same great Father and are alike his children. We all came from the same mother and were suckled at her breast. Therefore we are brothers, and as brothers should treat together in an amicable way, and should not quarrel and let our blood rise up against each other."

Micanopy spoke next. Osceola was seated beside the top chief, another indication of his new importance. Frequently he whispered advice to the chief. Micanopy said briefly, "When we were at Camp Moultrie we made a treaty, and we were to be paid our annuity for twenty years. That is all I have to say."

It was a good point. Jumper repeated it, then said the delegation sent to the west was only authorized to examine the country and report to the nation. The country, he admitted, was good, but surrounded by "bad and hostile neighbors." The delegates had been "forced" to sign the treaty, but "we considered we did no more than say we liked the land." Jumper concluded by saying, "My people cannot say they will go. If their tongues say yes, their hearts cry no and call them liars."

Charley Emathla mentioned that the Moultrie treaty still had seven years to go. (He was using the projected removal date of 1836.) He also stated that his people did not wish to leave Florida, and suggested a continuation of the meeting the following day.

Thompson concluded this session with an excited outburst that only served to insult the Indians. "When you come here again, come prepared to act like chiefs and honorable men; don't bring to me any more foolish talks. Men do not listen to the talk of a child; and remember that the talk I gave you must and will stand." With more patience, Thompson might have stopped the Second Seminole War during this meeting. But whatever virtues he may have had, restraint was not one of them, however "fatherly" he may sometimes have appeared.

On Saturday, Holata Mico opened the conference by saying he had never given his consent to go west. Jumper repeated that the Seminoles would not move until the Moultrie Creek treaty ended. And Micanopy said he had never signed the Payne's Landing Treaty.

"Abraham!" Thompson shouted at the interpreter. "Tell Micanopy I say he lies! He did sign the treaty for here is his name."

After this incredible insult, Thompson repeated that the Seminoles were obliged to go west. Still angry at Micanopy, he concluded by saying, "Micanopy doesn't tell the truth. He did sign the treaty at Payne's Landing."

"I did not touch the pen," Micanopy said. "I only reached over and pointed at it."

Thompson now launched into a long argumentative speech in which he said, essentially, that the Payne's Landing Treaty superseded the Moultrie Creek agreement, that the Indians were subject to white law, that they would be in a serious condition if they remained in Florida. "Your laws will be set aside; your chiefs will cease to be chiefs; claims for debts and for your Negroes would be set up against you by bad white men, or perhaps you would be charged with crimes affecting life . . . your condition in a very few years would be hopeless wretchedness."

At about this point in a tirade delivered at the top of his lungs, Thompson noticed Osceola whispering to Micanopy. This distraction caused him to lose his temper completely.

"I stand up for the last time to tell you that you must go!" he roared, "and if not willing you will be compelled to go! I should have told you that no more annuity will be paid to you here!"

Without bothering to rise, Osceola looked at the agent with what historian Cohen's source described as "withering scorn upon his upcurled lip." Clearly, the young Indian simply sneered at Thompson before saying something quietly. The sneer was for the agent's intemperate shouting.

"What did he say, Abraham?" Thompson cried.

"He says he doesn't care whether any more annuities are ever paid."

Thompson glared at Osceola, then finished his speech lamely with a threat to report the Indians to the President "as faithless to your engagements." He then sat down. He was startled to see Osceola rise from his seat beside Micanopy and step forward. Osceola raised his arm with fist clenched, then began what has been called his "Patrick Henry" speech.

"The sentiments of the nation have been expressed. There is little more to be said. The people in council have agreed. By their chiefs, they have uttered. It is well; it is truth, and must not be broken.

"When I make up my mind, I act. If I speak, what I say I will do. Speak or not speak, what I resolve that will I execute. The nation have consulted; have declared; they should perform. What should be, shall be. There remains nothing worth words.

"If the hail rattles, let the flowers be crushed. The stately oak of the forest will lift its head to the sky and the storm, towering and unscathed!"

There was a stunned silence. Osceola had virtually assumed leadership of the Seminole nation. Almost as one man, the chiefs turned toward Micanopy to see his reaction to this astonishing development. The chief rose slowly to his feet, then stared bleakly at Thompson, who was also rising.

"I do not intend to remove," Micanopy said simply.

Thompson managed to have the last word. He said, "I am now fully satisfied that you are willfully disposed to be entirely dishonest in regard to your engagements with the President, and regret that I must so report you. The talk I have made to you must and will stand. Retire and prepare your sticks to receive your annuity tomorrow." [7]

A man with greater vision than Thompson possessed would have realized he had just heard a declaration of war. But the idea of Seminoles fighting the United States was beyond this former militia officer's comprehension. Thompson now wanted further orders and, in accordance with past orders, he was willing to have the Seminoles prepare their tally sticks for the annuity division. Although the Seminoles could count, after the fashion of the Creeks, from one (*humpkin*) to 100 (*chopkihumpkin*) to 1,000 (*chopkithlucko*), it was customary to notch sticks to indicate the number of individuals in a band or to make other simple calculations. Sticks were also bundled sometimes for the same purpose, each stick representing one individual.

Thompson was apparently undisturbed a few days later when he observed that the Indians were buying unusually large quantities of powder and lead. Even whole kegs were purchased. To the Commissioner of Indian Affairs, Elbert Herring, Thompson wrote, "It may be proper to add that the chiefs and Negroes have a deposit of forty or fifty Kegs of powder, which I did not credit at the time."

President Jackson eventually read Thompson's report to Commissioner Herring, who had been appointed in 1832. He wrote, "Let a sufficient military force be forthwith ordered to protect our citizens and remove and protect the Indians agreeable to the Stipulations of the Treaty." [8]

In a way, this was another declaration of war.

6

Hostilities Begin

In his letter of October 28, 1834, Wiley Thompson had also told Commissioner Herring that Holata Emathla and Fuch-a-Lusti-Hadjo feared for their lives because of their general agreement to removal. The two chiefs had come to the agency secretly to say they and their families were in danger, and to plead for permission to visit friends far west on the Apalachicola River. Thompson lacked the authority to grant this request.

His views of Indian intentions shifted from month to month, ranging from pessimism to degrees of optimism. At this time, he felt the Seminoles were determined to resist the Payne's Landing agreement. He believed whites around the reservation had stirred up hostility to emigration among the Indians because they wanted to seize the Negroes in the Seminole country. If the Seminoles and their Negroes remained in Florida until the reservation came under territorial jurisdiction, it would be reasonably easy for fraudulent claimants to steal Indian Negroes through court actions.[1]

It was an ingenious argument, probably true at least in part. But as another thread in a perplexing situation, the Indian Negroes certainly did not want to move and were thus caught in a vise. Historian Sprague summed it up in clear, brief terms:

> The negroes exercised a wonderful control [of the situation]. They openly refused to follow their masters, if they removed to Arkansas. Many of them would have been reclaimed by the Creeks, to whom some belonged. Others would have been taken possession of by the whites, who for years had been urging their claims through the government and its agents. In Arkansas, hard labor was necessary for the means of support, while Florida assured them of every means to indulge in idleness, and enjoy an independence corresponding with their masters.[2]

Add to this the Seminoles' sincere affection for the Negroes among them, their love for their poor home, their fear of the Creeks; and one has all dimensions of the objection to removal.

The Indians remained outwardly peaceful during the remaining days of 1834, although Thompson's spies reported they were laughing at the idea that a handful of men at Fort King could compel them to remove. Osceola was not laughing, however. He knew clearly that the whites would bring in additional troops and that only a miracle could prevent an explosion. He still hoped for the miracle; meanwhile, however, he increased preparations for war by encouraging the storing of powder while maintaining outward friendship with the whites.

It was at about this time that Osceola married a second wife. As noted earlier, Seminole men could have two wives; and there is no question about the existence of this woman. Two wives were definitely present later in Osceola's life. Common sense suggests that he must have formed this second marriage prior to the outbreak of war. There is also circumstantial evidence in the writings of the contemporary historian, Cohen:

> Powell [Osceola] has two wives, as is common with the Indians, but they are rarely Trigamists. His two better halves live in perfect harmony, having one table in common, but occupying separate "lodges." They are both young and comely; one of them is particularly pretty [undoubtedly Che-cho-ter]. They yield passive obedience to his vigorous

intellect, and expressions which partake the character of his mind.[3]

It is regrettable that nothing more is known about this second wife. One of the most interesting suggestions is that she was part Negro. This seems to come primarily from the abolitionist Giddings via an antislavery magazine published in 1837.[4] In a remarkably fine effort to track down the facts, Kenneth W. Porter has concluded that an episode in which the wife was described as part Negro "rests on an unsupported assertion from a questionable source. . . ." Porter does say: "It should be kept in mind, however, that, whether or not Osceola had a part-Negro wife . . . Seminole Indians did have wives of Negro blood. . . ."[5]

It is probable that contemporary historians neglected to describe Osceola's wives fully because Seminole women almost always avoided contact with white men. It is true that they appeared at meetings such as the one described in Chapter 5, but they were present as a group, not as identifiable individuals. The beauty of Che-cho-ter appears well established, we can guess from Sprague that she was the first wife because he mentions no other,[6] and we know from Cohen's description that the second wife was also "young and comely." We also know from Sprague that Che-cho-ter bore four children, from Cohen that at least one was the daughter mentioned in Chapter 4. But there is no further description of the mysterious second wife.

Because of modern black interest in the racial background of the mystery wife, the present writers have sought information among Seminoles of today. A few admit frankly to the possibility of Negro heritage, thus agreeing with early historians that the Seminoles of Osceola's period sometimes married black women among them. But here the matter must rest.

Whatever the nature of Osceola's domestic affairs in late 1834, he was deeply involved in the public problems of the Seminole nation. He attended a December meeting at the agency, argued sharply with Thompson, then realized the futility of the discussion and told the agent, "I know you're my friend and friend to my people." Osceola's fight was with United States policy, not at this time with the man chosen to carry out the policy.

Early in the bitter winter of 1835, four companies of mixed artillery and infantry were ordered to Fort King under Brevet Lieutenant Colonel A. C. W. Fanning, who earlier had lost an arm in battle. (This was probably during the Creek War.) Already present was an infantry company under Captain W. M. Graham.

General Clinch, now fully in charge of troops in Florida, owned a four-square-mile plantation called Auld Lang Syne twenty miles north of Fort King and eight miles south of the long-established town called Micanopy. (This town was not Micanopy's residence. He lived south of Fort King.) A company under Captain Gustavus Drane was ordered to Fort King, but this unit was apparently diverted to General Clinch's plantation. Records for early 1835 are often contradictory. We know, at least, that Fort Brooke (Tampa) was reactivated at about this time with three artillery companies under Major Richard A. Zantzinger.

Osceola watched the strengthening of Fort King with a certain amount of amusement. Although there was frequent target practice, the whites were poor shots. This was due in part to the use of muzzle-loading muskets with an effective range of about a hundred yards. Rifles were rare in the Army of the time, but the Indians had fairly good rifles of Spanish manufacture.

The soldiers also conducted Indian-fighting drills in the woods and this, to Osceola, was even more amusing. Every Indian warrior learned in his youth to slip through the forests like a shadow; any good Seminole could literally disappear within seconds. But the white soldier attempted this kind of invisibility with the grace of a confused cow. Most soldiers came from the lowest social and economic levels; men of higher intelligence or better education could earn far more as civilians. (A soldier's wage was five dollars per month.)

Except for officers, the Army of the period was made up of impoverished farmers, city men from the slums, recent immigrants from Europe, and a thin sprinkling of reasonably intelligent adventurers. John T. Bemrose, a bright youth from England who served in the war as a hospital steward (medic in modern terms) and wrote an account of his experiences, later listed in his company Yankees, Georgia and Florida farmers, Germans, Scots, Frenchmen, English cockneys, Spanish, Minorcans, Poles, Swedes, Canadians, Nova Scotians, a few South Americans, and a large representation of Irish.[7] By no stretch of the imagination could these men be considered experienced woodsmen or "Indian fighters."

Osceola, whose sense of humor was strong, had to restrain himself from impolite laughter as he watched the men trip on vines, entangle themselves in underbrush, stumble over cypress knees, slap mosquitoes, scratch chiggers, and make enough noise to betray their presence half a mile away.

Moreover, it was cold during the early days of the soldiers' Indian-fighting games. They wore heavy coats over their blue fatigues, and Osceola carefully noted that these coats covered the men's cartridge boxes. He realized that a Seminole probably could fire twice while the white soldier was wrestling with his overcoat to get at his ammunition. (Indians in battle carried rifle balls in their mouths so that loading could be rapid.) He also noticed that white soldiers often marched with unloaded guns.

One pleasant spring morning, Osceola arrived at Fort King with his little daughter. The pretty child attracted the attention of Lieutenant John Graham, a twenty-one-year-old West Point graduate. Graham, understandably lonely, walked over to the handsome Indian and smiled at his little companion.

"Your daughter?" he asked.

"*Chits-hotes-teh*," Osceola replied in Creek. Smiling, he added, "Yes. Daughter."

"How do you say, 'You are a pretty girl'?" Graham asked.

Osceola understood enough of the English to say, "*Hocteh cheh elittah fon*." Graham grinned at the child and repeated the phrase. Osceola's daughter was enchanted by the handsome, uniformed white man.

"Where do you live?" Graham asked. Osceola, catching the meaning, said, "*Ista ma ehootah cheh*?"

Smiling radiantly, the little girl pointed toward the southwest in the direction of Osceola's village. Her father, laughing, suddenly picked her up and hugged her. Graham was delighted and somewhat surprised by this unexpected demonstration of affection. Like most whites, he had been led to believe that Indians never showed emotion. But here was a man who not only laughed easily but also obviously adored his child.

Graham shook hands with Osceola, then said, "I'm off duty this afternoon. May I visit your home?"

"*Inca*," Osceola replied. "Yes. You come."

From this gentle beginning, a strange friendship developed between the two men. Later in the day, Graham walked to the sutler's store to buy a little frock for the girl. He then hiked the three miles to Osceola's village, presented his gift to the delighted child, and talked until late afternoon with Osceola. Someone must have translated, for Osceola's English was monosyllabic at best and Graham knew no Creek or the Seminole variations of this tongue. But the day ended with Osceola agreeing to teach Graham some Indian words while the white man would attempt to improve Osceola's limited English.

Graham visited repeatedly to bring Osceola's daughter presents, smoke *hitchey* ("tobacco") with his host, struggle with the language problem, and glance occasionally at Che-cho-ter. Once, observing these glances, Osceola laughed and said softly, "*Hocteh ahcheh attanokah tamas cheh*."

"What does that mean, friend?"

Osceola smiled and changed the subject. Not until much later did Graham learn that his Indian companion had said, "I love this woman very much."

Graham and Osceola became such inseparable friends that they were seen together daily. Bemrose mentioned this friendship [8] and Cohen also commented in it.[9] There is no indication as to how Graham's commanding officer felt about the friendship, but he probably had no objections. Osceola was still popular with the officers; Thompson even gave him presents. As for Osceola's daughter, she loved the white officer. According to Cohen, she insisted on being dressed up whenever Graham came to visit her.[10] Evidently the little girl had her mother's charm as well as a bit of vanity.

The friendship between the two men was not in the least contrived. Graham, who was only a brevet second lieutenant, had no military information that could have been of any conceivable benefit to Osceola. Although Osceola had a great deal of information that would have been of value at Fort King, there is no indication that Graham ever tried to pry into Seminole secrets.

On March 27 and 29, Thompson and General Clinch held another meeting with the Seminoles at Fort King. Bemrose, who was there, said it was held "in the barracks" on a raised platform built about ten feet from the ground.[11] The main purpose of this session was to read a message from President Jackson urging the Seminoles to emigrate. Osceola, although present, said little.

The main speaker, according to Bemrose, was Holata Mico, tall, thin, and aged. Cudjo was translator. (Bemrose spells the name "Cudgo" and has the Negro interpreter talk in dialect.) Identifying himself as spokesman for Micanopy, Holata Mico said once more that the Seminole nation refused to agree to removal. The following is from Bemrose's account, as edited by John K. Mahon:

> "Tell him, Cudgo," said the agent, "if he breaks his word with us . . . I shall be obliged to call upon the White warriors to force him." Which being done, the noble fellow jumped up, speading wide his arms, and standing in the graceful attitude so easy to the savage, his eyes flashing fire, and his countenance at intervals taking a scornful look. Now and then he would burst into a derisive laugh!
>
> "What's he say, Cudgo?" was the agent's query, excitement depicted upon his countenance.
>
> "He say talk not to him of war! Is he a child that he fears it? No! He say when he bury the hatchet, he placed it deep in the earth with a stone over it, but he say he can soon unearth it for the protection of his people. When he look upon the White man's warriors, he sorry to injure them, but he cannot fear them, he had fought them before, he will do so again, if his people say fight."

The speech sounds like unadulterated Osceola, but Holata Mico was quite able to speak for himself. Arpeika, says Bemrose, was so angry that he stamped around in a great rage. And then, suddenly, the platform collapsed, dumping Indians and whites to the ground. Bemrose laughed to see "fat and lusty" General Clinch struggling out of the "medley of humanity." The council was adjourned until April 22.[12]

The April conference, already described in Chapter 1, produced three significant developments. Thompson struck five names from the roll of chiefs, one of them being either Fuch-a-Lusti-Hadjo or Coa Hadjo. (Sources conflict.) Osceola made his dramatic gesture with his hunting knife, stabbing the table in front of Thompson's nose. And the whites agreed to postpone emigration until January 15, 1836. This was exactly what Osceola and his group of intransigents wanted: more time to prepare for a war that was now inevitable.

Thompson had second thoughts about the large purchases of powder by the Indians. Sometime in April he prohibited the sale of arms, powder, and lead. However justified this decision may have been, it was considered by the Seminoles to be a hostile act. Sprague wrote that it was virtually a declaration of war. With the necessary equipment for hunting cut off, even the most peaceful among the Indians were enraged. As Sprague put it, "The passions of the friendly Indians, as well as others, were now aroused; indeed it was difficult to discriminate between friend and foe." [13]

A great deal of gunpowder had already been purchased, so Osceola was more concerned about the insult than he was by the cutting off of supplies. Having dressed carefully in full regalia, he strode to Fort King and stamped into the office of Wiley Thompson.

Ever since Osceola had stabbed the conference table and refused to sign the paper agreeing to the treaties of Payne's Landing and Fort Gibson, Thompson had expected an explosion. He probably knew it would come from Osceola, the man he had characterized earlier as a "bold, manly and determined young chief, who has perhaps been more violently opposed to removal than any other. . . ." But he certainly did not expect a confrontation in his office.

The two men eyed each other silently, antagonists between whom a serious breach was widening. Osceola was proud, defiant, blazing with anger, totally indifferent to Thompson's position as a representative of the United States government. Thompson, conditioned by his militia background, could not imagine that any Indian would defy him in angry, insulting language.

"I am told I may not buy arms and powder," Osceola said.

"That's right. Not at this time."

Osceola's face was transformed. No longer was this the friendly, laughing Indian who had played games with the Fort King soldiers. This was a man who obviously considered Thompson his inferior, and a man enraged at an insult.

"Am I a Negro?" Osceola roared. "Am I a slave? My skin is dark, but not black! I am an Indian—a Seminole! The white man shall not make me black! I will make the white man red with blood, and then blacken him in the sun and rain, where the wolf shall smell of his bones, and the buzzard live upon his flesh!"[14] (Thus goes the translation, which is probably nearly accurate. Indians used highly descriptive language.)

Thompson, watching Osceola stride from the room, could hardly believe what had happened. He had been threatened in his own office! Thompson clearly understood Osceola's puzzling reference to Negroes. He was not saying he was superior to blacks; he was, in fact, their outstanding defender among the Seminoles. But slaves obviously could not purchase firearms or ammunition. Osceola was simply saying he had been reduced to slave status in the eyes of the whites by being denied the right to buy arms.

"Let him calm down," Thompson told an officer who had overheard the outburst. "I must say, nobody ever talked to me like that before. But he's a fine man as well as a dangerous leader. When he thinks about it, he may even apologize. Then I'll give him a new breech-loading rifle."

Osceola, still raging, joined a meeting with Alligator, Micanopy, old Arpeika, Abraham, and Jumper. All were angry, for denial of the right to purchase arms was deemed an insult to all.

"I told the agent I would make the white man red with blood," Osceola said grimly. "What I say, we will do. But now, brothers, we must finish our preparations. We should be ready to fight during the last moon of this year.

"Brothers, tell your trusted young men to watch every movement of the white soldiers. We must know at all times where they are, where they come from, where they go, how many they are. We must know when they have the big guns with them, we must know when they ride horses.

"When the time of fighting comes, all crops must be taken to secret places in the swamps. The women and children must be hidden there. Cattle must be driven to the swamp ranges. When we start to fight, brothers, the white soldiers will be moving toward us with baggage trains. We must first seize these supply wagons. We will have to live and fight partly on what we capture."

"It is well," Abraham said. "Who will be our war leader?"

"That can be decided later. But he must be obeyed by all. Just as the whites have a *tustenuggee thlacko*, so must we. One chief warrior to direct. If the white soldiers have any secret, this is it."

"Do we attack the white settlers?" Alligator asked.

"Yes, if it serves a purpose. But we do not harm women and children. It is not on them that we make war and draw the scalping knife, it is upon men. Let us act like men." [15]

"It will be hard to restrain our young warriors," Arpeika observed.

"We can do it. There is one other matter at present, brothers. When fighting starts, I wish one white man spared. No one must harm the young John Graham. I will make the ground red with the blood of any warrior who injures my friend!" [16]

Osceola also suggested that the Indians stay away from Fort King, except when there was pressing need to visit the sutler's store. Top chiefs and subchiefs could and should visit to keep an eye on military activities and to allay any suspicions on the part of Thompson or the officers.

While the Seminoles prepared quietly for war, attention throughout the United States was turned to such matters as abolitionist agitation, inflated land values, labor unrest, and the agreeable fact that there was no national debt. *Niles' Weekly Register* for May 2, 1835, reported cheerfully that a Mr. Clayton of Cincinnati had sailed in a balloon for more than four hundred miles. Buried at bottom of the page was the following tiny item:

> The St. Augustine *Herald* states that there is no foundation for reports which have been in circulation, of apprehended difficulties in the removal of the Seminole Indians

> from Florida to the west of the Mississippi. The Seminole of the present day is a different being from the warlike son of the forest when the tribe was numerous and powerful, and no trouble in the removal of the remnant of the tribe is anticipated.[17]

Osceola was one of the Seminoles who continued to visit Fort King. Early in June, he called on Wiley Thompson for purposes that are unclear in the various contemporary accounts. Potter wrote that Thompson wanted to discuss a skirmish between whites and Seminoles, and that he had also angered Osceola by confiscating some liquor.[18] Sprague inferred that Osceola was still angry about the prohibition on the sale of arms and ammunition.[19] Giddings stated that Osceola had with him a part-Negro wife who was seized as a slave.[20] Other contemporary writers found different reasons for a furious row that broke out between Osceola and the agent.

Sprague was probably closest to the truth, although there is a good argument that the explosion may have hinged on Osceola's refusal to sign the document approving the Payne's Landing and Fort Gibson treaties. The liquor seizure may be discounted; Osceola drank but there is no indication that he was seriously addicted to alcohol. As for a half-Negro wife being seized by slave-catchers, the modern historian Kenneth W. Porter has successfully disposed of this possibility.[21]

Whatever the case, Osceola flew into a fury, abused Thompson, in one account brandishing his knife before leaving the agent's office. This was too much for Thompson. Lieutenant Colonel Fanning, apparently attracted by the uproar, was nearby.

"Colonel, will you arrest that man?" Thompson shouted.

Fanning obliged by ordering four soldiers to overtake Osceola, who was now some two hundred yards away. When they attempted to seize him, Osceola sent one man sprawling and literally shrieked with fury. But it was impossible to wrestle four desperate soldiers who were being watched by their commanding officer; and for some reason Osceola did not draw his knife.

As he was dragged back to the fort, he shouted in the Creek language, "I shall remember the hour! The agent has his day, I will have mine!" [22]

He was placed in irons and confined to the guardhouse, where, for hours, he raged at Thompson. To be imprisoned was the worst humiliation an Indian could suffer. For a top Seminole leader to be held in captivity was unthinkable. There is no adequate analogy except to suggest that Osceola's situation might be compared to the hypothetical arrest and shackling of a United States Secretary of War.

During the first hours, Osceola was nearly insane with anger. Trapped and confined like a wild beast, he reacted with the fury of an animal, straining at his bonds until the skin rubbed raw. His anguished cries could be heard far beyond the perimeter of Fort King as he called Thompson every name he could think of. Then, toward midnight, his fury abated and he began to think clearly.

Thompson would have to be killed, of course. There was no other choice. An affront of this magnitude could only be wiped out by bloodshed. But retribution could wait for a while. The immediate problem was to find some means of being released.

As Osceola reflected during the bitter hours, he saw clearly that Thompson wanted two things. One of his aims was obviously to punish Osceola. Very well, he would act humble and remorseful. He would be contrite, apologetic, the very image of a man who has seen the error of his ways. This would be a bitter brew, but somehow he could swallow it. The white men had been deceitful down through the years; now the Indian would also lie.

Thompson's other aim, as Osceola assessed his plight, was to force him to agree to emigration. Very well, then, he would sign the paper confirming agreement to the Payne's Landing and Fort Gibson treaties. It would be another lie as well as a further humiliation, but there was no other choice. He had to be free to fight for his people, free to repay Thompson for the terrible insult. If he had to crawl in the mud like an injured alligator in order to be free, then he would crawl.

In the morning, he asked humbly for a messenger. When the interpreter arrived, Osceola said, "Go to the agent. Tell him that if he releases me, I'll sign the agreement and go beyond the Big River. I'll even persuade others to sign."

Thompson sent back word that he needed some sort of guarantee that Osceola would keep his word. Osceola then asked that some of the chiefs who favored emigration be brought to him. If he could persuade them of his changed views, they could intercede for him with Thompson.

The consenting chiefs, including Charley Emathla, visited Osceola at the fort and listened as he told of his conversion to their views. It was a remarkable session. Thomas McKenney and James Hall, soldier and historian, described it in these words:

> He spoke of his past conduct in terms of regret and pointed self-condemnation; depicted in glowing language the hopes he had entertained of uniting the several factions of the nation, so that by organizing a firm opposition they might be permitted to occupy a little longer their present homes; and admitted the fallacy of these expectations. He spoke of himself as a martyr . . . but avowed a sincere determination to yield to what now appeared as unavoidable destiny, and remove peaceably to a new country.[23]

The friendly chiefs believed him and interceded with Thompson who agreed to free him on the promise that he would return in five days to sign the acknowledgment of the treaties. The irons were struck and Osceola, with bowed head, left the guardhouse in silence. Thompson returned to his office fully convinced that the last objective to removal had been overcome. Colonel Fanning was with him.

"You've made a mistake, General," Fanning said bluntly.

"That man should never have been turned loose. He's your enemy for life—yours or his."

"Oh, I don't think so," Thompson said mildly. "He's learned his lesson."

The door was open to admit the warm June air. Suddenly a peculiar sound came from the woods beyond Fort King. High and shrill, it seemed to be torn from the very bowels of hell.

"Yo-ho-e-hee!"

"As you very well know, General," Fanning said after a moment of silence, "we have just heard the Seminole war cry. May I respectfully suggest that your former prisoner hasn't learned any damn lesson at all." [24]

But Osceola returned as he had promised. With obvious relief, Thompson reported:

> True to his professions he this day appeared with 79 of his people, men, women, and children, including some who had joined him since his conversion, and redeemed his promise. He told me many of his friends were out hunting, whom he could and would bring over on their return. I have no doubt of his sincerity, and as little that the greatest difficulty is surmounted.[25]

Thompson was so delighted that he gave Osceola an expensive rifle. Osceola accepted it with expressions of appreciation. No one seemed to find it curious that few Indians were now visiting Fort King. If officers noticed this at all, they must have assumed that the Seminoles were busy with preparations for removal.

Now matters began to move rapidly toward an inevitable disaster. During October, the Seminoles held a secret meeting in the Big Swamp. This council, dominated by the group opposing removal and thus by Osceola, first agreed that the Seminoles would not remove and would resist with force. Thus, opposition to removal now spread to the entire nation with the exception of six chiefs: Charley Emathla, Holata Emathla, Conhatkee

Mico, Enconchatimico, Fuch-a-Lusti-Hadjo, and Otulkechala.

It was a solemn conclave with at least fifteen hundred Seminoles gathered to listen to Osceola, Micanopy, Jumper, Alligator, Abraham, and others of the antiremoval group. One terrible decision would be reached at this council. Osceola presented the issue.

"Brothers, I have said before that if any of our people want to go west, we won't permit it. They are our enemies and they must be treated as enemies.

"I say that anyone who prepares to move must be killed by the nation. I say that anyone who sells his animals as the white man wishes must be killed by the nation. Those who agree to move are no longer our brothers and must be condemned to death as enemies. What is the voice of the Seminole warriors? What is the voice of Micanopy? What is the voice of the chiefs?"

"I agree," Micanopy growled.

"You have heard our leader," Osceola said. "Who speaks against him?"

"It is sad to think of putting a Seminole to death," Abraham observed. "But who speaks against Micanopy?"

"I will not go west," old Arpeika muttered. "If I must raise the hatchet to my brother who dares obey the white man, then I raise it!"

The nation agreed to the death sentence for Seminoles who went along with the government's removal plan. A few days later, five of the chiefs agreeing to removal left quietly for Fort Brooke with about four hundred fifty of their people. Charley Emathla, fully aware of the danger, remained with his family at his village west of Fort King.

Clinch was now calling desperately for more troops. A number of companies arrived at his plantation where Captain Drane was ordered to construct a strong picket fort. In honor of the builder, this would be known as Fort Drane. As fear of an Indian uprising began to spread, settlers poured into this crude installation and the larger towns surrounding the Seminole reservation.

Late in November, Osceola's attention turned to Charley Emathla. Reports of what happened are contradictory and confusing, but it appears that this chief, who had come to believe in emigration, drove his cattle to the pens where the Indian cattle were to be sold. He then returned to his home. Hearing of this action, Osceola, Holata Mico, and Abraham led four hundred warriors to Charley Emathla's village where they surrounded the chief's lodge. According to Potter's account, which seems to be the best, the three leaders demanded that Charley Emathla pledge himself and his people to resist removal.

"I have agreed to go west," the chief replied. "I've lived to see the Seminoles degraded and almost ruined. The only hope of being saved from total destruction depends on going west. I've made arrangements to go, and I *will* go."

"You must die if you don't join us," Osceola pointed out. "You know of this decision of the nation."

"If I must die, I die."

"You'll have until the sun is overhead to consult with your people and choose."

"My mind will not be changed. But I ask for time to make some arrangements with the agent for the welfare of my family."

At this point, Osceola raised and aimed his rifle. Abraham, thrusting it aside, suggested that a council be held. While this was going on, according to the McKenney and Hall version, Charley Emathla went to the agency with two daughters, apparently collected some money for the sale of his stock, announced that he might be killed, and headed home. The daughters and an unidentified Negro were with him. The chief and the Negro were on horseback, the daughters probably riding with the Negro.

Suddenly, there was a war whoop. Osceola and twelve companions sprang from the underbrush and commenced firing. The Negro and the girls were not harmed, but Charley Emathla died from eleven bullet wounds. His handkerchief contained some gold and silver coins. Osceola seized it, then looked fiercely at his companions.

"This is made of red man's blood!" he cried, hurling the coins into the woods. The execution party now headed for Long Swamp, southeast of Fort King.[26]

When word of the killing reached Fort King, both Thompson and Colonel Fanning were seriously concerned. Thompson prepared a public warning in which he advised the citizens to guard against Indian depredations. Fanning wrote General Clinch, who was ill with fever in St. Augustine. After describing the murder and his disposition of forces to protect Charley Emathla's immediate family (most of this band later joined Osceola), Fanning called for immediate reinforcements and warned that the Army was trying to do too much with inadequate means.[27] A day later, in a second letter, he was even more forceful. He suggested that General Clinch raise up to a hundred mounted riflemen, collect all available regular forces, and march at once on the Indian strongholds in Big Swamp and Long Swamp. Otherwise, he warned, many settlers would be killed, along with the Fort King garrison.[28]

Clinch's Florida force was, indeed, weak. According to military records, six companies were supposed to be at Fort King; but Fanning's correspondence indicates he had two companies absent and "Drane's company" was apparently at Clinch's plantation. Three companies were at Fort Brooke, one at St. Augustine. On October 17, Clinch had ordered Major Francis L. Dade to move a company up from Key West to Fort Brooke. A mounted militia force was later formed under the command of Brigadier General Richard K. Call. But all of these forces were scattered in early December and, in the case of the regulars, inadequately supplied.

With the Seminole chiefs and warriors assembled at Long Swamp, another brief council was held. The first business was to select a head war chief, or *tustenuggee thlacko*. Osceola was promptly appointed,[29] with Jumper and Alligator as his top lieutenants.

"I want every move of the white soldiers reported," he ordered. "A message must also go to our brother, Philip, and his son, Coacoochee. When the sun has risen twenty-five times, they should attack the white man's plantations in their country."

Philip, known as King Philip, was about sixty years of age, and leader of the Seminoles east of the St. Johns River. According to Cohen, Philip had a force of two hundred fifty to three hundred warriors and about the same number of Negroes. He lived on an island in the middle of a large lake.[30] His son, Coacoochee (Wildcat), a few years younger than Osceola, was a furious, determined warrior with an excellent mind.

The council decided to move all Seminoles in the general Fort King area to the "cove" of the Withlacoochee (Ouithlacoochee) River southwest of Fort King. This incredibly wild, swampy area, known in modern times for Tsala Apopka Lake, was a fine military base for several sound reason. Except to the Seminoles, it was nearly impenetrable. It was also within striking distance of the military road connecting Fort King and Clinch's Fort Drane with Fort Brooke at Tampa. Concealing their trail carefully, Osceola and his forces moved rapidly to this wilderness where they were joined by the women and children. From this point, during December, Osceola launched a series of minor attacks on isolated farms or settlements.

He also ordered raiding parties to burn the bridges crossing the streams and rivers between Fort King and Fort Brooke. These bridges were essential for the passage of cannon or heavy wagons with supplies. They could easily be rebuilt by the whites, but the job of repairing bridges would delay soldiers and also expose them to attack during their weakest moments.

As for the menace of cannon, which Indians greatly feared, Osceola had learned the difference between canister shot and the six-pound cannonball. Canister fragments were the most dangerous, but cannon were not particularly effective unless the Indians bunched up.

"When we face the big guns," Osceola told Alligator and Jumper, "keep your warriors scattered. The white soldiers are most exposed when they load a big gun. Shoot at them then. But tell your warriors to lie down as soon as a big gun is loaded. Then few will be hurt."

The most difficult job confronting Osceola was to drill the concept of obedience into his warriors. In the heat of battle, Indians often fought according to individual plan, or whim, or no plan at all. One or two warriors might, for example, decide suddenly to leap from shelter and make an heroic but suicidal attack. Others would be shamed into following, the result being that many would be wiped out unnecessarily.

"If I am with you," Osceola told the various bands of warriors, "obey every order I give. Attack only when I give the signal. If I say to hide behind trees or lie on the ground, do it quickly. If I say to run away, obey me when you hear the words. Don't try to die foolishly. Stay alive so you can strike the white man again. And if I'm not with you, obey your *tustenuggees*. A warrior who fails to obey will be killed."

Osceola was remarkably successful in spreading the difficult concept of discipline among the Seminoles. There is no question about this; almost every contemporary writer mentions it. Perhaps remembering his own boyhood, Osceola even insisted that young boys throughout the nation be given daily rifle practice. In a remarkably short time, he had assembled a small but highly effective fighting force.

Terrified whites continued to seek safety at Fort Drane and other hastily built stockades, among them Fort Defiance at the town of Micanopy; Fort Crum, farther northwest; and Fort Gilleland at Newnansville on the St. Augustine–Pensacola highway. (This town was near modern Gainesville.)

General Clinch's problems were increased by the presence of these settlers and by a shortage of supplies so critical that whiskey sold for a dollar a drink, and a biscuit cost three dollars. But Florida forces were coming to his aid. General Joseph M. Hernandez, commanding the east Florida militia, was moving several companies under Colonel John Warren toward Fort Crum. General Richard Call was also in the field with his militia force of some five hundred men. These volunteers were to serve until sundown on December 31, 1835.

Sometime on December 18, Osceola learned of the movement of a wagon train west of the town of Micanopy. He lay in wait with eighty Seminoles, drove off the escort, and was plundering the wagons when a Captain John McLemore came up with a company of thirty mounted militia. McLemore promptly ordered a charge, but only twelve of his men obeyed. Forced to retire, he lost eight killed and six wounded. This was the first real battle of the Second Seminole War, an engagement called the Battle of Black Point.

Clinch, meanwhile, was centering his forces at Fort Drane where Call had joined him. He brought up all but one company from Fort King, which was to be strengthened by two companies from Fort Brooke. He decided to attack the Seminoles in the Withlacoochee swamp area before the militia's period of service ran out; this campaign was to start on December 28. (The volunteers had agreed to a few additional days of service.)

Osceola knew that Philip was now raiding plantations along the Atlantic coast according to the established schedule. He also knew that on Wednesday, December 23, two companies of 108 men had left Fort Brooke to relieve Fort King. From the moment the column departed under command of Major Francis L. Dade, Osceola had ordered its every move watched.

Now, in council, he told Jumper and Alligator, with Micanopy as nominal commander, to attack this slow-moving column when it was about halfway up the road from Fort Brooke. He indicated he would try to be there, but he had another job to perform at Fort King.

"The agent who put irons on me is *my* friend," Osceola said with a bitter smile. "I'll see to him."

Osceola's timing was little short of amazing, and his grasp of guerrilla tactics excellent. Strike the relief column in a favorable area where retreat to the swamps was easy, launch a diversionary attack at Fort King, and be ready to meet General Clinch's force on the Withlacoochee. At the same time, King Philip's raids to the east would tie down any reinforcement to Clinch from that direction. The military genius of Osceola became apparent during these late days of December.

He had one further order, surprising in view of what he had in store for General Wiley Thompson. He told Alligator, "When the white warriors from Fort Brooke are attacked, the bodies of the dead are not to be damaged. They must be left untouched where they fall. Just take anything that can be used."

Monday, December 28, 1835, was a cold but pleasant day. Birds chattered in the woods near Fort King, squirrels played in the pines, the usual woodsmoke drifted on a sharp breeze from the north, and no scene could have been more peaceful. Colonel Fanning had left with four companies to join General Clinch at Fort Drane. Captain Thomas Lendrum, with one weak company, remained at the fort.

Wiley Thompson had been spending his nights within the fort, but during the days he worked at his Seminole agency office. Despite the war atmosphere and the sporadic fights, he still believed the Indians could be forced into removal. There was the usual paperwork to be done, and Thompson was not the sort of man who feared greatly for his safety.

Erastus Rogers, the sutler, was engaged in moving some of his stores into the fort with the help of a clerk named Kitzler, a boy, Robert Suggs, and several Negroes. In the late morning, Rogers' elderly Negro cook began to prepare the heavy noon dinner of pork, beans, coarse bread, and molasses. Rogers, who believed the Indian alarms were exaggerated, proposed to eat as usual at his house and store. He had known the Seminoles intimately and was more fearful for his goods than his person. As he told Kitzler, the Indians were probably deep in the swamps.

Shortly after 1:00 P.M., Thompson strolled to the fort to join the officers' mess. This was a leisurely meal with Lieutenant Constantine Smith and Captain Lendrum. Lendrum said he was worried about the relief column from Fort Brooke. It should have arrived several days earlier. No one was able to account for the delay. Isolated as they were, they could only wait.

After dinner Lendrum excused himself while Smith and Thompson lingered over coffee. A little after three o'clock, Smith lit a cigar and suggested a walk to Rogers' store some six hundred yards to the northwest. It was too pleasant a day to be confined within the palisades of the fort.

Captain Lendrum had some defense works beyond the pickets in an opposite direction from the sutler's store. (Conflicting directions are given in the old reports.) He had stepped out to supervise the work and was not aware that Thompson and Smith had left the fort.

Suddenly, Lendrum heard a shrill *Yo-ho-e-hee!* followed by a heavy volley of shots in the direction of the sutler's store. Thinking this might be a diversion to cut him off, Lendrum immediately ordered his men to race toward the fort. There was a second, more distant war whoop and another splatter of shots.

"Lieutenant Smith!" Lendrum called as he reached the fort. "Smith, can you make out where they are?"

"Beg pardon, sir, but he ain't here," one of the soldiers said. "He an' General Thompson, they went out for a walk."

"Oh, my God!" Lendrum muttered.

Smoke now began to rise from Rogers' combined house and store. While Lendrum tried to decide how best to use his tiny force, a sentry called that some figures could be seen running toward the fort from the direction of the store. They turned out to be several Negroes, including Rogers' cook. The old woman, shaking with fear, had somehow managed to run the entire distance.

"They all dead!" she gasped. "Mr. Rogers dead! Mr. Kitzler, he dead! Mr. Suggs dead!"

The Indians had shot down the sutler and his clerks while they were eating dinner. The elderly black cook had concealed herself behind some barrels in the store section of the building. From this position, she watched as Osceola dashed into the room, cast aside furniture, and growled with anger when he found the store empty. He then gave a peculiar shrill yelp, evidently a signal, for the Indians raced into the woods carrying with them the bodies of Suggs and Rogers. The black cook guessed that about sixty Seminoles were with Osceola.

"Did you see General Thompson?" Lendrum asked. "Was he at the store?"

"Never seen him," the woman said.

At about this point, a Lieutenant Colonel Ichabod Crane galloped up to the fort with Lieutenant Joseph W. Harris, disbursing agent for the emigration, and six mounted militiamen. Their mission was to meet the relief column of two companies from Fort Brooke, under Major Dade, and hurry it on to join Clinch at Fort Drane. They had arrived by coincidence as the last war whoop sounded, and had even tried futilely to pursue the Indians.

A party was now sent out to search for Thompson and Smith. Their bodies were found about three hundred yards from the fort. Thompson had been hit by fourteen bullets, Smith by two. Thompson had also been stabbed, and both men had been scalped. As the killing was reconstructed later, one party of Seminoles had killed these men first, while a second group attacked Rogers and his clerks. There was a general agreement that Osceola had been the leader; several friendly Indians at the fort said they had recognized his terrifying war whoop, and the old black woman knew him by sight.

Kitzler's body, pierced by two bullets, was discovered

promptly. His skull had been smashed and he, too, had been scalped. The bodies of Rogers and Suggs, found on the following day, were badly mangled. Rogers had been struck by seventeen bullets, testimony to the fact that his Indian customers must have resented him. Young Suggs, killed by two bullets, was the only one to escape scalping.

Because Lieutenant Harris wrote an excellent account of the frightful episode, this event has been told from the white point of view.[31] Fortunately, Sprague presented the Seminole viewpoint through the words of Alligator reported at a much later date. Alligator said:

> We had been preparing for this more than a year. Though promises had been made to assemble on the 1st of January, it was decided not to leave the country but to fight for it. In council, it was determined to strike a decided blow about this time. Our agent at Fort King had put irons on our men, and said we must go. Oseola [*sic*] said he was *his friend, he would see to him*. It was determined he should attack Fort King, in order to reach General Thompson. . . .[32]

To whitewash Osceola would be ridiculous. He certainly hated Thompson, but it appears from Alligator's statement that the killing of the agent was a decision made in council, not entirely a matter of personal revenge. Thompson's afternoon stroll simply spared Osceola the problem of attacking Fort King.

We know Osceola was late getting to his next appointment, so we can assume he had watched the fort through all of Sunday, December 27. Then, after the killings of the twenty-eighth, he and his men raced south toward some startling events that were taking place forty miles below Fort King on the military road from Fort Brooke. We can guess that Osceola's party had lean Florida ponies hidden in the forest, for they arrived at a rendezvous in Wahoo Swamp later the same night. Osceola had discovered the uses of mobility; hereafter, the Indians often traveled on horseback.

Osceola. From a portrait by George Catlin (*Lent to the National Portrait Gallery by the Department of Anthropology, National Museum of Natural History, Smithsonian Institution, Washington, D. C.*)

Osceola. Engraving after a portrait by Catlin, date not recorded. (*Smithsonian Institution National Anthropological Archives. Neg. No. 1177–C*)

Osceola (Asseola). From a lithograph published by McKenney and Hall in *The Indian Tribes of North America,* 1836–44 and subsequent editions. (*Smithsonian Institution National Anthropological Archives. Neg. No. 45112–E*)

Osceola (Asseola) (*Smithsonian Institution National Anthropological Archives. Neg No. 1177–B*)

Nea-math-la. From a lithograph published by McKenney and Hall in *The Indian Tribes of North America*, 1836–44 and subsequent editions. (*Smithsonian Institution National Anthropological Archives. Neg. No. 45112–D*)

Micanopy. From a lithograph published by McKenney and Hall in *The Indian Tribes of North America,* 1836–44 and subsequent editions. (*Smithsonian Institution National Anthropological Archives. Neg. No. 45112–C*)

Tuko-see-mathla. From a lithograph published by McKenney and Hall in *The Indian Tribes of North America*, 1836–44 and subsequent editions. (*Smithsonian Institution National Anthropological Archives. Neg. No. 45112–F*)

Coacoochee, or Wild Cat, son of Ea-mat-la, or King Philip. From Joshua R. Giddings' *The Florida Exiles,* 1863. (*Smithsonian Institution National Anthropological Archives. Neg. No. 1176–D*)

Foke Luste Hajo. From a lithograph published by McKenney and Hall in *The Indian Tribes of North America,* 1836–44 and subsequent editions. (*Smithsonian Institution National Anthropological Archives. Neg. No.* 45112–A)

Chief Billy Bowlegs (Holatamico), 1861. From an oil on canvas by Charles F. Wimar (1828–1862). (*The St. Louis Art Museum*)

General Thomas S. Jesup (*U. S. Signal Corps photo in The National Archives*)

General Edmund Pendleton Gaines (*U. S. Signal Corps photo in The National Archives*)

General Winfield Scott (*U. S. Signal Corps photo in The National Archives*)

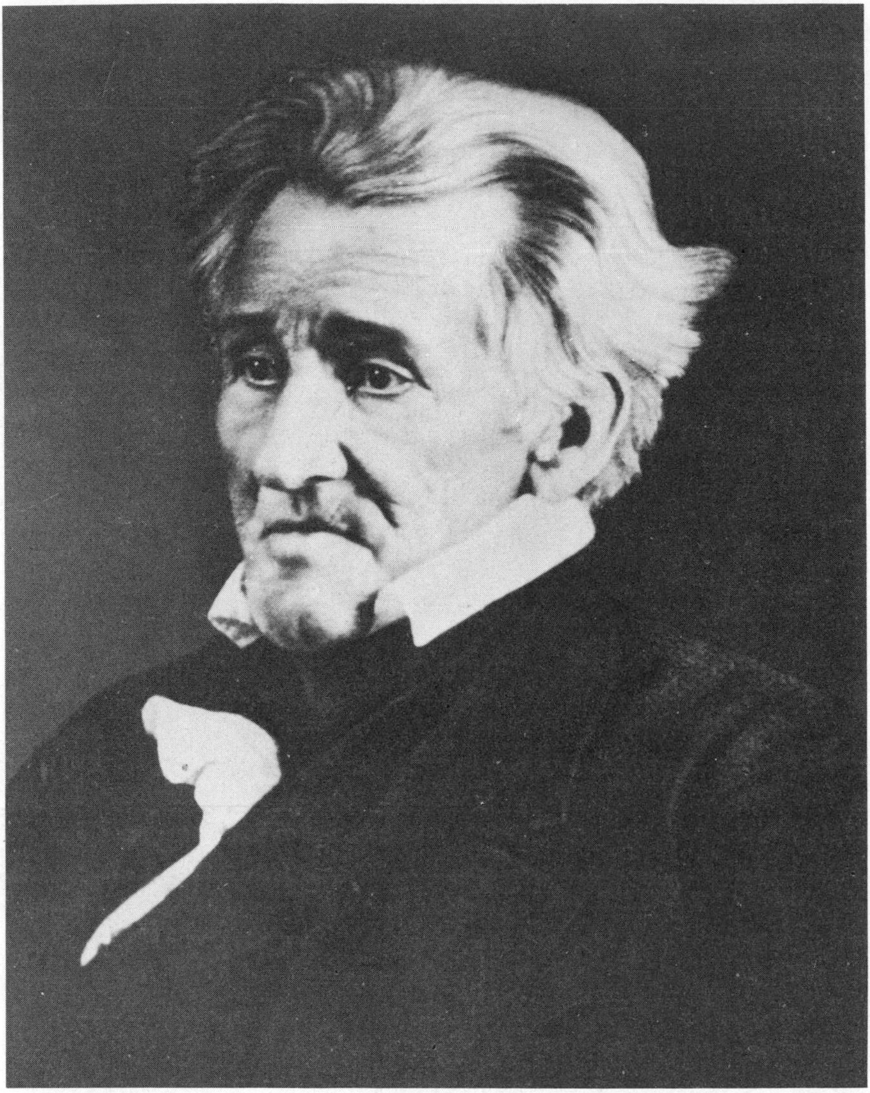

President Andrew Jackson (*U. S. Signal Corps photo in The National Archives*)

A beautiful Seminole girl sitting on a partially completed "dugout" canoe, which is hand-chiseled from a complete cypress log. They were made in many sizes, large enough to accommodate a family. Some Seminoles crossed the Gulf of Mexico or over to the Bahamas in years past in these canoes when all of Florida was their home. (*Florida State News Bureau*)

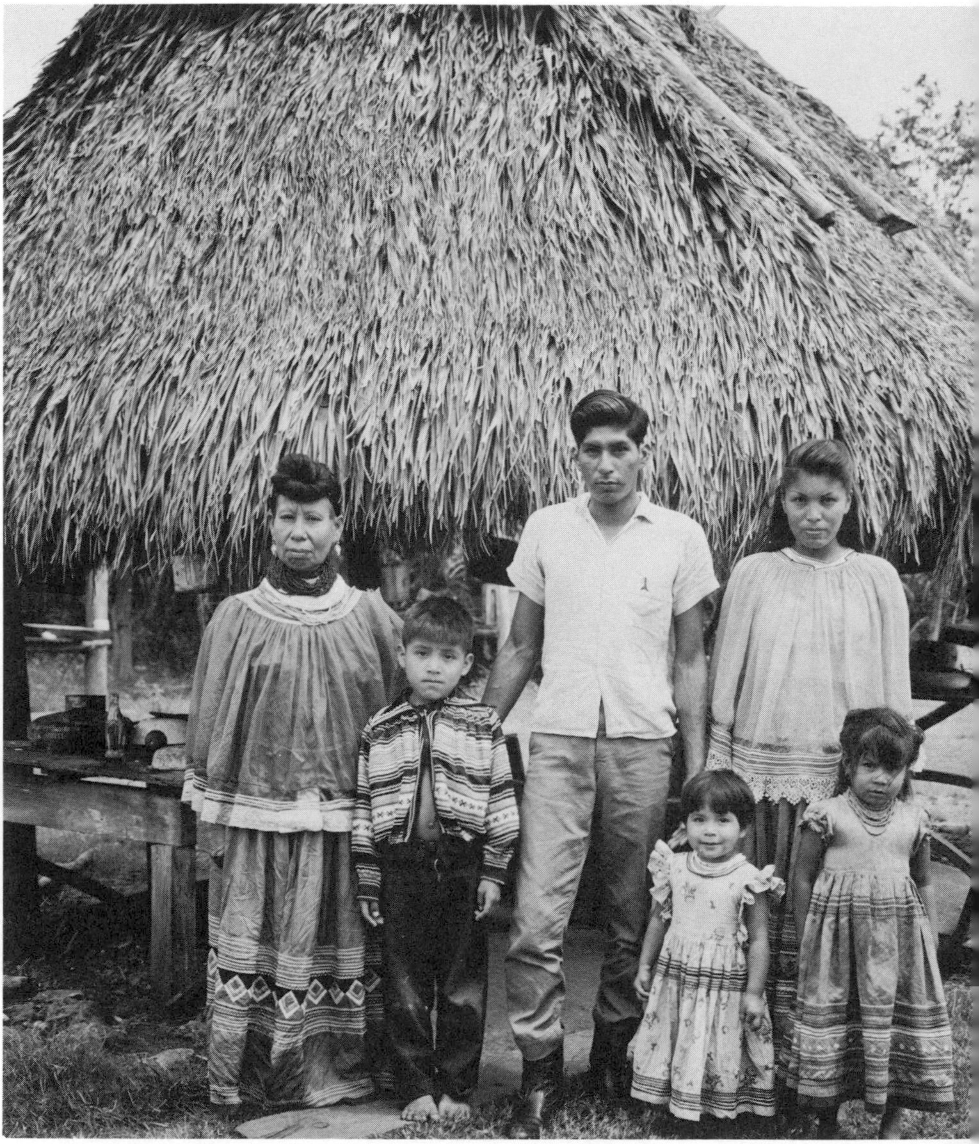

Typical Florida Seminole Indian family gathered in front of a *chickee* ("thatch-roofed hut"). Several *chickees* make up a family "camp" (residence), each *chickee* serving as a room, one for eating–living, others for sleeping, etc. (*Florida State News Bureau*)

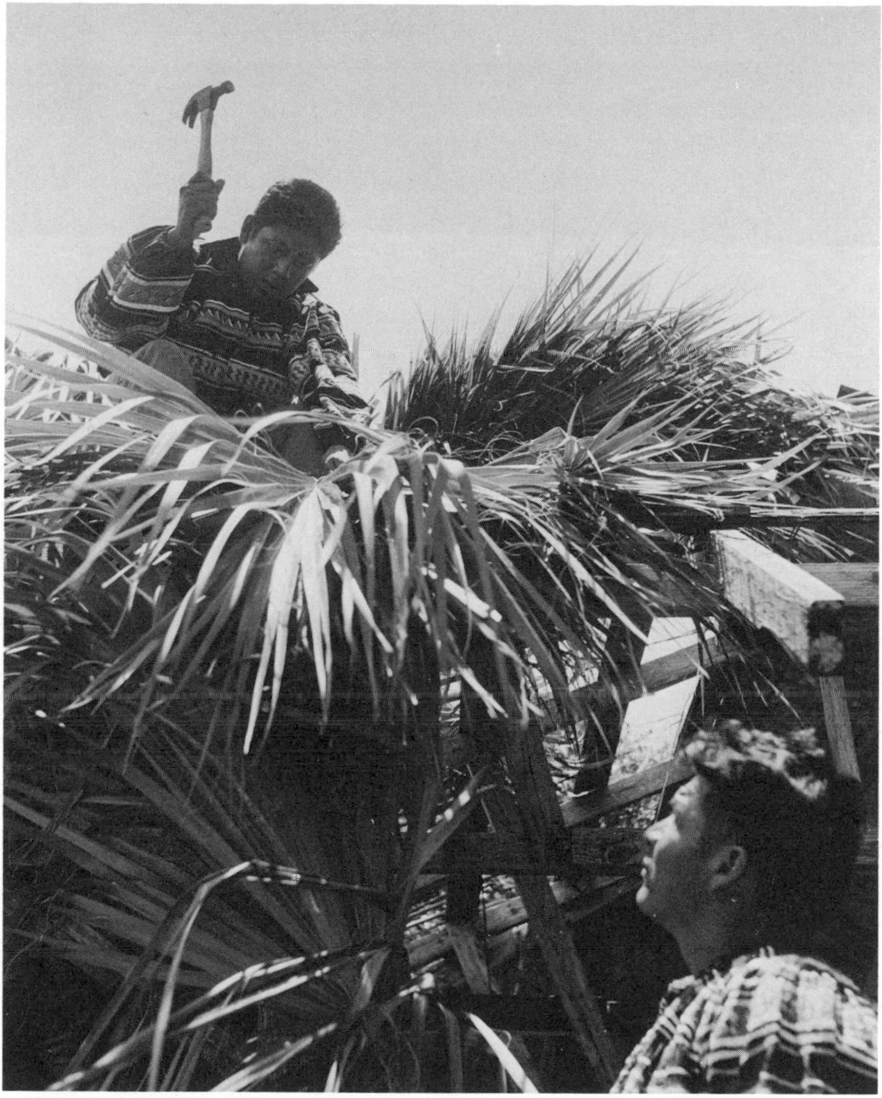

Florida Seminole Indian men in process of building a *chickee* with palmetto fronds. (*Florida State News Bureau*)

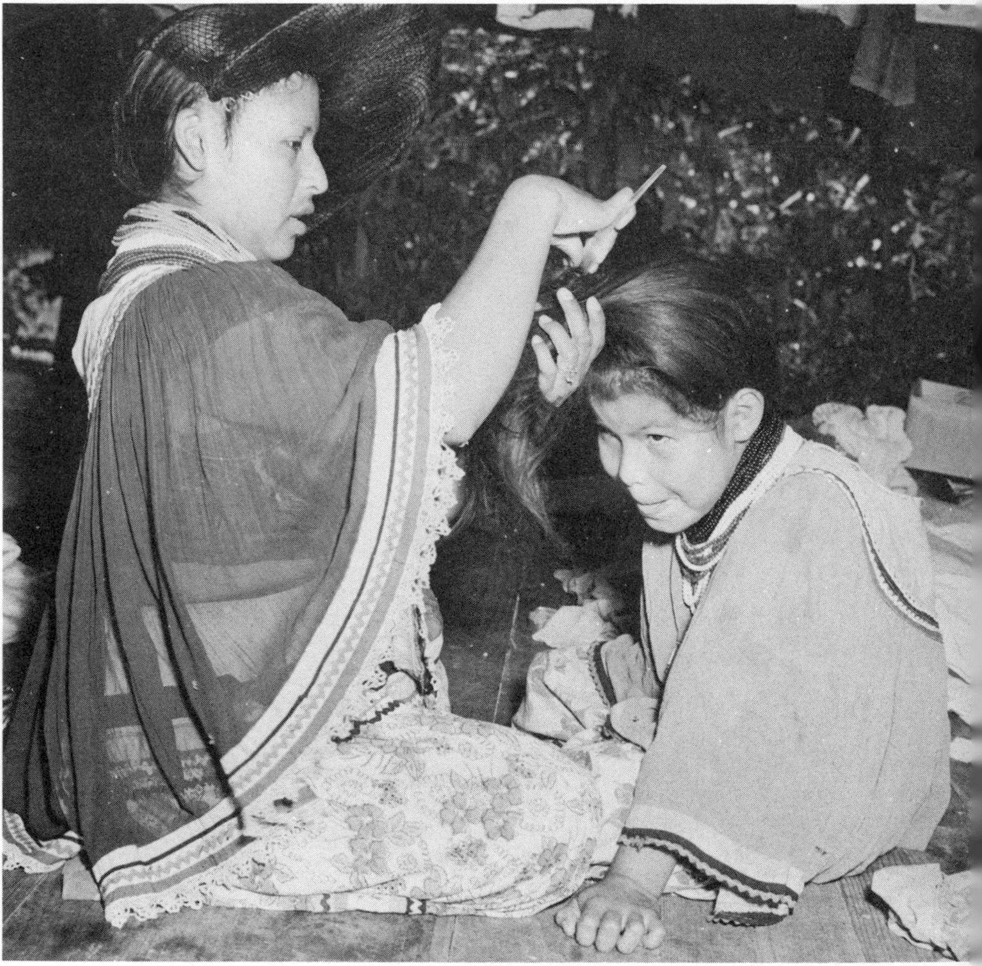

A Seminole mother combing her daughter's hair. Note lady's head-piece. Only a few of the older ladies now wear this hairstyle. (*Florida State News Bureau*)

7

Wahoo Swamp and Withlacoochee

At about 10:00 A.M., on the morning of December 28, 108 men and officers under the command of Major Francis L. Dade were marching from the north bank of the Little Withlacoochee River toward Fort King, forty miles away. At their rear, four horses dragged a six-pounder cannon and gun carriage weighing a thousand pounds. An advance party or "point" was about four hundred yards ahead and a rear guard directly behind, but for some reason the flanks were unprotected by scouts.

The men in this command were mostly artillerymen used as infantry according to military practice of the times. Dade, forty-three, was a Virginian and a competent officer formerly stationed at Key West, Florida. Of particular interest among the other officers was Captain George Washington Gardiner, a stocky, highly experienced West Pointer who was only five feet tall but a solid mass of chunky muscle. Another important officer was Lieutenant William E. Basinger, a Georgian with a fine West Point record. There was also a young surgeon, Dr. John S. Gatlin, not yet thirty. The other officers were of excellent caliber, although most were quite young and not seasoned in combat.

Captain Gardiner was present as the result of a peculiar set of circumstances. He had originally been assigned to command this relief column of two companies destined for Fort King, but his wife Frances was seriously ill at Fort Brooke. Major Dade had volunteered to replace him. Then an arrangement had been made to sail Mrs. Gardiner to the hospital at Key West, so her husband had galloped up to rejoin the column. (Officers were on horseback.) With him was a Negro, Louis Pacheco, who had been sent out as interpreter in case any Seminoles sought a peaceful parley. Pacheco was also a guide of sorts, although no guide was needed along the clearly defined road. Dade, who remained in command, had traversed the route before and was familiar with it.

From the start, the march was plagued by misadventures. First, the oxen tired at their job of dragging the cannon through deep sand. They were switched to pulling the supply wagon. A message was then sent back to Fort Brooke to bring up more horses, and the cannon was temporarily abandoned. It was brought up some hours later by an adequate number of horses from the fort.

Dade was properly cautious at the beginning. At night, logs were cut for stockades around the camp, and pickets (sentries) were posted beyond these barricades. Dade also used flankers during the earlier days of the surprisingly slow march, but failed to do so later. At the same time, he sensed that every move of his tiny force was being watched; and in this he was correct.

Osceola's scouts, under the disciplined leadership of Jumper and Alligator, were never more than a few hundred yards from the trudging column. The flank patrols, made up of soldiers mostly inexperienced in wilderness fighting, were often only a few feet from invisible Seminoles.

Sometimes, at night, owls sobbed in the woods, and night-hawks uttered their harsh, nasal calls. It seemed to the sentries, most of them city men, that a great many night birds inhabited the Florida wilderness. They almost sounded as if they talking to each other.

At the Hillsborough River Dade found the bridge burned. O Christmas morning his force waded through the icy water and tried to raft the heavy cannon across. It spilled into the stream. History indicates it might as well have been left there; but Major Dade had it dragged out at the cost of a man with a painfully injured back. This soldier was told to find his way back to Fort Brooke as best he could, and the column slogged ahead in cold rain. Soldiers who had thought of Florida as a warm tropical paradise found it miserably unpleasant on December 25, 1835. Dade's men suffered badly in their wet boots and soggy blue clothing that chafed their bodies and smelled moldy.

The bridge at the Withlacoochee River had also been burned but was only charred and thus passable. So far there had been no attacks; those familiar with the country knew that above the Little Withlacoochee the land was more open and thus less suitable for ambush. There were bad spots, of course, and this section of the road bordered dangerous Wahoo Swamp, but Dade was now reasonably certain he was out of trouble.

It was cold and wet on the morning of December 28. The soldiers gnawed at cold field rations of pork and tough biscuit, drew their overcoats tight (over their cartridge boxes or pouches), and plowed ahead through the mud. Among those in the advance party were Louis Pacheco, Major Dade, Lieutenant Robert Mudge, and a New Yorker, Captain Upton Fraser, who at forty-one was one of the oldest men in the unit. Dade, forty-three, was the senior in a command composed of men in their twenties and thirties. Except in Company B, Third Artillery, most of the soldiers were former laborers.

The column came abreast of a pond and grassy area to the east of the road with pine and palmetto thickets ahead and to the west. Major Dade rode back to check his column, then trotted forward to join the advance party. As he passed his men, he tried to encourage them with a comment about having a belated Christmas celebration at Fort King.

All of these movements were carefully watched by 180 Seminole warriors under Alligator and Jumper. As noted before, every step of Dade's march had been observed on orders from Osceola. Messages had been carried to Wahoo Swamp where the Seminole war party was hiding. There had been several good opportunities to attack Dade's party, particularly at the river crossings, but Alligator and Jumper had held back because of the absence of Osceola and Micanopy.

Finally Micanopy arrived and a council dominated by Jumper was immediately convened. Micanopy, never much as a leader, wanted to delay the attack until Osceola appeared to lead it. Some of the warriors agreed, but Jumper protested vigorously. He knew the pinelands farther north were too open for a successful ambush; furthermore, Wahoo Swamp and the wilderness behind it were readily available for a safe retreat.

"Any warrior who wants to hold back may do so," said Jumper. "But the rest of the warriors will be in position by dawn tomorrow. There's a good place by a pond. Our great chief, Micanopy, will fire the first shot. That will be the signal. But remember what Osceola said. Don't cut the bodies of the dead. You may take weapons but nothing else. Maybe their big coats."

An hour before dawn, the Seminoles moved out of the swamp and took up positions in the mist west of the Fort King road. Osceola's training had been so thorough that they even had a reserve force of horsemen stationed out of sight to the northwest.

Northeast of the proposed ambush site was a heavy palmetto thicket backed up by a dripping pine forest. If needed, this could also be a temporary retreat area. Alligator and Jumper had their own claims on genius; any military man, looking at the old maps, can see that if the Seminoles were driven into this pine forest their white pursuers could readily be attacked on the left flank by the Indian mounted reserve.

Indians usually stripped for battle, but it is unlikely that all followed this practice on such a wet, chilly morning. Alligator passed the word to load carefully, not carelessly as Seminoles often did. In this respect, the white soldier was better armed; his powder charge was measured in a paper cartridge while the Indian used a powder horn or pouch and guessed at the amount of the charge.

The trap was now set. A logical reconstruction of Indian positions would place Alligator, Micanopy, and a strong warrior band somewhat to the north, with Jumper and the main Seminole force opposite the pond on the west side of the road. Although the rain had stopped, the woods were still misty and dank.

Mapor Dade had almost caught up to the advance guard when the morning silence was shattered by the crack of a single rifle shot. Dade slumped in his saddle. As he fell from the horse, there was an ear-splitting crash from the pine barrens. One of the many accounts indicates this Seminole fire was at a range of twenty yards or less.

Half of Dade's command were killed within seconds of his death, many of the remaining soldiers were seriously wounded, others tore at their coats to get at ammunition, then fired blindly into the sky. Wounded men began screaming until the enraged, powerful voice of Captain Gardiner could be heard above the shrieks.

"Take cover! God damn! Basinger, get that damn gun in action! God damn it! God damn!"

The Seminoles watched almost with awe as the chunky little captain strode around waving his sword, cursing, roaring orders. This was the kind of bravery they admired, but admiration did not prevent them from firing repeatedly at Gardiner or any white soldier who could be seen. Most were now on the ground

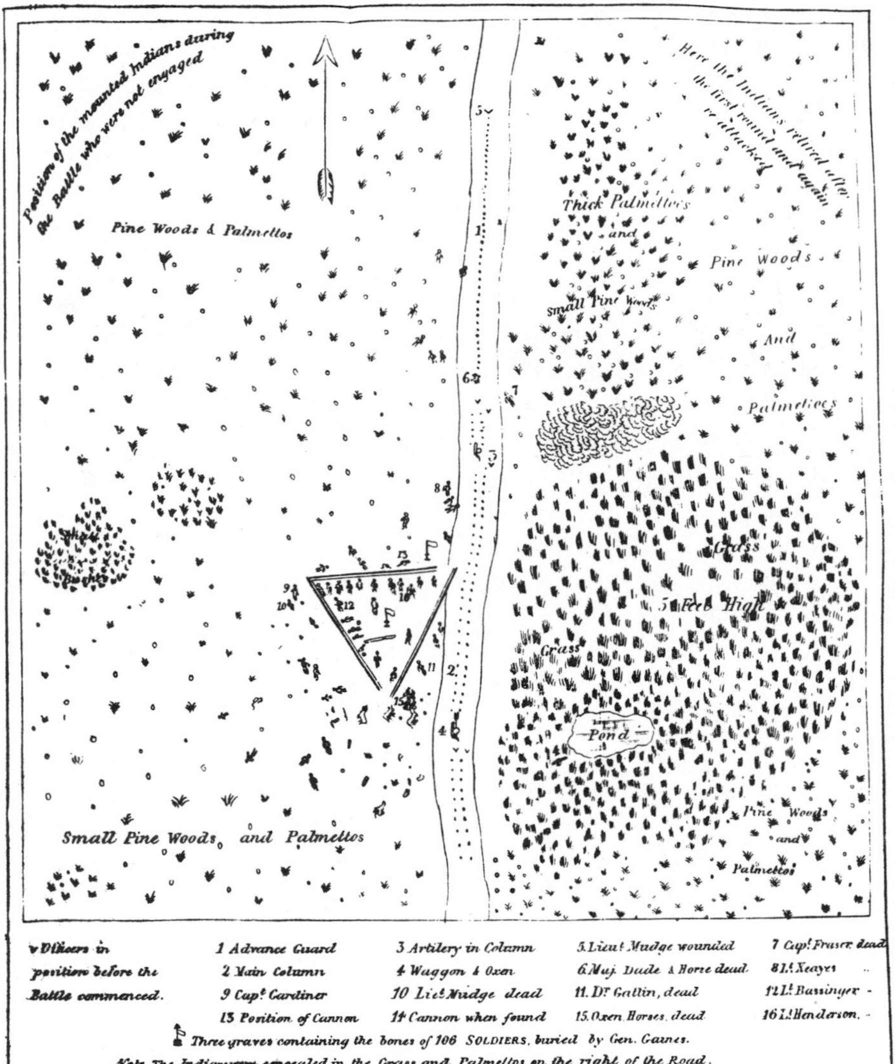

Site of the Dade Massacre

or behind trees to the east of the road. Gardiner, so far, had been unbelievably lucky.

The little six-pounder cannon was now manned and firing, but to almost no avail. Men in the unprotected gun crew were shot down one after another while the Seminoles generally remained unharmed. After about half an hour, Jumper passed the word to withdraw. It is not entirely clear why this was done.

Gardiner had about thirty men left, many of them wounded. He immediately ordered those who could move to start chopping down trees for a triangular barricade. Others staggered along the road to collect arms and ammunition from the dead. The cannon was placed just outside the tiny fort.

After about an hour, the Seminoles resumed their attack. This time the yells and war whoops were so loud that they drowned out the crash of gunfire. Surrounded, the whites gave up firing the cannon and retreated into the barricade, which was only a little more than two feet high.

Captain Gardiner died—on his feet as usual. Young John Gatlin, the surgeon, died before having a chance to use his last ammunition. Finally only three men remained alive within the enclosure. One was Lieutenant Basinger, who had somehow survived his earlier command of the six-pounder.

"I'm the only officer left, boys," he gasped. "Let's do the best we can."

Presently he was down, shot through the thigh. Ammunition was now gone. Still living was a man who seems to have been Joseph Wilson. Another was Ransom Clarke. Outside the enclosure were three wounded, Edward (Edwin) De Courcy, John Thomas, and Joseph Sprague. While these survivors watched, Jumper and Alligator with ten warriors approached to enter the enclosure.

As they were studying the ghastly scene, Joseph Wilson jumped to his feet and seized a rifle from one of the warriors. He smashed it down on the astonished Seminole's head, killing him, then jumped the barricade and rushed along the road. Two Indian horsemen gave chase and shot him fatally.

The Seminoles, obedient to Osceola's orders, did not abuse the dead or wounded, although they collected weapons and a number of greatcoats. Much later (April 2, 1836), *Niles' Register* carried this report of the battle scene:

> Major Dade's uniform coat was not found. With this exception, not one of these brave but unfortunate men had been plundered. Silver, gold, jewelry and watches were untouched—nothing seems to have been taken but arms and ammunition. To what are we to ascribe conduct so singular? It was not the effect of hurry and fear of an attack by a stronger party, for they [Seminoles] buried their own dead, as was ascertained, before leaving the field of battle. Was it forbearance, and magnanimity in the savages, or was it intended to show that it was blood alone they sought, and in the game of life and death they were playing they had no use for such baubles! Osceola [*sic*] is a master spirit, and must have acquired a wonderful influence over his followers, to induce them to forego the opportunity of gaining possession of articles of which they are notoriously fond. Our men were struck with awe and astonishment at the circumstance, and we fear that many a tragic event must be recorded, before the close of this war with an enemy capable of such determination and such self control.

Despite this report, some mutilation and looting was conducted by a party of fifty Negro allies who arrived as the Seminoles were leaving. It appears they were responsible for some scalpings and for the death of Basinger, who was struck with an ax when he asked for mercy. Eventually, they galloped off toward Wahoo Swamp, leaving poor Clarke desperately wounded but still able to stagger from the terrible scene.

John Thomas and Joseph Sprague managed to reach Fort Brooke with news of the battle. They thought they were the sole survivors, but there were two others. Ransom Clarke, with five serious wounds, found that De Courcy was still alive. The two men propped each other up and began to drag their smashed bodies toward Tampa Bay and the safety of the fort. Although they knew silence was important, they moaned at every step.

On the following day, they heard approaching hoofbeats. No white man would be fool enough to travel the Fort King road alone, so they scrambled into the brush, De Courcy to the left, Clarke to the right. The Indian horseman caught sight of De Courcy, wheeled toward him, and killed him as the soldier shrieked. He seemed to be in too much of a hurry to bother about Clarke.

Somehow Clarke managed to reach Fort Brooke with wounds in his right shoulder, right thigh, right temple, one of his arms, and his back. He later became a lecturer at twelve and a half cents per ticket. The remaining survivor was Louis Pacheco, the Negro interpreter who had joined the column with Gardiner. He played dead at the first volley and was later spared by the Seminoles because of his color. He may have been living as late as 1895.

At the time of the battle, the Dade command numbered 110 men. Three had been added—Gardiner, Pacheco, and one nameless servant—minus the injured man at the river crossing. A total of 107 were killed. Three soldiers and the interpreter escaped. The Seminoles lost three killed and five wounded.[1]

While buzzards began to drift over the scene and Clarke started to crawl toward Fort Brooke, the Seminole warriors assembled on one of the islands in Wahoo Swamp. Even Micanopy, usually stolid and glum, was pleased with the day's work. Food had been taken from the white soldiers' wagon, there were warm coats, many muskets had been seized along with the officers' swords, and there was even an adequate supply of liquor. The evening should be spent in celebration.

But where was Osceola, mastermind behind this victory? Had he somehow failed in his own mission on the important battle day? While Micanopy, Jumper, and Alligator speculated about him, their warriors began to eat by the great fires, drink brandy and other liquors, and start the typical boasting that followed any Indian fight. Micanopy ate and drank, too, but he was able to follow the conversation of Alligator and Jumper, who only drank moderately. They were worried about Osceola.

"Send one who hasn't had too much of the burning water," Alligator suggested. "He can ride a good horse almost to Fort King. Then he must return to tell us what happened."

A messenger was sent out. Meanwhile, a scalp rack was erected and the few scalps (taken by the Negroes) were turned over to the medicine chief Illis-haiah-Hadjo, who was a warrior as well as a prominent medicine man. He attached the scalps to a pole ten feet high and a victory dance began. The Indians were still in war paint, red smears on their faces and chests, and some wore soldiers' coats or caps. Except in the moments when a warrior could command attention for a story of personal exploits, most of the yipping and whooping was wordless. Gratifying sounds were more important than sense.

Into this chaotic scene rode the messenger sent out by Alligator. The flanks of his horse were heaving and the man was badly scratched from fast travel through the forest. But he was able to smile when Alligator asked him why he was back so soon.

"He comes!" the messenger cried. "He is ten breaths behind me!"

First to arrive in the circle of firelight was Osceola, haggard but calm, his horse smeared with gray swamp mud, rifle balanced on his legs, a bloody scrap of scalp tucked in his belt. His eyes, as he viewed the scene, conveyed no emotion. He glanced at the scalp pole, then nodded toward Micanopy who was drowsing from food and liquor.

"It is well," Osceola said in a harsh, dry voice. He tossed his bit of scalp to Illis-haiah-Hadjo. "This comes from the white men at Fort King. We cut every scalp into small pieces so more could share our victory. Hear me, my brothers! The agent is dead! A soldier is dead! The store man and his clerks are dead!

I'm sorry I missed what I see here, but we now fight as one man."

"Brother, we waited," Jumper said. "When there was no more time for waiting, we fought the white soldiers. All are dead."

"All?" Osceola asked incredulously.

"All. And we did not cut their bodies, except. . . ." Jumper glanced at some of the Negroes who were scattered among the Seminole warriors. "And we did not take from them anything but weapons and coats. We were cold."

"This is good. I would eat and drink."

"First, a gift," Jumper said. He picked up a uniform greatcoat. "This is a present from one of the white officers. He said he had no more use for it."

The grim joke started all of the warriors howling with laughter. Bits of the scalps brought in by Osceola and his warriors were thorn-pinned to the pole, and a ghastly program of mockery began. Thompson's voice was imitated by the interpreters.

"If you do not agree to removal, we will force you to remove. I have prohibited the sale of powder and lead. Colonel Fanning, seize that man! The Great Father in Washington says . . ."

There is no record of the extent to which Osceola, Micanopy, Jumper, and Alligator joined in this ugly scene. Probably they did; the situation was too heady for complete calm. At the same time, common sense suggests that Osceola did not stay up all night laughing at Thompson's gray hair. He was far too intelligent for that, as were Jumper and Alligator, and an early morning messenger on a dying horse brought interesting news.

General Clinch, who was not Osceola's favorite white man, and General Call, a man Osceola had never seen, were about to attack villages in the "cove" of the Withlacoochee, the general area of Osceola's western Florida stronghold and a place no white had ever entered.[2]

Osceola had expected this. We can assume he was desperately tired after the long watch at Fort King and the ride to Wahoo Swamp, but he promptly held council and then set out with a force of 250 to meet Clinch wherever he might be found. Alligator was his second in command; Jumper and Micanopy remained in the deep swamps with the other warriors and the women and children.

As usual, Osceola had the white soldiers at Fort Drane carefully scouted. He knew that Brigadier General Call had joined Clinch with some 550 mounted Florida volunteers and that Clinch had about 300 regulars. Of this total force, 460 volunteers and about 200 regulars left Fort Drane on the morning of December 29, with the intention of crossing the Withlacoochee River and attacking any force of Indians encountered.

"How do they travel?" Osceola asked his scouts.

"Big knives in the middle in pairs. [The regulars.] The soldiers on horses [volunteers] a long arrow shot to the sides of the big knives. Front men followed by the wagons. The big *tustenuggee* from Fort King [Clinch] at rear. Many warriors."

"Do they have many wagons?"

One of the scouts began to laugh. "Very many," he said. "They keep getting stuck in the dirt."

The white army was, indeed, having a troubled time. They traveled only twelve miles on the first day, a rate of progress that annoyed the horsemen. Wagons bogged down, heat on the second day was fierce, drinking water was muddied by the horses, and noise from the column could be heard a thousand yards away. The love of the American soldier for dogs was a serious handicap; this typical force was accompanied by scores of yipping, barking, howling pets. If Generals Clinch and Call had tried to give Osceola an hourly report of their whereabouts, they could not have found a better way.

It was clear that the white soldiers were heading for a convenient ford in the Withlacoochee River. Osceola proposed to ambush them there, but on the night of December 30, the whites seemed to be shifting toward a position several miles below the ford. When they encamped at night, this time without fires, they were still about three miles from the river.

Osceola considered the situation carefully. His scouts had located a remarkably fine site for an ambush south of the river, but how to get the whites to cross at this point? What would prevent them from retracing their steps upstream to the convenient ford? Osceola decided to take a long chance.

"Have an old canoe placed in sight where we want them to cross," he told Alligator. "Then have our messengers watch to see if they use it. If they start crossing, we can quickly get our warriors from the ford in position."

Young Bemrose was with Clinch's force. At 4:00 A.M. on the morning of the thirty-first, he was astonished to hear a militia bugler blow reveille as usual. This folly was characteristic of the whole expedition and, in fact, of much that happened later during the war. With a few notable exceptions, white officers had no knowledge of wilderness fighting, and their men, however brave, had even less. The usual march was in route formation, two abreast, so that a thin column could stretch for almost a quarter of a mile. Many such columns were either bogged down by supply wagons or desperately lacking in supplies. Camouflage was unknown, and would have been useless because of the noise. In general, the white concept of waging war, particularly during the early period of the conflict, was to use relatively large forces in European battle formations rather than smaller self-contained units capable of rapid movement through swamps and forests.

Osceola either knew or came to understand these failings quickly. In some of the early battles, he matched force against force. But he soon learned that one concealed Seminole was worth five white soldiers fighting in close order, that one guerrilla unit of thirty or forty men could be far more effective than a regular force of three hundred.

The young Englishman, Bemrose, was left with the wagons, the sick, and a guard under Lieutenant Francis Dancy at the encampment three miles from the Withlacoochee. He was disgusted, and modern historians might share his annoyance, for

Bemrose had a good eye for revealing detail. The dogs broke loose to help the bugler alert every Indian for miles to the whites' position. Finally the army, seven hundred men in all, crunched off in the fading moonlight. The regulars were commanded by Lieutenant Colonel Fanning, the militia by General Call, and the total force by General Clinch.

When they reached the river at the point where the canoe had been left, Clinch faced a mighty problem. The river was about a hundred fifty feet wide, running deep and black. Daylight was creeping through the top branches of the trees, and any element of surprise Clinch might have dreamed about was rapidly disappearing. If he were to spend hours getting seven hundred men to a ford, he might lose another day. The period of service for the militia was rapidly running out.

While Clinch was deliberating, a private swam the river without orders, bailed out the canoe, and paddled it back. Incredibly, some of the other soldiers cheered noisily. Osceola's scouts were already waiting to see what the white soldiers' next move would be.

Perhaps Clinch made the only decision available to him, although it was strange by any tactical standards. He began to move the regulars across in the old canoe, two paddlers conveying five men per trip, while Call and the horsemen cast around nearby to find a reasonable point for swimming the horses. While Clinch thus split his command, messengers hurried to report to Osceola.

On the far side of the river there was a kind of field or open space in the shape of a horseshoe or inverted "U" with the legs at the steep bank. The regulars, arriving in their tiny ferry, marched into this field where they were told to stack arms and await further orders. Meanwhile, horses for Clinch and several officers were driven across, and some twenty-seven Florida militia managed to reach the south side. Call, still on the north side with the main body of volunteers, thought a bridge could be built at a narrow point nearby; this job was started.

Osceola, meanwhile, arrived with almost all of his force and was watching the strange actions of the white men from the deep underbrush. He knew Colonel Fanning, detested him from the day of his arrest, but realized that Fanning was a wise, competent soldier. Why, then, this curious business of stacking arms and permitting soldiers to drowse when a strong enemy force was only a few hundred yards away?

It was about noon. The bridge was coming along fairly well; presently the main body of the militia would start crossing. Osceola, dressed for warmth in the Army greatcoat Jumper had given him, gave his warriors a hand signal to begin moving in for the attack. Surrounded on three sides and with their rear blocked by the river, the whites were adequately trapped.

The warriors advanced almost to the edge of a large hammock before one of Clinch's scouts detected their presence and raced toward the troops, screaming hysterically, "Indians! Indians!" At about the same moment, while soldiers barked their knuckles grabbing for stacked muskets, Captain Charles Mellon saw one of the warriors and fired. Several other muskets popped as other soldiers began to fire at real or imaginary targets.

Osceola's men were now in position on the edge of the hammock. Seeing that the soldiers were forming a double rank at close order, he gave the signal to open fire—his shrill, terrifying, "yo-ho-e-hee!" The warriors screamed in reply, then poured a withering blast into the half-formed ranks of the soldiers.

"Load and attack!" Osceola shouted to his men. Since the thickets were now gray with wisps of smoke and visibility would become increasingly poor, he knew that close action would be the most effective. All around him, warriors on the ground had rolled to the left after the first volley in order to free the right arm for reloading. Now, springing to their feet, they raced toward the white troops.

The soldiers had fallen back after the first volley. (Bemrose later wrote that this was a retreat of about a hundred yards.) But Osceola could see they were beginning to form again at the orders of their officers. Colonel Fanning, waving the stump of his arm in fury, was particularly active in this rally. Osceola had a fleeting moment of great respect for this slight, crippled man with gray hair who could whip his soldiers into obedience with words. But the moment passed quickly.

"Kill the officers!" Osceola shouted in Muskogee. He repeated the order in the Hitchiti tongue. Then he cried, "Get back! Reload! Attack again!"

The Indians obeyed, sweeping back into the thickets with their wounded and dead. Smoke now obscured much of the scene, but Osceola was able to see that the soldiers were still forming ranks at close order. One after another, they began dropping before the fierce Seminole fire. As it increased, Colonel Fanning could be seen ordering a charge; the soldiers, at least, were fixing bayonets.

"Fire on the middle!" Osceola cried in his high, piercing voice. He pulled himself up on a fallen tree in order to see through the smoke. The soldiers, smashed back, were beginning to huddle in small groups. Although Osceola could not know it, the constant Indian screaming was as terrifying to some of the white troops as the concentrated fire.

General Clinch was now visible on horseback. His voice could not be heard and officers had to repeat his orders, but the soldiers were no longer bunching up. They had spread out to left and right and were advancing in a charge led by the indomitable Colonel Fanning. Osceola's warriors slipped into the shelter of the hammock underbrush.

Osceola knew instinctively that he could terrorize and ultimately destroy the force of regulars if he could turn either flank and attack from the rear. The soldiers on the far side of the river represented no threat; many of the ones who could be seen had their backs turned to the action. (General Call, fearing an attack on his rear, had ordered this formation. Later, he attempted unsuccessfully to move his troops into action across the river.)

Calling to Alligator, Osceola ordered an attack on the right flank of the troops. When this was countered by General Clinch, the Seminoles were ordered to strike the left flank. Clinch, with a bullet through his cap, managed to drive back this attempt; but his horse was shot from under him and his men began to withdraw before another Seminole charge. Osceola, standing on his tree, saw Clinch stem this retreat and get the remains of his force back into line.

"Try them over there again," he said to Alligator, pointing to the right where there was a heavy thicket. Alligator, stripped to a breechclout and smeared with war paint, nodded and turned to leave. Suddenly Osceola cried out and clutched his arm.

"Are you hit?" Alligator shouted.

"Nothing. *Chehsak pah.* My arm. *Stonekus.* Nothing wrong."

Alligator saw that the sleeve of the Army uniform coat was turning red with blood. As Osceola jumped down from the fallen tree, Alligator scooped up dirt to plaster on the wound. Part of a coatsleeve made an adequate bandage. Osceola repeated "*Stonekus,*" but his voice was grim.

Once again, the white troops were charging. Brave little Colonel Fanning, well in the lead, was screaming encouragement and brandishing a sword with his good arm. Alligator fired, loaded, fired again, then looked to Osceola for orders. The Indian leader saw that the thicket to the right was under heavy attack. (According to Bemrose, this action was led by Captain Mellon and Captain Lemuel Gates.) Osceola could see that the Indians in this quarter were retreating.

"Have the warriors draw back," he told Alligator. "The fight is over. We've hurt them enough, brother."

The Seminoles had lost five dead and five wounded. (Bemrose claimed thirty Indians killed, a highly unreasonable number.)

General Clinch lost four killed and fifty-two wounded, one of whom later died. Only a few of the volunteers crossed the river to engage in the battle. The volunteers later said their presence was a deterrent to the Seminoles who might have massacred Clinch's regulars if Osceola had not known of the strong force on the north bank of the Withlacoochee. This was sheer nonsense; if anything, Osceola and his men were heartened by the reluctance of the militia to cross the river and engage in a fight.

As for who won the battle, both contemporary and modern historians disagree. The Seminoles, under Osceola, withdrew, having stopped General Clinch's abortive campaign. General Clinch also withdrew, knowing full well he had met Osceola and gained little or nothing. His troops limped across a bridge belatedly constructed, leaving some guns and ammuniation behind, cursed the militia, and returned to Fort Drane, where, on January 6–7, the Florida volunteers went home to boast of their victory. Although seven volunteers were wounded, making the total white casualties sixty-three, only twenty-seven had crossed the river. Most had never been within range of a stray bullet.

Osceola's wound was not serious. Deep in the swamps again, he summed up this battle perfectly. He asked Abraham to write a letter to General Clinch, a note that could be passed along by sympathetic slaves or "friendly" Indians who often served as spies within the white camps.

"Tell this to the white chief I have known," Osceola said while Abraham dipped a pointed stick in black vegetable paint. "Say this to General Clinch: 'You have guns and so do we; you have powder and lead and so do we; you have men and so have we; your men will fight, and so will ours until the last drop of the Seminoles' blood has moistened the dust of his hunting grounds.' "[3]

Osceola added that he could hold out against the total forces of the United States for five years. This was a calm assessment rather than a boast. He had knowledge of the terrain, his people were united, his warriors were obedient. So far, the white soldiers had suffered severely while Indian losses were slight. Most important of all, Osceola could fight when and where he chose; the initiative was his.

The regulars at Fort Drane under General Clinch were no longer an effective force, although they had not been sorry to see the militia go home. Bemrose wrote, "Their departure was a boon to us all, and not much less to the government, as they were apparently a strength when in reality they were a weakness, taking up the time and room of more useful men." [4] Clinch wondered what had happened to his reinforcements from Fort Brooke. (News of the Dade disaster did not reach him until about January 20.)

Meanwhile, Philip and his son Coacoochee were terrorizing eastern Florida. One plantation after another was struck—sixteen during January in east Florida. New Smyrna (south of modern Daytona Beach) was burned down, and attacks were made as far south as the present site of Miami. (White refugees paddled out to Key Biscayne, Richard M. Nixon's modern shelter, and hid near the Cape Florida lighthouse until removed to the safety of Key West.)

On January 14, 1836, James Gadsden wrote an almost hysterical letter to President Jackson. Parts of it reflect the general feeling of Floridians at the time:

> . . . I must say that we the People of Florida are in a most distracted and distressed state—We are literally without a Government; without concert of action . . . a universal distrust seems to pervade the whole Community . . . all seem distracted in the general cry of something must be done, while all oppose every measure which can be suggested. . . .
>
> . . . The Army of volunteers & Regulars have met the Enemy at the Withlacouchey & after a sharp contest for one hour separated, as it were by consent—The Army retiring to their old Camp at Lang Syne, & the Indians remaining on

> the field of Battle—Since when the Volunteers have returned home leaving Clinch with his regular force reduced 40 or 50 by death or wounds in position on the frontier—In the meanwhile the Indians have been encouraged & have burnt & destroyed the whole country to the St. Johns River. . . .
>
> Thompson the Agent I presume you have heard has been killed & the whole country of Tomoka, Lower Allachua, &s Destroyed & laid waste—the Peopel [*sic*] of the East are in in truly deplorable state & something must be done & that speedily to relieve them—Yours &c.[5]

The name of Osceola (usually called Powell by the whites) was now mentioned constantly in Florida and throughout the country. It is strange and perhaps unprecedented that many whites, including Army officers, viewed the Seminole leader with tremendous admiration. It does not appear that this was some sort of public *mea culpa* reaction; most Americans were not deeply concerned about the injustice of Indian removal. They also howled with rage and frustration at the many stories of Indian cruelty—often exaggerated but sometimes true. The Seminoles *did* scalp and burn, and they may not be excused on the basis, well established, that the whites also scalped, chopped off ears and other parts of Indian bodies, and burned Seminole villages.

Osceola won respect among his enemies for a broad variety of reasons. Despite the killings at Fort King, he clearly disliked bloodshed and wanted peace. Although he permitted scalping and could not, in fact, have stopped it, he detested mutilation and torture. Historian Coe quotes Andrew Canova, a soldier during the war, as saying:

> The fiendish instinct which led the wild tribes of the West to prolong the death of a captive over a slow fire, was totally lacking in the red men of Florida. Through all of the long and bloody strife which preceded the settlement of Florida, no well-grounded tale was ever told of a Seminole putting a captive to death in an unnatural manner.[6]

The assessment of Osceola by historian (and Army officer) Sprague is interesting. Sprague said:

> In Oseola, or Powell, was combined a nerve, activity, and intelligence, which seemed to diffuse itself among all classes. The women gave a most hearty cooperation, and though obliged to abandon their homes, they cheerfully encountered fatigue, and congregated in places of safety, where they supplied provisions indiscriminately to the warriors, as they went to and from the field of battle.[7]

Buried in this observation is another key to Osceola's genius: the ability to achieve a total involvement of his people, and to turn the women into a functioning, communal commissariat. Among all Indians, women were often close to war parties; but Osceola apparently capitalized on this custom. Sprague, a thoughtful man, would not have mentioned this unless it was unusual.

Osceola's qualities were even described in *Niles' Weekly Register* during early February. Quoting from the *Floridian,* the *Register* said:

> Oceola, or Powel, the head chief of the hostile Seminoles, is likely to figure in history with Philip of Pokanokee or Tecumseh, possessing all their noble daring and deep love of country, with more intelligence, and perhaps, more ferocity.[8]

Historian Coe quotes the St. Augustine *Herald* of January 13, 1836:

> The character of this chief is but little known and not sufficiently appreciated. He is represented to be a man of great tact, energy of character, and bold daring. . . .[9]

Many whites not only admired Osceola but also proclaimed his cause. The following, appearing in *Niles' Weekly Register,* is described as a letter from a writer in Washington, D.C. to the *Journal of Commerce*:

> . . . this is the last and most desperate struggle of the Indian. He fights now gloriously and gallantly, with the spirit of a thousand lions in his breast—for the soil on which he was born, and which was a just inheritance from his ancestors. We, by a forced and corrupt treaty, call it ours. We send armed men—men armed with a whiskey bottle, a weapon more terrible than the rifle—to persuade them to abide by a treaty which they never made, and to cross the Mississippi never to return. The spirit of their tribe—the Great Spirit walking in the sky—tells them they must perish. The voice of their fathers calls them to their home—the only home which the white man has left them—the grave. . . . Preparations are making—not for the defeat of the Seminoles, but for their extermination.[10]

This grim and somewhat emotional assessment failed to take into account the fact that Osceola was winning his war. But this gave him scant pleasure. Almost without exception, every contemporary account indicates that Osceola truly hated a war that virtually had been thrust upon him. The killings were stupid, but they had to go on until the whites recognized Seminole rights. If they ever did. . . .

Osceola's camp in the Withlacoochee swamp was primitive even by Seminole standards. Huts of palmetto thatch sheltered his wives, his beloved daughter, and a new baby. Deerskins were spread on the ground and some thin blankets covered the women and children. A low fire burned nearby, corn gruel with a little meat bubbling in the iron kettle. Fish, speared by the women, smoked above this fire.

On a January night, Osceola stepped from the circle of firelight to stare at the evening star. His people were all around him in their own camps. Children, women, warriors, all driven by the white man toward potential destruction. And none of it made any sense. The land was large enough for all. The Indian had never asked for more than a chance to exist in peace.

A cold wind sent sparks dancing from the Seminole fires, and beyond the swamp the skeletal wolves howled their song of desolation. White soldiers, huddled at Fort Drane, shuddered at this dirge, and their pet dogs yipped back nervously. Clouds, driven by the wind, blurred the moon. A tissue of frost was forming on the brush, and the swamp waters were smoked with mist.

Osceola, turning back toward his camp, felt the indescribable loneliness of leadership. He had wanted to be leader, he had even seized at leadership with passion. Now he was the main figure in a cruel pageant of decisions that might be wrong. Among the Seminoles, no one had his influence. The war was his, the courage to fight came primarily from him, the spirit of his people depended on him.

"We will win," he told himself. "We may die to win. But the children of my children's children will walk this land."

Che-cho-ter, silent at the camp site, may have wandered why the husband she shared with the second wife no longer laughed. Osceola had not laughed since the afternoon of December 28.

8

The Second Battle of the Withlacoochee

Osceola and his Seminoles were reasonably comfortable in their hiding place in the cove of the Withlacoochee. There was enough to eat—at least there is no record to the contrary—and they were safe from attack. The initiative was still theirs. Philip, across Florida on the east coast, was driving settlers to the dubious safety of St. Augustine. A steady flow of Negro spies informed Osceola that all of white Florida was in a state of panic.

Spy reports also indicated that the situation at Fort Drane was close to critical. Young Bemrose later told of the suffering of the wounded and the kindness of General Clinch who could be seen "sitting upon the earth floor, giving counsel and comfort to a poor dying private soldier. . . . He was plain in dress and in all his surroundings, living in a simple tent like unto others."

Bemrose also remarked on the thinking of the soldiers:

> The daily tales of murder and scalping, first in one direction and then in another, possibly 100 miles apart, showed plainly the enemy was terribly on the alert, nothing escaping his vigilance, causing us to be filled with many forebodings. Now all began to see we had got into a hornet's nest, many miles from the seaboard, and consequently not over safe in keeping our scalps. Tales of horror filled all minds, discipline

> became most rigid, for all saw the necessity of proper care.
> The outside sentinels were placed more thickly around so as to prepare for the creeping Indian, and, you may depend, the outside sentinels had not very pleasant reflections when on their stationary posts, none being allowed to move, if so doing being a sure mark for the Indian rifle. What nights these poor fellows must have passed, surrounded by the croaking of bullfrogs and the yelling of apparently 10,000 wolves.[1]

Osceola was, in fact, engaged in a form of psychological warfare that may have been intentional. All Seminole warriors used terror as a weapon, smearing their bodies with red war paint, sometimes providing a contrast with black, thus achieving an almost inhuman appearance that was supposed to frighten the enemy.

The war whoop, moreover, inspired a terror almost impossible to describe. The Seminole cry, "*Yo-ho-e-hee!*" was not the "gobble" or shrill "wa-ha-ha" usually associated with the Northeastern Indian of earlier times. It was a shriek, a banshee wail, an unearthly scream of rage. The many incoherent accounts of the Seminole war whoop suggest that when it was rendered by two hundred determined Indians it sounded like a holiday in hell. Soldiers as well as civilians shuddered.

While Osceola sat comfortably in the swamps, watching the small boys practice marksmanship, listening to reports from spies, sometimes even drilling his warriors in an approximation of white practice, the United States government flailed around in bureaucratic confusion. By the end of January, however, Congress had appropriated more than six hundred thousand dollars for conduct of the war in Florida. General Clinch was authorized to call upon South Carolina, Georgia, and Alabama for any forces he required. Brevet Brigadier General Abraham Eustis, stationed at Charleston, South Carolina, was ordered to proceed with militia and regulars to St. Augustine, defend the east coast, and place himself under the command of General Clinch.

To confuse matters, Brevet Major General Winfield Scott was ordered to assume overall command in Florida, thus relegating the unhappy Clinch to a lesser position. Scott, tall and good-looking despite a chin like a piano leg, was not a West Pointer. Possibly as a reaction, he was more of a West Pointer than any graduate. (He is the old "Fuss and Feathers" of American military history.)

When he finally arrived at Fort Drane on March 13, he brought with him a fine military band, three wagons full of furniture, excellent wines, and, according to Bemrose, "other luxuries." Bemrose shrewdly observed: "Thus had he decked everything with the grand panoply of war, very becoming to a man, who was certainly one of nature's finest specimens of the genus homo, yet quite unsuitable for Indian bush fighting." [2]

Historian John K. Mahon reminds us that Scott had fathered a new manual, *Infantry Tactics*, the contents of which were borrowed from French drill guides.[3] It may not yet have been in use, having only been published in 1835, but Winfield Scott's tactical orientation and that of most of the American military leadership was European.

A simple key to European military theory of the time may be found in the word "battlefield." Battles were fought on fields with opposing soldiers stationed in neat lines. Engagements were carried out with the precision of a macabre waltz. Nothing could have helped Osceola more than this kind of white military thinking.

To complicate matters further, the estimable General Scott profoundly disliked one of his fellow officers. This was Major General Edmund Pendleton Gaines, the rawboned, gaunt, ill-tempered commander of the Western Department of the Army. Scott and Gaines (who hated Scott) had long feuded for top position in the Army. Gaines's Western Department also extended a considerable distance into Florida, thus causing some confusion in military responsibility.

Hearing on January 15 about the troubles in Florida, Gaines

assembled eleven hundred men and set off from New Orleans on February 4. He was poorly supplied and acting without any clear orders (he should have been in Texas), but he knew shortly after his arrival at Tampa Bay on February 9 that Scott had sent stores of rations to Fort King. What to do? Turn around and go back where he belonged? Nonsense!

On February 13, Gaines and a command of about a thousand men headed for Fort King where General Scott's rations were supposedly waiting. Gaines's little army marched in three columns with an appropriate point or advance guard and an adequate rear guard. They moved slowly, for it was not until the twentieth that they saw buzzards circling above the remains on the Dade battleground.

Pausing to bury the dead, Gaines then hurried to Fort King, arriving on the afternoon of February 22. To his chagrin, he found only enough rations to maintain the company occupying the little fort. Now almost desperate, he wrote to Clinch at Fort Drane that he was returning to Fort Brooke by way of the cove of the Withlacoochee and required some rations. He said he also hoped to engage the Seminoles on or near General Clinch's recent battleground.

Clinch mercifully sent him twelve thousand rations, or enough for about seven days; and on February 26 General Gaines began his march. Osceola was following all of this with deep interest. When it became apparent that Gaines was heading for the Withlacoochee, he held a meeting with Alligator, Jumper, and Micanopy.

"They may try to cross at the ford," he said, "but it's farther than they would want to go. I'd guess they would try to cross more toward the rising sun. But this time we won't let them go over. Every available warrior is to be waiting on our side of the river.

"A good hammock rises three miles from this part of the river. Have the women assemble there with the food, powder, and lead. They're to make bullets as they've been shown, and keep food cooking. This time the white man's going to know he's been met."

When the women, boys, and old men had assembled on the hammock, the atmosphere was joyful. Boys wrestled and pummeled each other while the old men stared fiercely in the direction of the river and the women occupied themselves at the cooking fires or with the running of shot. After the coming battle, the white man would think twice before attacking Osceola and the Seminoles! [4]

General Gaines reached the river on the afternoon of February 27, missing the ford by a little more than two miles. Osceola was waiting on the far shore with part of a total force of almost a thousand warriors. Dense vegetation and some high sandbanks gave his men excellent cover. From his position in some deep grass, he could see two officers and a small party of men wading toward a tiny island in the middle of the river.

"I know one of them," Jumper said. He was lying beside Osceola. Sweat had smeared the red war paint on the faces and chests of both men. "He's General Gaines. I saw him many moons ago."

"They won't cross here," Osceola said, pointing. "The water's too deep on this side. But we'll let them know we're waiting."

He gave his terrible war cry and fired. The signal brought a chorus of fearful whoops followed by the roar of several hundred rifles. The Indians directed most of their fire toward the troops on the far shore, so Gaines and his scouting party were able to splash back unharmed. Osceola kept up the attack until a fieldpiece, dragged along by Gaines' men, began to splatter the area with canister shot. He then withdrew to await developments.

After Gaines had ordered his men back from the river to camp for the night, Osceola began to shuttle his warriors to and from the hammock for food, ammunition, and rest. For his part, he walked to the edge of the river and stared across the black water toward the campfires of the whites. Many fires, he told himself.

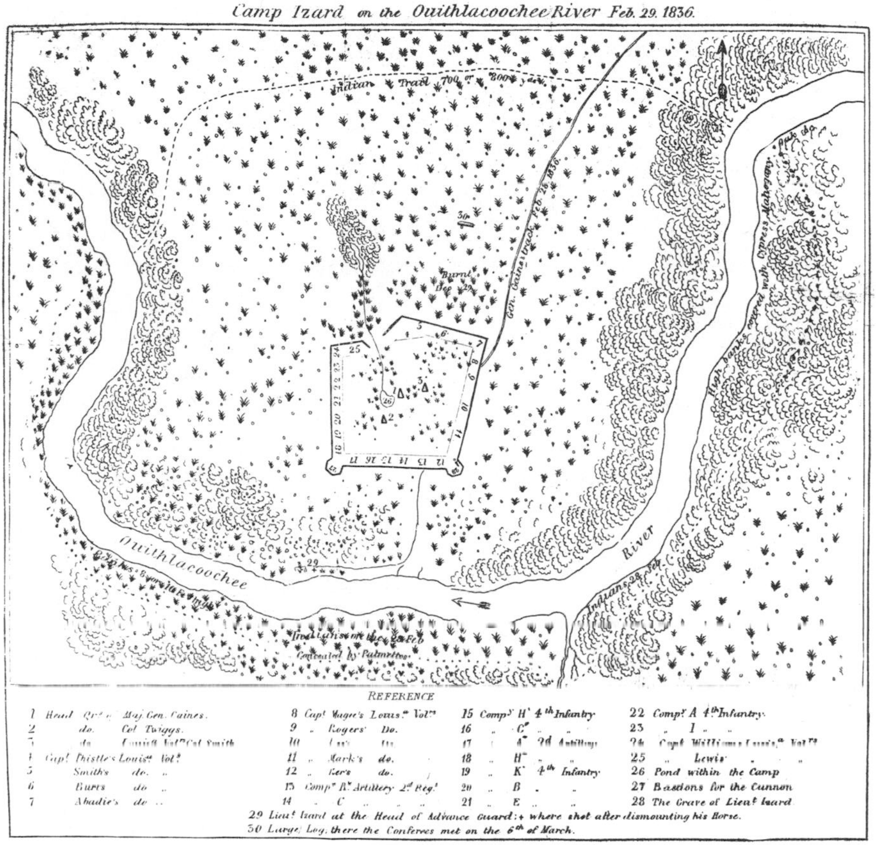
Camp Izard on the Ouithlacoochee River Feb. 29. 1836.
Indian Trail 700 or 800 yds.
Burnt
Ouithlacoochee
River
REFERENCE
1 Head Qrs of Maj. Gen. Gaines.
2 do. Col Twiggs.
4 Capt Thistle's Louisa Vols
5 Smith's do.
6 Burts do
7 Abadie's do
8 Capt Magee's Louisa Vols
9 Rogers' Do.
11 Mark's do.
12 Ker's do.
13 Compy R. Artillery 2d Regt
14 C
15 Compy H 4th Infantry
16 C
18 H
19 K 4th Infantry
20 B
21 E
22 Compy A 4th Infantry.
23 I
25 Lewis
26 Pond within the Camp
27 Bastions for the Cannon
28 The Grave of Lieut Izard
29 Lieut Izard at the Head of Advance Guard: + where shot after dismounting his Horse.
30 Large Log, there the Conferees met on the 6th of March.

Site of the Second Battle of Withlacoochee

The tally sticks received earlier had been right; Gaines had about a thousand soldiers with him.

In the morning (February 28), Gaines began to move downstream toward the ford while Osceola quietly duplicated this move along the south bank. At about 9:00 A.M., the soldiers reached what was supposed to be the ford, but found the water still too deep for crossing. The Indians opened fire and Lieutenant James F. Izard, a regular on leave who had volunteered for the expedition, was shot through the head. Somehow this brave man managed to live for five days.

The river handicapped Osceola as much as it did General Gaines. To the Seminoles' immediate right and left were high banks covered with cypress, mahogany, and oak. Osceola had concentrated his warriors in a palmetto thicket directly across from the point at which Izard had been killed. Until about 1:00 P.M., he kept up a fierce fire on the whites; but they then moved out of range and began building a quadrangular breastwork in the middle of a pine barren. Woodburne Potter, who was a staff officer with Gaines, wrote that it was 120 yards from the river and indicated that it was built around a small pond or spring.

Osceola was delighted by Gaines' choice of a defense position. As shown in a map of the period, the river here formed an almost perfect "U." Osceola could cross his warriors out of range and hammer from the north or from the heavy river foliage within the "U." He proceeded to have two crossings scouted to the east and west while Gaines, apparently unaware that the was boxed in, wrote General Clinch saying he had the Seminoles concentrated and suggesting an attack on their rear. This astonishing message, sent out at 10:00 P.M., was a bit like the mouse saying he has the cat cornered.

On the morning of the twenty-ninth, Osceola quietly moved his force over the river and placed his warriors to the east, west, and north of what the whites now called Camp Izard. Each of the Seminoles was well armed and supplied with abundant powder and ammunition. (Potter commented on the excellent quality of Indian weapons.)

"Don't shoot until you hear me fire the first shot," Osceola had told his men. For his own station, he had chosen the north or top of the "U." Here the cover was mostly pine with some cypress around a second small pond.

At about ten o'clock, he slipped up to this cypress stand, which was about a hundred yards from the breastworks, fired, and gave his war cry. The response was startling; almost a thousand rifles shattered the morning quiet. With pauses for loading, the firing continued for the rest of the morning; but the range was generally too great for effective shooting. After an hour, Osceola noticed the breeze was from the north.

"Build a fire," he ordered one of his warriors. When this was done, he fashioned a torch from twisted grass and began to race from the cypress stand toward the eastern bend of the river. Every few yards, he paused to ignite the winter-dry grass. Musketballs hummed around him but he managed to hurl himself into the safety of the thickly wooded bank. To the warriors there, he shouted, "Move up behind that smoke! You'll get close before they see you!"

The Indians obeyed the order, but to Osceola's dismay the wind shifted and the fire was turned back on the burned ground where it quickly died. It was now almost noon and ammunition was running low. Since supplies would have to be brought up from the hammock, Osceola ordered all of his warriors back across the river until late afternoon, when he launched a brief attack from the river woods.

The two days had been costly for General Gaines. Two men were dead, thirty-five wounded. (The low death rate was due to the small caliber of Indian rifles.) Again Gaines wrote to Clinch suggesting that an attacking force be marched directly to Camp Izard where the enemy appeared to be concentrated.

The two messages went through, but Clinch was in a strange position. General Scott, by now at Picolata (west of St. Augustine on the St. Johns River), was the top commanding officer in Florida, and orders for a major attack had to come from him. On March 1, Scott wrote to Clinch to keep his hands off Gaines' problem. Gaines would have to get out of his own mess.

Osceola, meanwhile, was having his own problems. Although he had nearly a thousand warriors, Gaines held the advantage of the breastwork in the middle of the pine barren where cover was limited. In order to attack, Osceola felt he required a stronger force. He had reinforcements on the way; some eight hundred Seminoles and one hundred seventy Negroes were preparing to join him and would reach the Withlacoochee on March 6, when Osceola hoped to launch an all-out assault.

"Then we'll crush the white man like a bug," he told his followers.

But the delay created a curious situation. Osceola had to keep the white soldiers occupied while waiting for reinforcements. He did so by daily attacks in varying strength. They did little damage but kept the whites pinned down.

Toward noon on March 3, Osceola had a strange but clever idea. The white soldiers had always said the Indians were undisciplined savages who could never obey their leaders. White officers were proud of parade and drill, symbols of discipline. Osceola smiled slightly as he considered his plan.

At 3:00 P.M., one of the sentries on the north side of Camp Izard blinked his eyes and suddenly exclaimed, "My God!" Then he shouted, "Bedamn if the Injuns ain't holdin' a parade!" Soldiers and officers not at post along the breastworks rushed to the north side. The spectacle before them had never before been seen in America; and, as far as the writers of this book know, would never be seen again.

Osceola had divided some six hundred Indians into two forces of approximately three hundred each. He had sent one force to the east, another to the west. Now, out of range but in clear view of Camp Izard, these two units marched toward each other *exactly like regular troops.* Each was preceded by an ensign bearing a large red flag. Most of Gaines' men missed the significance of this astonishing parade, but a few of the officers had wits enough to know what they were seeing. "Undisciplined" Indians could be formed into a disciplined force.

"Look at that!" one of the officers exclaimed after considering this startling thought. Osceola's lieutenants had given orders to countermarch the two units. Complete military precision was missing, but the order was obeyed promptly and without confusion. During all of this strange show, a horn of some sort blared mockingly.

On the evening after the Seminole parade, food was beginning to run out. Two horses were slaughtered and part of the meat distributed to men in the greatest need. Woodburne Potter tried some of the cooked liver and found it excellent. (As time passed, a quarter of a butchered dog brought five dollars; one biscuit, the same; a piece of horse entrails, six dollars.)

Firewood was in short supply within Camp Izard. On the morning of March 4, a detail was sent out to gather wood. Osceola's warriors wounded two of these men, also killed a man behind the barricade. Except for some mild shooting on March 5, little happened until evening when Osceola ordered some fires built along an Indian trail to the north. He then had them put out. This was simply a distraction designed to mystify the beleaguered, cold, starving whites.

Osceola now had some annoying news that had been carried by relays of runners from Fort Drane. General Clinch, with four hundred fifty infantry and one hundred fifty cavalry, had left at noon on the fifth to relieve Gaines. (He had done this on his own initiative, not knowing Scott had relented and sent him an order on the fourth to act as he thought best.)

Osceola knew white infantry moved slowly. Clinch had thirty-two miles to cover; at the usual rate, he would not reach Camp Izard until evening of the sixth. If the Seminole reinforcements arrived early on the sixth, the Indians could strike well in advance of Clinch's arrival; but if they did not, Osceola would have to devise some other plan.

At 10:00 P.M. on the night of March 5, the guard at Camp Izard heard a distant hail and some indistinct words. The speaker was told he could safely come closer. Potter and apparently others familiar with the Seminoles thought he was the interpreter Abraham; he was really Micanopy's Negro, John Caesar, who thought highly of himself because of his association with the chief. Caesar, incredibly enough, was visiting the whites without authority or permission of Osceola, Micanopy, or any Seminole leader.

"What do you want?" the captain of the guard called.

"How far are your sentinels posted out?"

"You can come closer. They won't fire on you."

Caesar came within a hundred yards. Then he asked if Colonel Twiggs (Lieutenant Colonel David Twiggs) was in the camp. Told that he was, Caesar said, "Tell him we don't want to fight anymore. As tomorrow [Sunday] is a good day, we'll come in and shake hands, and be good friends."

"Very well," the captain of the guard shouted back. "If you come in with a white flag, you won't be harmed."

"We'll come in after breakfast tomorrow morning, about nine o'clock. Good night."

Caesar returned to the Seminole camp where he found the chiefs in conference with Osceola. He cheerfully announced what he had done, then cringed and began to slobber excuses as the chiefs rose one by one to glare at him through eyes that gleamed red in the firelight. There was the silky whisper of knives being drawn. The ring around Caesar began to tighten.

"Kill him!" one of the chiefs suddenly screamed. "Kill the fool! Cut him to pieces and throw him to the dogs!"

"Wait!" Osceola roared. "Caesar has done no real harm! He's a fool, but he doesn't deserve death! My brothers, think for a while. If our friends don't join us tomorrow, we won't be able to attack. In the meantime, the fat general, our old enemy, is coming from Fort Drane with six hundred soldiers. The tally sticks say so. What then? We'll have to retreat.

"Why not bargain with the white man? It would be wise to see what he has to say. If the killing can be stopped with honor, I say to stop it. Why rage like animals when we should think like men? Caesar was wrong, but no damage has been done. We can meet the white man with honor. At present, he's our prisoner, so why should we fear to meet him?"

Most of the chiefs grumbled agreement, but a few strode away haughtily. It would later take all of Osceola's powers of persuasion to placate warriors who felt Caesar had betrayed them. He had, in fact, gravely damaged the Seminole position by saying that the Seminoles did not want to fight anymore; and Osceola had shown remarkable restraint in saving his life.

At 8:30 A.M. on March 6, Abraham, Jumper, Osceola, Alligator, and Caesar advanced under a white flag to be met by a Major Barrow, an interpreter, and several other whites. The meeting took place about a hundred yards from Camp Izard, with a log serving as a seat.

"What is it you want?" Major Barrow asked.

"To stop fighting," Jumper said through Abraham. "We have spilled a great deal of blood, and we have had enough revenge. . . ." At this, Osceola nodded agreement. Jumper continued, "We have fought the white men because we were badly treated by them. We have killed many of their men, but we will stop if we withdraw our warriors to the other side of the river and the white soldiers remain on their side."

"I'll tell this to General Gaines," Barrow agreed. "We'll meet here again in half an hour."

At the appointed time, Captain Ethan Allen Hitchcock came out with several officers and a soldier named Chamberlain who had known Osceola at Fort King. Osceola shook hands vigorously with the soldier, then glanced curiously at Hitchcock. Meanwhile, Holata Mico joined the parley.

"How is Lieutenant Graham?" Osceola asked, referring to his Fort King friend.

"I heard he was wounded in the first battle on the river," one of the whites replied.

"No, that couldn't happen," Osceola protested. "I told my warriors not to hurt him. They would never disobey." *

Captain Hitchcock now said that General Gaines had no authority to make a treaty with the Seminoles. They must cease killing whites and retire to the south side of the river to await the arrival of United States commissioners. A large force was coming to "operate against them," and every armed Indian would be shot down.

To this, Jumper said, "We know you have many men marching toward us, but our people are opposed to going away from the lands of their fathers. We're sorry the white people forced us to fight them, but they oppressed us and deprived us of our rights, and we could not bear it."

After some additional conversation, it was decided to meet again at about 4:00 P.M. In a curious side conversation, Alligator revealed that the Seminoles now numbered sixteen hundred men. If true, this suggests that some of the reinforcements had come in. Osceola might have attacked at once, but he wanted to honor the truce and also decide how to meet the threat of General Clinch.

The meeting at 4:30 P.M. was a virtual repetition of the earlier ones. Hitchcock repeated that General Gaines had no authority to treat with the Indians, that they should remove to the south side of the Withlacoochee and remain there peacefully until the arrival of United States commissioners. If they did so, they would not be disturbed.

To this, Osceola and the chiefs agreed. But just as a truce seemed to have been achieved, shots were heard to the north and Osceola's rear guard began whooping. Clinch's advance

* Woodburne Potter denies that this conversation took place, but there is repeated confirmation by other contemporary writers.

guard had arrived. Not knowing about the parley, they had simply opened fire. The Seminoles melted into the woods, crossed the river, and awaited developments. Osceola realized he had not been betrayed; he had known Clinch was due to arrive about evening, and he understood Clinch had no way of knowing about the conference.

Clinch, who had brought forty head of cattle and two days' extra rations of bread, pork, and sugar, fed Gaines' starving army. On Monday, March 7, some of the soldiers splashed or fished in the river. Osceola ordered his warriors not to molest them.

"Leave them alone this time," he said. "They're going to retreat with their wounded. They have no more taste for battle, and we also gave our word to stay on the south side of the river."

Gaines had lost five dead and forty-six wounded. His men would have starved without the arrival of Clinch, who also prevented the imminent destruction of Gaines' force. On March 9, Gaines turned his command over to General Clinch after making some remarks to the effect that the Seminole War was over. He had won it. At noon on March 10, a day following heavy rains, the combined command began to slog back to Fort Drane with the anguished wounded. Shortly after they reached the post, General Scott arrived to peer disdainfully at Gaines' battered army and stare silently at an invisible object six inches from the commander's left ear.

General Gaines departed on March 14 for Tallahassee where he was received as a hero. Mobile and New Orleans wanted to honor him with public dinners, but he decided to push on to Texas where he was supposed to be. He sincerely thought he had defeated the Seminoles and somehow mysteriously won the war.

M. M. Cohen, the contemporary historian, summarized Gaines' remarkable campaign in these words:

> After a careful investigation of all the circumstances, we think that every impartial mind must arrive at the conclusion that Gen. Gaines' victory at the Ouithlacoochee is not an event the repetition of which is greatly to be desired. We regret the results of some of his movements. . . . The Indians were not only able to hold their own ground, and keep the whites within their entrenchments, but also succeeded in moving off unmolested, after Gen. Clinch arrived with 500 additional troops, many of which were mounted. Another such victory would be more than the reputation of any one General could stand without detriment.[5]

Scott had been so infuriated by General Gaines' campaign that he had written the adjutant general on March 2: ". . . it would be better for the public interests that the Indians should drive Major-General Gaines, than that he should drive them. . . . The lives which he has lost have promoted no end." It is difficult, in historic perspective, to take a different view of the second battle of the Withlacoochee, which Osceola clearly won with the loss of three dead and five wounded.[6]

Meanwhile, Winfield Scott had a master plan for crushing Osceola and the Seminoles. Reduced to its essentials, it consisted of attacking the Indians in the cove of the Withlacoochee with three converging wings or columns, and hopefully driving Osceola into open terrain more advantageous for traditional white fighting.

The right wing, commanded by General Clinch and accompanied by Scott, consisted of about two thousand regulars, plus Georgia and Louisiana volunteers who would march from Fort Drane to the general location of Camp Izard on the Withlacoochee. This was the hammering wing—the one supposed to drive Osceola into one or both of the other two wings.

The center wing, with about twelve hundred fifty men, including Alabamians, Louisiana volunteers, and a small body of regulars, would move north from Fort Brooke to a position near Chicuchatty (Checuchatty), southwest of the Withlacoochee swamps and roughly in the vicinity of modern Brooksville. This wing would be commanded by Colonel William Lindsay.

Brigadier General Abraham Eustis, a stern-looking officer, commanded the left wing and had the toughest job. Eustis, with a force of South Carolina volunteers and four artillery companies totaling fourteen hundred men, was assigned to move from St. Augustine to Volusia on the St. Johns River, then cross to the Indian town of Pelacklakaha (Pilaklakuha) near the Dade battleground. Eustis would be crossing terrain much of which is difficult even today.

The columns or wings were supposed to reach their destinations at approximately the same time, and to keep track of each other by firing cannons. A total of 4,650 soldiers would be involved in this campaign, and even the Navy would be guarding the Gulf Coast against Cuban supplies for the Seminoles or any attempt on the part of the Indians to retreat by water.

Osceola knew General Scott's plan shortly after it had been formulated. He heard about it on a cool, pleasant afternoon when the winter sun sent warm shafts down through the cypress branches. He smiled at the messenger and then, for the first time in weeks, began to laugh aloud. After sending the messenger to be fed, he called in his strong, shrill voice for Alligator and Jumper.

"Brothers, come here! Laugh with me! The white man wants to catch water in a net for fish!"

9

Osceola's Guerrilla Tactics Pay Off

In his own way, Winfield Scott was a fine man and a worthy officer. He had served with distinction during the War of 1812, receiving a severe wound, and later had spent a year studying military affairs in Europe. In 1841, he would become supreme commander of the United States Army. The Mexican War would make him a national hero, and cast him in the role of unsuccessful candidate for President.

This was the man Osceola faced in 1836. He was the best the United States Army had to offer—probably a far better commander than Andrew Jackson, certainly a more thoughtful planner than Edmund Pendleton Gaines. His liking for comfortable living did not make him less sympathetic toward the men under him; he was generous and compassionate although insistent on discipline. His only real deficiency was a total lack of understanding of Indians and Indian fighting.

The one possible way to describe the clash between Osceola and Scott is to recount briefly the movements of the three wings. Events naturally overlap, but a reasonably clear picture may be sketched. Osceola's side of the story is the more difficult one to relate; it is clear what he planned and did, but the exact timing is elusive.

He certainly told his lieutenants, "Let the white soldiers come from north, east, and south. We'll hit them when we have an advantage, then let them pass by. And we'll fight in smaller bands, about two hundred in a group. Most important of all, messengers must keep every *tustenuggee* aware of what the others are doing. And I must always know where and how you fight. If I say to fight elsewhere, do so. If I say to leave the white man alone or hide from him, do so."

So far, Osceola had made no mistakes. There had been the unfortunate affair of Caesar, but that could be overlooked; no warriors had been killed because of it. During the entire war so far, few Seminole lives had been lost, the women and children had been safe, and there had been enough food. Because of the careful planning, powder and lead were in abundant supply. The Indians found it easy to obey a leader with Osceola's record of success.

Scott wanted adequate supplies in position before he moved. Because of incredibly bad roads, this was an almost impossible job; but it was accomplished to his satisfaction by mid-March. He ordered Lindsay and Eustis to leave their jump-off points on March 25, then departed with Clinch and the right wing on March 26 for the short march to Camp Izard on the Withlacoochee. Troops were in their winter clothing but there were enough rations for eighteen days and Scott felt confident of a successful campaign. Two large flatboats were carried on a trucklike device that constantly bogged down. There were two six-pounder cannon on carriages, also unwieldy and easily mired.

Scott reached the river on March 28, and cheered up his men by ordering the band to play during supper. Osceola's warriors, attracted by the musical interlude, applauded it with a volley of shots that killed two soldiers.[1] At 4:00 A.M., the crossing of the river began. A man named Foster Blodget swam over with a rope that would serve as a handline for ferrying. (Thereafter, the place, near modern Dunnellon, was called Blodget's Ferry.) The crossing was unopposed until the end, when the Seminoles opened fire on the rear troops. Presently, after a minor exchange of shots and some bayonet charges, the Indians withdrew.

This was about what Osceola had planned. Depending on the swamps to slow the soldiers, he had only a small force at the river crossing. There was no point in fighting almost two thousand men when the swamps would do the job for him.

What happened thereafter was particularly frustrating to the white troops and typical of much of the war. Scott found the cove of the Withlacoochee a maze of dense cypress swamps and lonely hammocks. Water and mud were everywhere; wagons and cannon could be moved only with the help of sweating, cursing men. Everyone including the officers was immediately soaked and smeared with mud. No scene could have been more desolate; in the semidarkness, Spanish moss drooped wetly like the beards of ghostly old men, cold rain hissed or spattered on the water, strange birds glided suddenly and silently beneath the trees. The soldiers feared alligators and snakes in the murky waters; and at all times they sensed the presence of the Indians. There was little talking as the men slogged ahead, but occasionally someone would mutter, "They're out there, ain't they?" And they were.

Flanking the river was a chain of island-dotted lakes then called Oloklikaha. Late in the morning of March 30, a band of Seminoles was spotted on one of these islands. The soldiers groaned when they were ordered to attack.

"Now they tell us to go swimmin'," one man muttered.

But they started for the island in force, having left three hundred men to guard the wagon train. This took bravery, for the soldiers had to plod through mud, water, and reeds with gun and ammunition boxes held above their heads. The Indians welcomed them with sharp fire, then retreated through shallow water to shore and deep woods. In a kind of running fight for which they were totally unprepared, soldiers stumbled after them, sometimes stopping to fire at shadows. The whites were soaked with sweat, plastered with mud, plagued by insects, shaken by the occasional war cries that now had a mocking tone.

"If we could only see the devils!" an officer complained. As if to underline his protest, a shot rang out and a soldier, screaming, stumbled to the ground. Again the mocking cry.

The whites camped for the night; the Seminole band, pleased by this kind of fighting, settled down on a nearby island. No one knows who was in this group, but if Osceola was present he must have said, "This is what I've wanted. Let's play with them again tomorrow."

There was certainly no happiness in the white camp. Fires smoked and stank but gave little heat, men cursed their rations of the soggy flour and pork provided instead of the hard bread and bacon that kept better and was more edible, wolves howled, and in the cold hours after midnight there was the gnawing, sour fear of the unseen enemy. When they could sleep in their wet, stinking clothes, the soldiers dreamed of the hideous war cry, the crackling of shots, the visceral thud of a rifle ball against breast or belly. (Men would sometimes become helpless from fright, almost paralyzed, or even insane.)

After a cold, wet night, two columns of troops started for the island where the Seminoles were clearly visible. The battle was a repetition of the one the day before; when the soldiers were within range, the Indians fired several volleys. One of the columns of soldiers had managed to drag a six-pounder to firm ground. This was fired and the Seminoles headed for a dense cypress swamp, shooting at the pursuing troops as they ran. Repeatedly, their mocking laughter mingled with the wild cries of disturbed birds and the screams of the wounded. The two days cost the whites four dead and thirteen wounded; there is no record of Indian losses.

Scott was frustrated. This wet, dark hell was no place for white men, certainly no place for wagons and cannon. You could not catch Osceola here. The Seminoles could move through the islands, a trick unknown even to the "friendlies" who served as guides for the white soldiers. These friendly Indians were always getting lost.

Dismayed, Scott set out for Tampa and Fort Brooke. A Georgia battalion under a Major Samuel Cooper was left at the south end of the chain of Withlacoochee lakes with the sick and wounded, seventeen days' rations, and a promise to be relieved in nine days. About three hundred fifty men stayed at "Camp Cooper."

On April 5, the right wing limped into Camp Brooke with one hundred fifty sick men. Lindsay and his center wing had arrived from their excursion the day before. Both wings were a cheerless sight to each other; Scott now saw clearly the failure of his plan and the scar on his reputation.

Lindsay, with his volunteers from Alabama and Louisiana, and two companies of regulars, had built a stockade on the Hillsborough River and called it Fort Alabama. On March 27, the garrison of some seventy men was hammered by a band of Seminoles. One white was killed. In the meantime, Lindsay had marched to Checuchatty (Chicuchatty), while small bands of Osceola's warriors spattered him with gunfire from the underbrush. The fire was heavy on March 26, but the Indians were driven off at a cost of one white killed and one wounded. On the following day, the Alabamians lost another killed and two wounded. Unable to find Scott, Lindsay turned back to Camp Brooke—where, a day after his arrival, the colonel finally met his commander. Through no fault of his own, Lindsay had also accomplished nothing.

The left wing, under Brigadier General Abraham Eustis, had the toughest job. The history of this wing is recorded in considerable detail, particularly by M. M. Cohen, who was one of General Eustis' staff officers. Cohen made the most of his experience in a delightful narrative, but unfortunately left the wing engaged in more hard marching than dramatic or significant fights. It was also commanded by a severe but just and unusual man. Eustis was profoundly disliked by his South Carolina contingent of volunteers because of his abrupt manner, his failure to praise them, and his odd habit of wearing civilian clothing and never carrying a sword.[2]

Eustis reached Volusia on the St. Johns (south of Lake George) on March 17, and began to cross the river four days later. When a few companies were over, a band of Seminoles opened fire. These warriors may have been attached to Philip or to Euchee Billy, who lived some miles to the south, but Osceola had arranged for harassment of General Eustis' force. Cohen wrote that the soldiers, in their excitement, fired into their own troops. Three whites were killed, six wounded. Cohen says the Indians lost at least six, one supposedly being Euchee Billy. (This identification was a mistake.)

Eustis began crawling west at 4:00 P.M. on the twenty-sixth. Any modern gas station map shows what he had to contend with; he was obliged to cross the present-day Ocala National Forest, then far wider than now, and find a passage through the lake country west of the modern town of Eustis. In one day, he made only seven miles.

The Oklawaha River had to be bridged for crossing on the twenty-ninth. This miserable job took until long after midnight, with the wagons being hauled by wet, cursing, weary men. Baggage had to be carried across on their backs. Finally they were able to stagger into camp a mile southwest of the river and collapse, sometimes without shelter. There were only three tents per company.

Earlier, just before dusk, fires had been seen at a distance and a party including General Joseph Shelton had gone out to investigate. Shelton, a remarkable man and a militia brigadier general, had attached himself to the Carolina troops as a plain volunteer private.

When he caught up with the Indians, he fired and struck one of them in the neck. He then drew a pistol that misfired, giving the Seminole a chance to shoot Shelton in the hip. The duel was concluded when one Barclay Gibson rode up and killed the

Indian. The episode would be of minor significance except that on the following day the body of the slain Seminole was identified as that of Yahahadjo, signer of the Payne's Landing Treaty and one of the delegation to Arkansas. This is more evidence that Osceola was watching Eustis' progress carefully; for Yahahadjo had associations with Micanopy and doubtless was influenced by Osceola. The signal fires seen by the whites were certainly repeated and read far to the west.

After Yahahadjo's body was viewed, the soldiers explored the area and found a small Indian village where, according to Cohen, there were forty or fifty pieces of scalps attached flag-like to small pine sticks. Cohen was upset because some of the hair was soft, bright, and of fine texture, suggesting it came from women.

He was probably right; despite Osceola's objections, a number of white women were killed and scalped by Seminoles. Rumors multiplied these cases far beyond the actual number, just as stories of white atrocities on Indians were also exaggerated. But Indians sometimes *did* scalp, as did whites; and whites sometimes mutilated Indian bodies just as Indians and Negroes occasionally mutilated white bodies.

After several more skirmishes, General Eustis arrived at Pelacklakaha (Pilaklakuha), the town where Micanopy and Abraham had once lived. Eustis burned the town, then dragged his force into Tampa Bay and Fort Brooke where he found Scott and Lindsay. Bemrose probably summed up this entire campaign as well as anyone else. He said, "The Indians were not so dull as to be swallowed up by an overwhelming force! Their mode being to attack only small bodies, and to allow the larger companies to pass through." [3]

The time had come for Osceola to attempt new tactics. There had been losses during the tripronged Scott campaign, but much lower than the whites optimistically claimed. (The exact number is unknown.) Now Osceola sketched in the sand while his lieutenants watched.

"The white man has built many little camps and forts," he said. "Here is the one called Camp Cooper at the edge of our country. And here is Fort Alabama. Fort Drane is weak until General Clinch returns with his soldiers. We must strike at all of these places with small bands of warriors."

"There's one other place," Alligator said. "The blockhouse the white man built near the white water on the lower Withlacoochee." Major John McLemore (the McLemore of the early Battle of Black Point) had established a supply base for Scott on the river, then had built a blockhouse and left a force of forty to fifty Florida militiamen under Captain James M. K. Holloman.

"I'll attack the blockhouse," Osceola decided. "Meanwhile, you strike the other places. Shake them like a dog with a rat, but don't waste warriors or gunpowder."

The story of the blockhouse is best told from the white point of view. Records conflict on dates, but it is possible to reconstruct much of the action. The blockhouse had just been completed and a spring dug when Osceola reached the area with about two hundred warriors. Camping at a distance, he scouted the fort and decided to attack on the morning of April 9. (Cohen said it was the twelfth.)

There had been no signs of Indians while the blockhouse was being built, but Captain Holloman had wisely posted sentries. Just before dawn, one of them saw some movement from the direction of the river and shouted, "Indians! Indians! Turn out!" While the soldiers rushed to their posts, Osceola ordered a heavy fire poured on the blockhouse. This made sense; however the place was built (and no record exists), there would have been firing ports at which the Indians could shoot.

Nothing much happened during this engagement of about two hours. The blockhouse was probably surrounded by a stockade made of pine logs that would have been proof against small-caliber bullets; this would be a strong defense with ten or twelve men to a side. Whatever the case, an angry Osceola attacked on the following day, killing a soldier named Eli Sealy.

He also noted a flatboat drawn up in the riverbank in front of the blockhouse, and guessed correctly that this was the only means of escape for the whites except for a battered, leaky canoe. Fort Drane was forty miles away through country where Seminole bands were operating; escape to the north or south was equally impossible.

"That boat must be destroyed," Osceola told his warriors. "When we fight again, I want seven men to help me get it off."

On the fifteenth, he struck the fort with an estimated force of about four hundred fifty warriors. (White estimates of Indian strength were much too high; one account foolishly puts the number of attackers at fifteen hundred.) Three soldiers were wounded and at least five or six Indians were either killed or wounded.

While this three-hour engagement was going on, Osceola led a group of warriors in a dash toward the heavy flatboat. Musket-balls spattered around them but they managed to inch the heavy boat into the river where the current carried it down-stream. Later they found and destroyed it.

The Indians were mystified by the resistance of the soldiers and attributed their success to witchcraft. Osceola probably shared this superstition; there is no reason to believe he was less superstitious than other Indians or, in fact, many whites of the period. According to historian Cohen, the Seminoles made silver bullets in an attempt to overcome the witches. (They could have been made from ornaments or coins, but the story seems unlikely.)

Silver bullets or not, Osceola had a more logical idea. On the twenty-third, he had some of his warriors gather pitch while others made crude bows and feathered arrows. This was easily done, but the Seminoles thought their leader was insane. Then the idea dawned on them: fire-arrows. Years earlier, their ancestors had used them.

"I want twenty-six warriors to shoot arrows at the blockhouse roof," Osceola said. "The others will use rifles."

The idea was effective when tried the following day; the roof was completely burned away. That, however, was about all that happened. Two soldiers were wounded while the Indians suffered badly—or so the whites said later. Osceola, thoroughly disgusted, decided to get on to more important matters. He would leave a small band to harass the blockhouse and cut down the militiamen if they attempted to escape.

In a strangely magnanimous gesture, he approached the blockhouse that night to make a short announcement. "Soldiers!" he called. "You white men in there! I'm going away in the morning. I won't trouble you again."

This is exactly what he did, but the affair of the blockhouse was not over. Captain Holloman was killed on May 3, while improving the fortification. Ammunition was low, food was running out, and the small Indian band reminded the soldiers of their presence by launching a few volleys at least once a week. The rest of the time, Seminole guards watched the blockhouse.

By May 10, the situation was desperate. Lieutenant L. B. Walker, who had assumed command after Holloman's death, called his men together and explained what had to be done. "Our only chance is the old canoe," he said. "We need three men to get away and remind the government we're here. We'll choose by lot."

This was done, and shortly before midnight three soldiers slipped from the blockhouse to put the canoe in the water. Two paddled while the third bailed furiously; water poured in at the seams. Although the Indians saw the escape and fired a number of shots, the party managed to reach the Gulf and head north toward the mouth of the Suwannee. This would give them a route to civilization.

But the Seminoles were waiting for them. After a few shots, the soldiers decided to remain in the Gulf. They paddled all the way to St. Marks, arriving on May 20 to tell the story of the blockhouse. A rescue party reached the defenders on the twenty-fourth and found them alive. No shots were fired.[4]

While all of this was going on, Camp Cooper had been under attack off and on from about April 4 until the seventeenth when Clinch arrived on his way back to Fort Drane. One soldier was killed, a number of others wounded. The camp was evacuated and the united force set out for distant Fort Drane. At one point, General Clinch, waiting for a party with some cattle, removed his sword and belt to rest beneath a tree. When he had left and was four miles away, he discovered he had forgotten his gear. A Major Holmes and five horsemen went back to retrieve it, found six Indians—one of whom was wearing the sword, fired on them, and were forced to retreat when a larger body of Indians appeared. The story is more revealing than amusing; Osceola's warriors were never far away from any white force. Clinch was home at Fort Drane on April 24, where he was promptly harassed by small bands of Osceola's warriors.[5]

Several days later, some seven hundred fifty men left Fort Brooke to relieve Fort Alabama and destroy the place. This they did, but on the return march they were attacked sharply by one of Osceola's bands. Cannon and a bayonet charge finally drove off the Indians, but the whites lost four dead and eighteen wounded.[6]

Cohen devoted a certain amount of his purple prose to the beauties of Tampa ("Come with me, and note this romantic grove of lofty trees—these venerable oaks, crowned with streaming locks of grey. . . ." and later departed with the left wing and General Scott for Volusia. There were a few skirmishes, but nothing of significance happened. Scott and Eustis left Volusia by water for Picolata. Cohen, back in St. Augustine and seated comfortably in Allen's Hotel on May 2, deplored the fruitless campaign: ". . . the Campaign has turned out a failure. For, though it went forth whizzing and shining like a rocket, it has come back like the rocket-stick, falling low, a dull, heavy, inert, burnt-out thing."

Cohen blamed the nature of the country itself, the climate, poor transportation, the conduct of government, and the generals in the field. He said the government, including the Presidency, was either wholly ignorant, erroneously informed, or criminally apathetic as to the affairs of Florida. He also said that everyone had seriously underrated the Seminoles. He quoted Scott as having said, "In less than twelve days from the time he left Fort Drane, he would have the pleasure of shipping off the hostiles, and disbanding his army." [7]

On April 15, Scott was ordered to Alabama to put down an uprising among the Creeks. Later, before a court of inquiry at Frederick, Maryland, he discussed "The Failure of my Florida Campaign." He managed to blame Gaines and others, as well as climate, terrain, transportation, and the supply problem, but the court charitably held him guiltless.

Richard Keith Call became Florida's governor on March 16. (He was the same Call who had been with Clinch during the first battle of the Withlacoochee.) Ten days later, General Clinch resigned after turning his command of fifteen hundred men over to Lieutenant Colonel James Bankhead.

President Andrew Jackson refused to accept the resignation and offered Clinch command in Florida, but Major General Thomas S. Jesup was supposed to be arriving eventually. Clinch had been superseded once by Scott, and he had no wish to go through the same bitter performance again. He pleaded the need for his motherless children and private affairs, so the President made his resignation effective as of September 21, 1836, when a leave of absence would run out. Clinch was later knocked about badly in politics, but nothing would ever tarnish his reputation as an outstanding white leader during the Second Seminole War.

Everything was now stalemated. Osceola launched a few

minor attacks on Fort Drane, where fever had broken out. Bankhead, on leave of absence, left Lieutenant Julius Heilman in command, but Heilman died of fever on June 27. Meanwhile, Osceola continued a series of skirmishes particularly in the vicinity of Micanopy where Fort Defiance was located.

Sickness during the summer of 1836 mounted to epidemic proportions. Fort King was closed down in late May. In July, it was decided to evacuate Fort Drane in favor of Micanopy and Fort Defiance. On the nineteenth, a long wagon train of stores was moved out of Drane under an escort of sixty men. Osceola, knowing of this movement, ambushed the column near Micanopy, killing five soldiers and wounding six. Relief from Fort Defiance finally drove off the Indians.

Early in August, Fort Drane was completely evacuated. This provided Osceola with a magnificent windfall of standing corn—more than ten thousand bushels. The only remaining effective fort in the area was Fort Defiance at Micanopy. Except for Newnansville and Fort Defiance, Osceola ruled the western Florida peninsula north of Fort Brooke. He also occupied abandoned Fort Drane. Shrewdly, however, he kept the women and children in the swamps along with the largest body of warriors and most of his supplies.

During July, Lieutenant Colonel Ichabod Crane became commander in northeastern Florida. (This was the same Ichabod Crane who had galloped up to Fort King after the killing of Thompson and Smith.) Thinking it wise to evacuate Fort Defiance, which was now dangerously isolated, he sent Major Benjamin K. Pierce and one hundred twenty-five men to close the place. Pierce arrived on August 20, and was tempted to assault the Indians at Fort Drane while he was in the area. For this chore, according to Sprague, who mixed up the dates, he departed at 2:00 A.M. on the morning of the twenty-first with 110 men and one cannon. The ten-mile march was concluded shortly after dawn.

Osceola, of course, knew Pierce was coming. He had some

three hundred warriors outside the fort, but quickly retreated to a large hammock where he ordered a heavy fire on the soldiers. Pierce banged away with his cannon, then gave up after an hour when he decided he was seriously outnumbered. His losses in this futile fight were one killed and sixteen wounded. A few days later, he evacuated Fort Defiance, the last stronghold in western Florida.

The Seminoles at Fort Drane and in the Withlacoochee swamps gloated over their successes during the past eight months. Not only had the whites failed to conquer them, but white forces had been driven from the country. Small bands of warriors had found they could injure large forces of soldiers by striking quickly, then retreating. It was sad that warriors had fallen, but the Seminoles as a nation were still intact.

One Seminole was not deceived by the victories. Osceola knew the white soldiers would be back. He realized some of the fighting would have to be conducted outside the Withlacoochee swamps. He also knew, from spies, that the white government in Washington had appropriated huge sums of money to fight the Indians—almost two million dollars, whatever that meant. Money like grains of sand to buy weapons and men and supplies. Strange that the whites would use all that gold to kill Seminoles, and only a handful of gold to buy their land or give them help. Was a man more valuable dead than alive? Toss him a few coins for food, but use great riches to kill him.

If only the white man could believe in a fair peace. Enough blood had been spilled, enough warriors had fallen, enough white soldiers had been slain. Osceola hated the impersonal aspect of war. It was one thing to avenge an insult, to kill and scalp a personal enemy. But Osceola had known the men at Fort King, the Irish, the English, the other white men who spoke in strange tongues. Could these men be enemies? Killing them was meaningless, senseless. It gave no satisfaction.

There was another reason for wanting peace. Osceola knew his Indians, knew clearly that nothing was more tiresome than success. The Seminoles had won repeatedly, at least in terms of holding their enemies in check. To the Indian mind, victory meant that war should stop. Many Seminoles could not believe that they must now fight again, again, and again. Osceola realized they would eventually tire, not from lack of courage but simply from diminished interest. An honorable peace must come before the Seminole will to resist began to disintegrate. No warpath could be endless. The Indian would turn aside in dismay when he saw no ending.

For a while, Osceola could keep spirits high. He had great influence among the chiefs and warriors, he was the leader, his was the vision. He had heard that even whites respected him as a leader, an Indian general. But it would not be easy to hold the Seminoles together, firm in their conviction, in times of distress or defeat. It would also take anger to keep the Seminoles fighting, anger as well as determination to struggle for the Florida homeland. A victorious man is not an angry man.

Osceola faced another problem. He had picked up the fever that caused the whites to evacuate Fort Drane. This was probably one of the many forms of malaria, although it is almost impossible to identify it properly from a distance of more than a hundred years. The whites called it "country fever" and noted that it peaked after five days with heavy bleeding from the nose. Bleeding was almost of ritual importance to the Indians, but only when caused by ceremonial scratching or cutting.

"I am sick," Osceola told Che-cho-ter. "A blackness comes over me and I grow weak."

For days, she sat beside him, cooling his face with water, calming the moments of delirium, feeding him the juice of wild grapes mixed with sassafras. When he was conscious, Osceola bled himself by slashing the skin of his legs; this was supposed to let out poison and renew his strength. He would never recover entirely from this fever, but he sometimes could look into Che-cho-ter's lovely face and say, "*Hinclamas cheh.* Very good."

During all of this period following Scott's ill-fated campaign and his removal from Florida, the white troops had no supreme commander. There were only about a thousand regular troops in the area, the volunteers having served out their enlistments and gone home. Regular general officers were not anxious to follow in the stumbling footsteps of Gaines and Scott. Public attention was turned toward the Southwest where Texans were caught up in their war of independence. One man, however, was deeply interested in leading the whites to victory over the dangerous Seminoles. He was Richard K. Call, the new governor of Florida.

Call, forty-four in 1836, had served as a young volunteer in the Creek War where he met Andrew Jackson. Later, he served as aide to Jackson, toured the North with him, served as acting secretary of west Florida under Governor Jackson, became a prominent lawyer, was commissioned as a Florida militia brigadier general, served in the Eighteenth Congress with Jackson, and actively supported him for the Presidency. When Scott's campaign failed, Call insistently asked Jackson for command of forces in Florida. He said that if Osceola could be beaten once, the Seminoles would stop fighting. Everything hinged on defeating Osceola.

His plan was to attempt a summer campaign during which supplies would be placed on the Withlacoochee River in support of an attacking force that would probe the cove of the Withlacoochee and presumably eliminate Osceola and his warriors. All Call's predecessors had justified their failures by pointing to the lack of nearby supplies. Call apparently had found a way around this problem, so Jackson on May 18 gave him command of the militia in federal service *and the regular Army* in Florida until General Jesup could take over.

The regulars were not enchanted by the idea of being commanded by a civilian, no matter what he had done in the Creek War. They also remembered Call's first visit to the Withlacoochee when he was unable to get his volunteers across the river. As for the tiny militia, numbering less than two hundred fifty men, most did not want to fight in summer, particularly disliked the idea of fighting Osceola, and were unhappy about leaving their homes unprotected.

Call expected fifteen hundred mounted volunteers from Tennessee, but they were held in Alabama to fight the wayward Creeks. Call, meanwhile, suffered "bilious fever" and was confined to bed in Tallahassee. He had encountered trouble in getting food and ammunition to Suwannee Old Town, one of his supply points, and he was furious about the evacuation of Fort Defiance at Micanopy, an installation on which he had counted as a supply depot.

Weeks passed before the arrival of the Tennessee troops in Tallahassee on September 18, 1836. Call, in the meantime, had written Major General Thomas Sidney Jesup offering him command in Florida; but Jesup, knowing Call had planned a campaign, politely refused. Jesup would not take over until Call had been given his opportunity. So Call, rising from his sickbed, set out from Tallahassee on September 19, with one hundred forty Florida militiamen as well as the Tennessee brigade. His first destination was Suwannee Old Town, which was reached on the twenty-fourth. (This had been Billy Bowlegs' village during the First Seminole War.)

General Call's supply program had gone awry; ships were late or had been diverted to other purposes. Thus, on the twenty-ninth, he ordered General Leigh Read to take the Florida militia and some regulars to the mouth of the Suwannee where a steamboat, the *Izard*, was waiting with some other vessels. All were to proceed to the mouth of the Withlacoochee, some thirty-five miles distant, where the vessels would sail up the river about twenty miles and establish a depot. The *Izard* would haul two large barges behind her.

After this arrangement was made, General Call set out for Fort Drane with the remainder of the force. He hoped to find corn for the horses at the abandoned fort, but the Indians had stripped the fields of everything but sugarcane.

Call waited there for a few days until joined by Major Benjamin K. Pierce and a small force of regulars. On October 9, very short on rations, the army set out for the Withlacoochee, which was reached by October 13. When a crossing was attempted, Osceola's warriors harassed them with heavy rifle fire. The river was deep and in flood, so the only possible way of crossing would have been by rafts. But only a few axes had been brought along.

Supplies were running short. An advance party, sent out to locate Read's supply point on the river, found that Read had mysteriously disappeared. Desperate for supplies, and with horses dying of hunger, Call headed back for the comparative safety of Fort Drane. Here he could feed his horses sugarcane, and send messengers for rations.

It turned out that the *Izard* had grounded and broken up as she moved up the Withlacoochee. Read had made a desperate effort to get the supplies to their destination, but had arrived too late to help General Call.

Meanwhile a body of Creek volunteers had been sent to Florida under the command of Colonel John F. Lane. Arriving at Fort Brooke by ship, they marched to join Call at Fort Drane on October 19. Colonel Lane killed himself as a result of fatigue and was replaced by Lieutenant Colonel Harvey Brown. Finally, on November 10 an army of almost twenty-five hundred men left Fort Drane for the Withlacoochee. Among them were the Creek Indian volunteers, the mounted Tennesseans, some regulars, and a body of Florida militia. The Withlacoochee was crossed on the thirteenth without opposition.

Because of the size of this enemy force, Osceola was in trouble. He first ordered the large villages in the north part of the cove abandoned, then withdrew toward the south. The white soldiers had never before been persistent in pursuit; perhaps they would follow the usual procedure of fighting briefly and then seeking shelter back at Fort Drane.

Osceola also had a psychological problem on his hands. His warriors were infuriated by the intrusion of the Creeks and wanted desperately to fight them. (The Creeks wore white turbans to distinguish them from the Seminoles.) In this atmosphere of hatred, Osceola could expect some outbursts of bad judgment on the part of his warriors.

Call found and burned three of Osceola's deserted villages. Then he recrossed the river with the Tennesseans and the Florida militia, while Benjamin K. Pierce, now a colonel, and Colonel Brown moved south on the Seminole side of the river with the remainder of the force. The plan was to bring the two columns together in the vicinity of Dade's battleground.

Call fought several battles as he moved south. Osceola had his first serious losses: forty-five dead and an unknown number wounded. The spirit of his warriors was unshaken, however, as they moved to meet the white force at Wahoo Swamp near the Dade battleground. Here Pierce joined Call on November 20, 1836.

Both the Indians and white troops started moving toward each other at dawn on the twenty-first. Osceola planned to fight first from a hammock at the edge of the swamp, then to move back to the far side of a creek where there was excellent cover in the form of stumps and fallen logs. (Although Osceola is not mentioned in any of the white reports and, indeed, could not be identified in a wild battle of the sort that developed, the tactics clearly bear his signature: Attract the enemy and invite him to follow you to the place where you want to fight.)

When four columns of General Call's troops came in sight of the hammock, Osceola and his warriors screamed their war whoops, then threw themselves on the ground to wait for the soldiers to come within range. For his part, Colonel Pierce, who was in command of the whites and Creek volunteers, made none of the errors so common among white military leaders. He spread out two lines composed mainly of Floridians, placed a reserve of two companies fifty paces behind, put the Tennesseans on the right and the Creek volunteers on the left. This attacking force was almost a mile long.

Both the Seminoles and the whites held their fire until they were within range. The scene had an ominous aspect; soldiers advancing silently, morning sunlight gleaming on their weapons, while the Indians in war paint watched them over the sights of their rifles.

Presently Osceola gave his war cry and fired. The soldiers advanced in a full charge, firing as they ran; the Seminoles moved backward, shooting as they withdrew from tree to tree. Whites invariably called this kind of movement a retreat when, in fact, it was usually a planned tactical withdrawal.

"Back to the water!" Osceola shouted, and the Indians slipped shadow-like toward the chosen position about a mile and a half to the rear. They had the advantage of knowing how to get there and were able to avoid the worst of the terrain. The whites with their Creek allies were able only to splash in pursuit through mud and swamp water.

In parts of this swamp, water was almost up to a soldier's chin. Stumps and the swamp rubbish of roots and decayed vegetation made the footing uncertain, so that men sometimes stumbled and went under, came up gasping and spitting, and wondered if they would die by drowning. Every soldier was aware of the foul, sulfurous odor of the water; each man also feared the creatures that might be living in it. Incredibly, they still advanced.

The Creeks were in the lead. At the far edge of the morass, the ground rose to a dry, heavily wooded strip along the edge of a stream about thirty feet wide. It was on the far side of this little river that Osceola had distributed his men. They met the arrival of the Creeks with heavy fire and screams of rage. The warriors were so well concealed behind logs and stumps that repeated volleys by the Creeks and whites had little effect on them.

Among the government troops was a Major David Moniac, who was a Creek Indian and a West Point graduate. Moniac carefully examined the stream separating the Seminoles from the white army. The water was black and looked deep, but Moniac knew swamp water was often deceptive.

"I'm going to try it," he called to Colonel Harvey Brown, commander of the Creeks.

He had just stepped into the stream when he was killed by a Seminole rifle ball. There were a few other attempts to cross the creek, but Osceola and some chosen warriors shifted to the critical points and discouraged the attempts with heavy fire. Meanwhile, the remainder of General Call's force dragged up to the creek bank and opened fire when their wet guns could be used. The men were soaked with water, smeared with mud, tired of struggling through the swamp, and very hungry.

The battle across the water raged until about 3:30 P.M. Above the crackling of muskets and rifles could be heard the whoops of the Seminoles and the angry shrieks of the Creek volunteers. Among the Creek chiefs were Paddy Carr, John O'Poney, and Jim Boy. These men fought bravely, but so did the Seminoles. Finally, following a conference among the officers, General Call decided to retreat toward a source of supplies. He must not have known that General Read had finally left supplies on the lower reaches of the Withlacoochee, for he headed toward Volusia some sixty miles away over the route General Eustis had covered earlier. He finally reached there on November 27.

Osceola had won again, but this time with appreciable losses. Even so, he had compelled a strong force to withdraw. Historian Sprague summed up the campaign in these words:

> The result of the expedition to the Wahoo Swamp was a lesson to other commanders. To force so large a body of troops, horse and foot, into the enemy's country, without a base of operations, is a sacrifice of human life, without attaining the end, besides encouraging the enemy. The horses of the Tennessee brigade died for the want of food. The men, dispirited by exhaustion and fatigue for which they were unprepared, with scanty food, lost that fortitude

> and resolution so indispensably necessary in this peculiar warfare. The enemy was vigilant and independent; he lived upon the wild productions, and knew the swamps and hammocks, while the soldier, as he waded them without food or rest, looked upon these fastnesses as his sepulchre, more than as a field of battle.

Sprague went on to say that the black stream, "which was so resolutely defended," was only three feet deep. "The water was black and sluggish, deceiving those who ventured to approach." The stream could have been crossed; if so, the way would have been clear to a settlement where two hundred Negro men and four hundred twenty Seminole warriors with women, children, ponies, horses, and abundant supplies had been living since the outbreak of hostilities.[8]

Shortly after his arrival at Volusia, General Call received a belated letter from the Acting Secretary of War, B. F. Butler, criticizing him for his early "retrograde" movements and saying harshly that "the President deems it expedient to relieve you from the command." Major General Thomas Sidney Jesup was ordered on the same day to assume command in Florida. Poor Call was bitterly shaken, but on December 9, 1836, he turned over the command to Jesup, who had arrived at Volusia with a force of four hundred men.[9]

Osceola, meanwhile, had again split his warriors into small bands numbering about two hundred men each. Among the leaders were Micanopy, Philip, Jumper, Alligator, Osceola himself, and Osuchee (Cooper). Abraham also had a band. At this time, Coacoochee seems to have been with his father, Philip. (Other Seminole leaders will be mentioned later.)

Nothing had changed greatly for Osceola in late December. Another white commander had been driven away. There had been deaths—too many deaths. There were wounded in the swamp villages; however, the sacred medicines worked well and many of the wounded would fight again. But there was the prime difficulty that only Osceola could see clearly.

"What troubles you, brother?" Jumper asked him when he saw the leader staring somberly at the ground.

"Twelve moons have passed. A year. We have fought for a year."

"We have fought well," Jumper said.

"Our warriors are brave. But a year is a long time. Will they fight for another year? Another? Will they fight to the last drop of blood?"

"I don't know."

"And I don't know. I can only hope that our children will see the sun rise on the same forests and the same waters. If we fight, perhaps the white man will talk of peace to our children."

10

Flight from Camp Mellon

The orders received by Major General Thomas Jesup were explicit. On November 4, 1836, Acting Secretary of War Butler had written him in part:

> The hostile Indians having been discovered in considerable force on the banks of the Wythlacoochie, and it having been also ascertained that their principal Camps and settlements are situated on the south side of the river, you will immediately make all suitable arrangements for a vigorous attack upon their strongholds, and for penetrating and occupying the whole country between the Wythlacoochie and Tampa Bay. . . . The above direction to attack the enemy in his strongholds and to possess yourself of the country between the Wythlacoochie and Tampa Bay, you will regard as a positive order, to be executed at the earliest practicable moment. . . .[1]

General Jesup was a colorless officer who could be expected to do his duty. He was quartermaster general of the Army between 1818 and 1860, a circumstance that placed him in an important position for a number of small wars. He was also a good combat general with a stubborn streak and a flair for occasional small outbursts of independence. In Alabama, some months earlier, he had defied one of Winfield Scott's orders when he thought it unreasonable. Very few of his mannerisms were recorded by contemporaries, but he obviously had a wholesome capacity for phrasing unpopular thoughts. Army surgeon Samuel Forry quoted him as saying: "The Indians are a persecuted race, and we are engaged in an unholy cause." [2]

However perceptive that observation may have been, Jesup evidently believed that the end justified the means—unholy cause or not. For one of his acts during the Second Seminole War, he became the personification of treachery throughout much of the civilized world. In parts of the United States and much of England, no man would be more despised than Thomas Sidney Jesup.

But Jesup, up to a point, was a good commander and certainly the most effective man the Seminoles had encountered during the war. He had the orderly mind necessary for a competent quartermaster general, and troops apparently liked him—perhaps because he at least kept them adequately supplied. Scott was also orderly, Gaines was erratic, Clinch approached the heroic, Call was an inexperienced romantic; but Jesup was a plodder, a workhorse. He also had the capacity for acting rapidly on his decisions.

On December 12, 1836, Jesup set off from Volusia for the Withlacoochee with his fresh unit of four hundred men and the Tennessee volunteers who would shortly conclude their enlistment period. At the Dade battleground, he had his men erect an installation named Fort Armstrong. Fort Foster was built on the site of Fort Alabama; Fort Clinch rose at the mouth of the Withlacoochee. Fort King was still in existence, and Fort Drane was again reopened. At the crossing of the Tampa–Fort King road and the Withlacoochee, Jesup ordered Fort Dade to be built. Many of these small forts, calculated to surround the Withlacoochee area and provide readily available supplies, were manned by Navy marines and sailors.

Osceola had expected another concentrated attack on the cove of the Withlacoochee. In conference with the chiefs, he suggested that the bands spread out and move gradually toward the south. Jumper, Alligator, and Micanopy would shift toward the headwaters of the Oklawaha. Osuchee would operate in the vicinity of Lake Apopka (near modern Winter Garden). Philip was already considerably south of St. Augustine, although raiding parties often struck close enough to the city to terrify its occupants.

As for his own plans, Osceola decided to move to the Panasoffke Swamp on the Withlacoochee where there was a large Negro village. (Lake Panasoffke appears on modern maps west of Leesburg.) He was still ill; and he believed he and his family would be more comfortable with the Indian Negroes who virtually worshiped him.

This devotion was due to Osceola's unswerving defense of the Negroes, whether maroons, Indian slaves, or runaways. He had thought carefully about the position of the Negro; perhaps, to some extent, he agreed with Jesup who had once written, "This is a Negro not an Indian war."

To Osceola, the desirable Seminole policy toward the Negroes was as clear as the water in the Silver Spring: No Negro should ever be surrendered to the whites. This applied as much to runaways as it did to the Indian slaves or the free maroons. The dilemma was a clear one: If the Seminoles moved to the west by themselves, their Negro allies in Florida would either perish or be captured for slavery under the lash of the white man. If Negroes went west with weakened, submissive Seminoles, the story would be exactly the same; slave-catchers would seize them, and any who escaped would be wrested away by the Creeks.

Osceola was not hesitant about bringing these possibilities to the attention of the Negroes, who were quite aware of them. "Your only hope," he told them, "is to fight the white man.

Stand beside your Seminole brother when he takes the warpath. Stand beside me! We fight not only for the Seminole and his rights, but also for you!"

It was not surprising that the Negroes, predominantly male, were glad to fight as warriors of Osceola. Not only could they accept discipline, but the forefathers of many of them had been fierce warriors in Africa. Most of the Negroes, caught in a war they could not escape, fought bravely. They had more to lose than the Indians, and they also had more to remember. The overseer's lash in Georgia, the Carolinas, or northern Florida, the wife sold in the New Orleans market, the child crying because no doctor was called, the raped sister, the endless future of work in the fields until the slave was kicked aside to die. Fighting beside the Seminole might be a form of suicide, but at least the Negro could take a few whites with him.

Osceola's fever rose, broke, rose again, his strong body becoming thin until the muscles stood out like vines on a slight tree. In his lucid moments, he was able only to worry about the progress of the war. No longer could he control all bands, but his lieutenants had been well trained and would fight wisely. Negro spies said the new American, Jesup, would have great numbers of troops.

There was no reason to doubt this, and it would be foolish to fight when the Seminoles were badly outnumbered. The scattered bands could move quickly and harass small bodies of white soldiers. No alligator ate the whole calf; the *halpatter* rolled and churned to rip off pieces he could swallow. Eventually, Osceola told himself, the calf disappeared.

He had a visitor early in January, a cantankerous, bad-smelling, lean old man with dirty white hair and the skin of an aged turtle. Arpeika (Sam Jones) was as brusque and ill-tempered as ever. With him he had another Mikasuki, Halleck-Tustenuggee, who was quite young. This man, along with Thlocklo-Tustenuggee (Tiger Tail), would later be an important Seminole war leader.

Brushing aside the customary salutations, Arpeika said, "I'm going to lead warriors. Many young Mikasukis will follow me."

"As you say, brother," Osceola said, smiling a little.

"As you say, as you say!" Arpeika mimicked furiously. "I can still fight better than most young fools!"

"It is well." Osceola was serious. "You haven't changed your mind about moving?"

"Never! If I die, I die on my own soil!"

"And I, as well," Osceola said.

"No." The old medicine man and prophet stared at Osceola out of glassy, red-veined eyes. "I don't think you die on this soil. And I don't think you die beyond the Great River. But you die."

"A story!" Osceola exclaimed irritably. "Perhaps I die right here from weakness!"

"I heard of this and came," Arpeika growled. He ordered Che-cho-ter away, adding to Halleck-Tustenuggee, "And you, too!"

Alone with Osceola, the old man administered some boiled herbs and began the ritual chanting that was the important part of every medicine man's business. Medicine men such as Arpeika were not only priests or warrior-priests, as in Arpeika's case, but were also practitioners of curative medicine. Herbs such as snakeroot and sassafras were used along with many others (white settlers also depended on medicinal herbs) but the medicine man was more concerned about what he said in the chants than what he did. The medicine man's ritual drove out the disease; the herbs were only of minor significance.

Osceola slept and dreamed after Arpeika left. In the dream, he raced after a deer, running at full speed, until he reached a lake where snags probed from the water like black, broken fingers. The deer swam between them, spreading ripples on the dark water, and Osceola plunged in to follow. On the far shore, he pursued the deer to a strange place where a great cave gaped in the side of a hill. When the deer entered the cave, he shuddered at the idea of following. But he entered the cave, where suddenly, in the blackness, there was a loud popping sound. . . .

He wakened to find his two wives bending over him. Three Mikasuki warriors stood behind them. The popping continued—shots at a distance of about five hundred yards. Che-cho-ter and the second wife had swept up bundles of blankets, food, and cooking gear. The children were clinging to their skirts.

"Soldiers near," one of the warriors growled. "Too many. Can you walk, brother?"

"I can walk," Osceola said, staggering to his feet and seizing his rifle. "One of you ahead, the other behind. The third beside me if I falter. My family behind me."

One of Jesup's probing battalions had attacked the Negroes, capturing fifty-two. Osceola had been the real target of these raids in early January, but Arpeika's medicine had given him strength enough to escape. He circled to a new hiding place on the Withlacoochee while Jesup wrote to the adjutant general "that he [Osceola] can collect about a hundred warriors." This was probably an understatement. Jesup, in the meanwhile, turned his attention to mid-Florida where he would "proceed against Micanopy and Jumper, who, I have reason to believe, are on the headwaters of the Oklawaha." [3] (This would have been around modern Leesburg.) Osceola, in somewhat improved health, also turned toward the Oklawaha with about fifty Seminole and Negro warriors. Families accompanied the band; there were hundreds of places in the central wilderness of Florida where women and children could hide. Supplies were still adequate, for many of the hammocks in the Cove of the Withlacoochee had been cultivated during 1836. The white soldiers had burned some villages, but there is no record that they had been able so far to destroy any appreciable amount of supplies and ammunition.

When recurrent attacks of fever made it impossible for Osceola to be in charge, the Seminoles took several beatings. Osuchee was killed in the vicinity of Lake Apopka along with three of his warriors; and eighteen women, children, and Negroes were captured. These prisoners said most of the Indians were moving south toward the headwaters of the Caloosahatchee River, not then competently mapped but west of Lake Okeechobee.

Jesup arranged a pursuit. Near modern Kissimmee, cattle were found in large numbers and there were numerous trails showing that Indians were in the vicinity. Scouts reported them near the Hatcheelustee creek, a stream entering Tohopekaliga Lake, in the Great Cypress Swamp. (Not the one in southwestern Florida. This one was roughly in the wilderness of present Osceola County.)

Colonel Arch Henderson traced a body of some fifty Seminoles and Negroes (apparently under Abraham) to the edge of the swamp, where twenty-five, mostly women and children, were captured after a brief fight. More than a hundred horses were also seized. The whites then pursued the Indians across the Hatcheelustee creek and as far into the swamp as they could manage. This was a typical running fight in which the Seminoles fought from tree to tree, helped by the Negroes, while the white soldiers resolutely splashed through the mire and attempted to shoot down an invisible enemy.

This fight was not particularly costly in Indian lives, but the Seminoles lost valuable supplies, horses, some baggage; and twenty-three Negroes. Two Indian women were also captured, always a distressing event to Seminoles. (If Osceola tried to prevent harassment of white women and children, the white officers had no compunctions about seizing the wives and children of Indians. Although they did no fighting, Seminole women were regularly captured and held by the whites.)

Now there was a strange turn of events. Prisoners revealed that the Seminoles in the area were led by Micanopy, Jumper, Alligator, and Abraham. On the morning of the twenty-eighth, a prisoner was sent to the chiefs with an offer of peace if they fulfilled the treaty. On the thirty-first, Abraham visited Jesup and promised to bring in Jumper and Alligator. They arrived on February 3, and agreed to meet at Fort Dade on the eighteenth for a conference. Until then, hostilities would be suspended.

Jesup was mightily pleased by this unexpected armistice, but he was also depressed by the war that had been thrust upon him. Hurrying back to Fort Armstrong ahead of his army, he wrote to the adjutant general:

> As an act of justice to all my predecessors in command, I consider it my duty to say that the difficulties attending military operations in this country can be properly appreciated only by those acquainted with them. . . .
>
> This is a service which no man would seek with any other view than the mere performance of his duty: distinction, or increase of reputation, is out of the question; and the difficulties are such, that the best concerted plans may result in absolute failure, and the best established reputation be lost without a fault.
>
> If I have, at any time, said aught in disparagement of the operations of others in Florida, either verbally or in writing, officially or unofficially, knowing the country as I now know it, I consider myself bound, as a man of honor, solemnly to retract it.[4]

This was probably the most revealing statement made by a white officer during the entire Second Seminole War.

Word of the truce moved to the Indians and the soldiers slowly. On the morning of February 8, 1837, Lieutenant Colonel A. C. M. Fanning was encamped on the south shore of Lake Munroe (modern Lake Monroe) with a force partially composed of recruits. Low breastworks had been thrown up the day before; a little steamboat, the *Santee,* was nuzzled into the shore. This boat and another, the *Essayons,* had brought the soldiers up the St. Johns River.

"Lie on your arms," Fanning had ordered his men, so they slept with weapons at hand. This precaution probably saved their lives. King Philip and his son Coacoochee had been watching Fanning's movements. Shortly before dawn, they slipped up toward the encampment with a force variously given as three hundred to six hundred warriors. A nervous sentry heard a rustling in the bushes. It could have been a wild hog or a cow, but the sentry decided against taking any chances.

"Indians!" he screamed, firing at the sky, and at that moment the bushes sparkled with gun flashes. Captain Charles Mellon was killed at once. As the soldiers jumped to their posts, the Indians surged forward in a charge. Then they saw the breastworks which, for some reason, their spies had not mentioned. Coacoochee shouted, "*Tohopekee* ("fence")!" and the horde swung back. The white recruits were still firing wildly, according to what Fanning wrote later, but their officers managed to quiet them down for several hours of battle.

At one point, Second Lieutenant George H. Thomas bravely dashed to the steamboat *Santee* and turned a six-pounder on the Indians. This drove back the Seminoles' right flank; but Coacoochee maintained a strong attack until about 8:00 A.M. He and his father then withdrew, having killed Mellon (who left a wife and four children) and wounded fifteen soldiers, some seriously.[5]

Coacoochee was an unusual warrior. While other Seminoles usually howled with rage during the heat of battle, Coacoochee sometimes burst into laughter. During swamp fighting, he would watch the soldiers stumbling through deep water, start laughing, and even forget to shoot. To his strange but brilliant mind, death itself was apparently funny.

The battle at Lake Munroe was significant for a number of reasons. Fort Mellon, named for the dead captain, was established near the site of the battle where the town of Sanford now stands. This fort would be of great importance later in the war. Fort Mellon could be reached by water along the St. Johns River; thus it could be adequately supplied. Also of importance, this was one of Coacoochee's first truly important battles. Later he would associate himself closely with Osceola.

Osceola's reaction to the truce was one of skepticism. He wanted an honorable peace; he would also be guided by the will of the nation. A truce was welcomed by both sides, and there was wisdom in hearing what the whites would have to say. Osceola, however, remained doubtful about white intentions.

Soldiers at Fort Dade prepared for the meeting on February 18, giving everything the best possible military appearance. But on the eighteenth no Seminoles appeared. Four days later, a party of Seminoles was spotted on the Fort King road approaching the fort. Among them were Alligator and Yaholoochee (Cloud) who promised to bring others for a meeting on March 5. (Martin Van Buren would become President of the United States the day before.) Finally, on March 4, Jumper, Yaholoochee, Abraham, and Holatoochee (Davy) came in and stated they represented Micanopy as the top chief. They agreed to a capitulation that stated (Article 4) that the Indians would immediately withdraw south of the Hillsborough river where they would assemble in camp (Article 8) prior to April 10. Most important of all (Article 5), "the Seminoles and their allies, who come in and emigrate to the west, shall be secure in their lives and property [and] their Negroes, their bona fide property, shall accompany them to the west. . . ."

As Osceola had anticipated, the Seminoles were growing tired of fighting. By agreeing to this treaty capitulation, Jesup had removed one of the great obstacles to emigration—the status of the "allies," or free Negroes, and that of the Indian-owned slaves. It was not entirely clear, however, what would happen to the runaway slaves who had joined the Seminoles after the beginning of the war. Were they to be considered "allies"?

The capitulation troubled Osceola deeply. Had all the fight drained out of the Seminole leaders? The whites apparently had changed their position in regard to the Seminole Negroes, a concession of great value, but why had so many leaders suddenly decided to agree to emigration?

"Too much time," old Arpeika growled. He and his band had met Osceola's group in mid-Florida. "They don't tire of being brave, they tire only of fighting. The long rain of war has put out the fire, but the coals are still there."

"And if we blow on them?" Osceola asked.

"Not yet. The time will come later. For now, we only watch. But I will tell you one true thing, brother, Arpeika is not moving!"

"Nor I," Osceola agreed. "Not until I see exactly what the white man plans to do."

General Jesup believed sincerely that the war was over. On March 18, he wrote to the adjutant general:

> Several Mickasukey Indians have come to camp today—Micanopy has heard from the Chief of that band, Abi-a-ca (Sam Jones), also from Oseola (Powell). [Abi-a-ca for Arpeika.] Those Chiefs are both between Apopka & the St. Johns; and Micanopy and Alligator have no doubt of bringing them in early next month, perhaps sooner—
>
> I now for the first time have allowed myself to believe the War at an end. The same errors, however, that renewed the War in Alabama would renew it here; I mean the imprudent violence of the Citizens. Should they attempt to seize any of the Indians either as criminals or as debtors the scenes of the last year will be renewed. If it should become necessary to protect them from such annoyance, I shall not hesitate to declare Martial law, and send every individual not connected with the public service out of the Country.[6]

Jesup saw part of the problem but not all of it. He was afraid the citizens might attack the Seminoles; he should have feared seizure of the Indian Negroes. Gradually he began to see this danger. He met it first by ordering that no whites could go south of Fort Foster (old Fort Alabama) on the Hillsborough River. The ruling could not be effectively enforced; Floridians were furious about it.

Bowing to pressure from the slave interests, Jesup began to

retreat from his position on the capitulation agreement by April 8. He wrote the new Secretary of War, J. R. Poinsett, on the ninth: "The Chiefs entered into an engagement yesterday to surrender the Negroes taken during the War. They will deliver them to the commanding Officers of the Posts on the St. Johns." [7]

When Osceola heard about this, he was furious. He realized he must again assert himself and seize control, but the problem was difficult. Micanopy, Holatoochee, Alligator, Jumper, and some others were already assembling at Tampa Bay. Over at Fort Mellon, Coa Hadjo, Philip, and Coacoochee had come in. Meanwhile, to aggravate matters and upset a delicate balance, slave-catchers were beginning to harass Jesup, who wrote the Secretary of War on May 8:

> Nothing is now to be apprehended unless it be the imprudence of Citizens of Florida—The officious interference of some of them has already embarrassed the service; and from the public papers I discover that certain citizens of Florida, who, I presume, were unwilling to trust their persons nearer to the Seminoles than Charleston, are denouncing my measures. I have only to say in reply to them that I can have no agency in converting the Army into negro catchers, particularly for the benefit of those who are evidently afraid to undertake the recapture of their property themselves. . . .[8]

Arpeika and Osceola were puzzled about what to do next. The idea of turning in runaway slaves was inconceivable, even worse than any agreement about going west. Meanwhile, in the late days of April, they were isolated from the rest of the Seminole nation.

"We have one choice," Osceola told the old medicine man. "Philip and Coacoochee have gone to Fort Mellon. I think they might agree with us to resist the whites. They can't come out to join us without causing a great deal of trouble, but we can go in to join them. Then we'll see what happens."

On May 3, Osceola and Arpeika arrived at Fort Mellon and

reported to Lieutenant Colonel William S. Harney that they were prepared to emigrate. Osceola, although thin and weary from illness, organized a ball game and was his usual charming self. (Presumably, Arpeika was as dour and irritable as ever.) Reportedly, twenty-five hundred Seminoles were in or near Fort Mellon, but they reported to the camp slowly. Over at Tampa Bay, the move to assemble was even slower. Measles broke out in the detention camp, frightening the Indians into a smallpox scare. According to Jesup, many of Alligator's people dispersed because they heard they would be executed. Someone, probably a white interested in seizing Negroes, spread the rumor that the Seminoles would all be herded into the twenty-six waiting transports and drowned at sea before reaching New Orleans en route to Arkansas Territory.[9]

To Jesup's profound irritation, a Georgia company with designs on the Indian Negroes sent slave-catchers toward the Tampa area armed with powers of attorney.[10] Perhaps a dozen other factors, including nothing more dramatic than reluctance, slowed the assembly of Seminoles at the detention points. And some, without question, still expected Osceola to pass a miracle.

It was about this time, according to Army surgeon Samuel Forry, that Jumper proposed to General Jesup, "Put us even down among the capes, below Charlotte's Harbour." He went on to say that the Indians could live on Koonti roots, game, and fish.[11]

Annoyed by the Seminoles' delay in assembling, Jesup wrote Colonel Harney:

> If you see Powell again, I wish you to tell him that I intend to send exploring parties into every part of the country during the summer, and that I shall send out and take all negroes who belong to the white people, and that he must not allow the Indians or Indian negroes to mix with them. Tell him I am sending to Cuba for bloodhounds to trail them, and I intend to hang every one of them who does not come in.[12]

At least in Jesup's mind, Osceola was still the most influential leader among the Seminoles. Jesup would soon find, to his dismay, that this was correct. He also learned quickly from the national press that most citizens objected to the use of his bloodhounds.

On a warm evening late in May, Osceola and Arpeika sat beneath a tree on the shore of Lake Munroe and watched the fish snap at the swarming bugs. They had the freedom of the area; the commander of Fort Mellon realized it was impossible to confine any of the Seminoles. Osceola listened to a bugle from the fort where soldiers were lined up before the white man's flag. It was a peaceful scene, and Osceola felt better than he had for weeks.

"You sleep," Arpeika snarled, spitting at the water.

"No, brother, I don't sleep. But perhaps I dream."

"You sleep and dream. Go to your women."

"My women are going away to a safe place," Osceola said, smiling. "I think your kin should join them."

Arpeika watched an alligator glide through the water, eyes alone showing on the surface. The old man muttered to himself, scratched his chest, laughed, stared at Osceola fiercely. At last he said, "I'll hear your dream."

"Very well. Tomorrow night I take my warriors to Tampa Bay. When everyone sleeps, we free Micanopy and the others. A word to Coacoochee and the people here will scatter, too. I think Micanopy will no longer be chief over all. I think there will be a new chief."

"Philip?" Arpeika grunted.

"Not Philip. A great warrior but too cautious. The new chief should be a Mikasuki. His name must be Arpeika."

"We will leave tomorrow at the middle of night," Arpeika growled. "Now we blow on the fire. After it's over, we'll talk about Arpeika."

There was no difficulty about leaving Camp Mellon. Not only

did the Seminoles have their weapons with them, but stores of ammunition were hidden in the forests. After sending their families into the wilderness and telling Coacoochee of their plans, Osceola and Arpeika set out with two hundred warriors for Tampa Bay.

Incredibly enough, Jesup knew they were coming to kill or abduct Micanopy and other chiefs in the detention camp. The general alerted Captain William Graham, in charge of a mounted company and one hundred twenty Creek warriors, to guard Micanopy's camp. Creek spies were placed among the Seminoles, but they failed to make any reports. Samuel Forry wrote that the Creeks were angry at their white employers. Women and children, left in Alabama under white protection, had been mistreated, so the Creeks were no longer anxious to obey any white commander's orders.[13]

Micanopy, comfortable and fat with the white men's rations, slept well on the night of June 2, 1837. (He always ate and slept well.) Jumper, the sense-bearer, may not have slept well. Jumper and Alligator had obeyed Micanopy in agreeing to removal, but they had also betrayed everything for which they had fought for a year and a half.

At midnight, Micanopy was wakened by a yank on his plump leg. He sat up, snorting and gulping, and was pulled from his blankets into the dim light of a dying fire. He could make out the figure of Jumper, also under guard with his arms pinned, and the familiar faces of old Arpeika and Osceola. Behind them stood a score of armed warriors.

"You are surrounded," Osceola said softly. "You will come with us."

"I gave my word to go west," Micanopy protested. "I must keep my word."

"Come with us or be killed," Arpeika said.

"Then kill me now."

"Put the old fool on a horse," Arpeika snarled, turning to the warriors behind him. "He'll change his mind tomorrow."

"Where's your horse?" Osceola asked Jumper.

"I sold him."

"Then walk. We'll talk to you later."

"I only obeyed Micanopy."

"Later!" Osceola said sharply. To his warriors, he called, "You men, get them moving! Get them all moving!"

It was not difficult to stir up the entire camp, order belongings packed quietly, and get the Seminoles traveling toward the north. Many had secretly hated the idea of removal, while others had feared it. Under the firm influence of Osceola, old Arpeika, and their determined warriors, it was easy to accept a decision to flee. After all, the Seminoles were going home—about seven hundred of them. They were well clothed by the whites, food was waiting for them in caches, secret crops could be harvested in a few weeks, and the white soldiers would not wish to fight during the summer "sick season."

Osceola aimed his mob of men, women, and children—about nine hundred Seminoles in all—toward Long Swamp near Micanopy's old town, Pelacklakaha. Here they could be divided up and scattered effectively over central Florida. Osceola and his people planned to operate with Arpeika near Volusia on Lake George, while Jumper, Micanopy, and the others would be sent south to the area below Casseeme (Kissimmee).[14]

General Jesup's reaction to what he called an "abduction" was one of bitter dismay. On June 5, he wrote the adjutant general asking to be relieved of his command. Later, angry about attacks on him in the press, he decided to stay. Jesup never put it in so many words, but most of his future actions showed that he had one goal in mind: Stop the war by stopping Osceola. Other Seminole leaders were important, but all were mere shadows when compared to Osceola.

For his part, the great Seminole leader was content to wait for the fall of 1837. He was still ill periodically, and the entire conduct of the war had to be reviewed. One important job remained, however. It was accomplished quickly and easily. An election was held, Micanopy was deposed, and Arpeika became top chief. Osceola felt far more comfortable with the old firebrand by his side.

There was a curious sidelight to the events of this period. Jesup managed to send ninety Indian Negroes to New Orleans en route to Arkansas. In New Orleans, there was an attempt to seize them as runaway slaves. General Gaines stepped forward to defend them and the Indian rights to these Negroes. Coe concluded his description of this affair by writing:

> The General finally proved to the satisfaction of the court that the negroes, "found in the service of the Seminoles, and speaking the same language," had never been captured from the whites, but were descendants of former slaves of the whites, who had been free for upwards of a century. They were therefore released, and soon after proceeded on their way in charge of one of our army officers.[15]

11

The Seminoles Succumb to Jesup's Treachery

In Florida, the summer of 1837 was marked by widespread sickness and almost no military action. Dysentery was common, but typhus, yellow fever, and malaria also troubled Indians and whites alike. There were many fevers of "unknown origin"; probably these were of viral nature. Some illness among soldiers was certainly due to inadequate food.

The government promised Jesup Indians to fight Indians, a development that disgusted some military personnel as well as civilians. Surgeon Samuel Forry, stationed at Fort King, wrote to a friend on August 6:

> The head of the War Department has granted Gen. Jesup the following Indian force: four hundred Shawnees, 200 Delawares, 200 Choctaws, 100 Kickapoos, and 100 Sacs and Foxes. We shall then have war to the knife. Every warrior shall be killed, and all the women and children become slaves to the captor! How magnanimous is a civilized and enlightened Republic of the 19th century! In the catalogue of earth's nations, the name Seminole shall be erased! They have been weighed in the balance, and found wanting! The edict has gone forth! [1]

Forry could have spared himself his indignation; only a few of these Indians were ever used, and then not effectively.

Jesup planned his fall campaign on the premise that most of the Seminoles were moving toward the south. One army wing or column would go up the Caloosahatchee River toward Lake Okeechobee (which still did not appear on many maps of the period). Another would operate along the St. Johns, while a third would comb the Indian River country of the east coast, and a fourth would attempt to meet the Seminoles along the Kissimmee River.

Indians were coming in to some of the posts, particularly Fort King. General Jesup agreed to a conference in late August with Coa Hadjo, John Hicks (son of the earlier John Hicks or Tuckose Emathla), and Tuskeneho (about whom not much is known). Osceola and Arpeika stayed away but sent representatives. (Coa Hadjo said the main obstacle to emigration was Arpeika and that even Osceola might be persuaded to leave Florida.[2])

One session of the conference was described by Forry who wrote that it started out with a vituperative harangue by Jesup. The general said he extended the time of emigration to October. He also said he would never acknowledge Arpeika as a chief. He then threatened to execute Seminole prisoners "the moment fresh depredations are committed. . . . If you spill a drop of blood, I will execute them man for man." He stated he had a thousand Indian warriors ready to kill the Seminoles, a reference to the government's western Indians.[3]

In his own report of this affair, Jesup said he agreed to a cessation of hostilities provided the Indians stayed south of Fort Mellon, west of the St. Johns River, and east of the Fort King road. Coa Hadjo promised an early council of warriors and said runaway Negroes would be turned in, but warned that Arpeika and Osceola "controlled the young men, were opposed to [emigration]; and that the former had threatened with death all who favored it." [4]

During the summer, Osceola again waited to see what the whites would do. He was willing to accept the armistice arranged at Fort King, although he and Arpeika, Philip, and Coacoochee had no intention of staying within Jesup's boundaries and, in fact, did not do so. So far, Osceola's war had been defensive and he planned to keep it that way. Attacked, he would fight. But during the summer of 1837, no one attacked him. If more fighting became necessary, it could wait until General Jesup began his operations in November.

Osceola also increasingly wanted peace. Jesup had said the Seminoles must agree to emigration before there could be any discussion of peace, but Osceola could see no justice in such a concept. The war had been caused by the emigration problem and the status of the Indian Negroes; how, then, could the Seminoles accept the white man's priorities? Peace would have to be a first step toward any discussion of the Seminoles' future.

Fort Mellon was closed down in June for health reasons and the garrison was withdrawn. Early in September, four Negroes appeared at Fort Peyton, a new installation on Moultrie Creek some eight miles from St. Augustine, and stated that Philip with a party of warriors was encamped near Bulow's plantation, a deserted ruin north of modern Ormond Beach, Florida. General Joseph M. Hernandez, a native Floridian, decided to strike the Seminole band with a force of one hundred seventy men. Thus he put in motion a chain of events that led to the most important episode of the Seminole War.

Starting at dawn on September 7, the soldiers rode thirty miles to Bulow's where they bivouacked for the night. Army surgeon Jacob R. Motte was along on this expedition and wrote a fine account of the night scene, "the river Halifax smoothly gliding nearby through green meadows of pastoral beauty."

On the morning of the eighth, a number of Negroes appeared at the camp. One, called John Philip, was a fugitive slave who belonged to Philip, the Seminole chief. He wanted to join his wife who had recently fled from the Indians. He said Philip and his party were south of the Tomoka River near the Dunlawton Mill, another ruined plantation, and he agreed to guide the soldiers to the site, twenty-five miles away.

Motte described a difficult march during which horses bogged down to their bellies in one of the swamps. At about sunset, smoke from campfires was seen in the distance. From the edge of a heavily wooded hammock, the soldiers watched Indians moving through the old ruins of the plantation. Presently they departed and the whites advanced cautiously to the ruins where, at a distance of about a mile, they saw the night fires of the Indian encampment.

Shortly after midnight, the soldiers moved out to surround the camp. Dismounted men took positions on two sides while the others, still mounted, circled to the rear of the Indians. For some strange reason, no Indian dogs barked to warn Philip of the intruders.

The attack exploded at dawn. Philip, naked except for his breechclout, was knocked down by a charging horse; apart from this indignity the raid was not marked by any violence. About a score of Indians were captured, including one called Tomoka John. He said that Euchee Billy was camped some ten miles away with a party of his warriors. (This was the Euchee Billy who had been mistakenly reported slain months before when General Eustis was crossing the St. Johns.)

General Hernandez could not pass up so magnificent an opportunity; if Euchee Billy could also be seized, the expedition would be remarkably successful. After securing the prisoners, the entire force set out for this new conquest.

At about 4:00 P.M., Tomoka John brought the soldiers to a dense stand of cabbage palm. One hundred men were dismounted while the others remained with the horses. Surgeon Motte, a brilliant reporter, described the advance in these words:

> Silently and cautiously we wended our way through the old woods, where possibly a civilized being had never before

> voluntarily ventured. A deep and beautiful serenity pervaded nature; for all was silence, save when at long intervals the cry of some solitary bird broke on our ears with startling shrillness; or when a rustling among the dry branches made us pause in breathless silence, till a deer, bounding across our path, would plunge into the opposite thicket; while we dare not send a bullet after him, lest the report of our guns should alarm the wily enemy. . . .

The attacking force moved forward until midnight when Tomoka John whispered that they had reached Euchee Billy's camp. The force was then divided, the soldiers crawling to circle and surround the Indians. Motte wrote later that they managed to get within a hundred yards of the Seminole fires, a remarkable feat for white men.

Before dawn, however, the Seminole dogs began barking and the fires in camp were quickly extinguished. Although Motte does not say so, the breeze that often springs up just before dawn must have carried the scent of the white men to the dogs. Whatever the case, the Indians were alerted.

When the attack signal came at dawn, Euchee Billy's warriors whooped and began firing. The battle was over quickly, however, with one Indian killed and a white lieutenant, John McNeil, mortally wounded. After litters were constructed for McNeil and several wounded Indians, the entire party set out hurriedly for distant St. Augustine. McNeil died on the way.

The prisoners were placed in Fort Marion, the great old Spanish fortress, and, according to Lieutenant J. W. Phelps, a notable celebration was held in St. Augustine. There was also a number of balls and fetes, and (says Phelps) General Hernandez got drunk.[5]

At the request of Philip, whose dignity was not injured by his capture, Tomoka John was sent out to ask Philip's family to join him at Fort Marion. It was arranged for General Hernandez and a mounted battalion to meet them at the ruins of the Bulow plantation on or about September 24.

Surgeon Motte, who had stepped firmly into history for some important moments, went along with the escort party. He wrote that it was raining furiously but "nothing daunted by the wild and dreary aspect of the weather" the battalion plodded on horseback to Bulow's camp where the soldiers made leaky shelters of palmetto fronds and pine boughs. It was wet, nasty, boring, but Motte thought it was picturesque. He said his companions looked like brigands in their secret haunts; probably they looked like wet soldiers the world over.

The Indians did not appear until the afternoon of September 26. Under a white flag were Coacoochee, Philip's son, who was called Wildcat by the whites; Blue Snake who was an associate of Coa Hadjo; Tomoka John; and two Seminole warriors. Despite the foul weather, the party left for St. Augustine at 5:00 P.M. From Motte's description of the journey, a minor hurricane had blown in from the Atlantic and the battalion had to camp for the night in a dismal pine forest.

The weather cleared in the morning. Before reaching Fort Peyton, Coacoochee insisted on dressing up. Motte wrote:

> He soon reappeared in all the pomp of scarlet and burnished silver; his head decorated with a plume of white crane feathers, and a silver band around his gaudy turban. His leather leggings were also superceded by a pair of bright scarlet cloth. He insisted on being mounted on a spirited horse; and attired in his picturesque native costume, he rode with a great deal of savage grace and majesty.

Motte's description could have applied to any of the younger Seminole chiefs.

Coacoochee was paraded through St. Augustine and taken to Fort Marion [6] where he and Blue Snake were detained despite having come in under a white flag. This was the beginning of Jesup's battle with the devil of treachery—a battle he would eventually lose. Every event from the moment of Philip's capture contributed inexorably to Jesup's disgrace and a grave tragedy for the Indians.

Over at Fort King, Samuel Forry heard about Coacoochee. On October 3, he wrote to his friend:

> We have received intelligence of Coa-cuchee's [*sic*] being enticed into St. Augustine—that he came under the protection of a white flag, which secured him a position in the old Fort. Can such things be enacted by men who call themselves civilized? I do not, however, credit this report.[7]

It was true, however. Coacoochee managed to talk his way out by serving as a message bearer for Philip, his father, to others of Philip's family and various chiefs under his control. Basically, however, Coacoochee was temporarily paroled while his father was held as hostage to assure his return.

Coacoochee came back on October 16, bringing with him Philip's brother and youngest son. Of the greatest interest to General Hernandez, Coacoochee said Osceola planned to arrive near St. Augustine in a few days for a conference with the whites. About a hundred warriors would be with him.[8]

Osceola and Coa Hadjo had talked matters over after meeting with Coacoochee, and had decided to negotiate for the release of Philip. They also wanted to discuss a possible peace. They would arrive under a white flag of truce. (The whites had already provided the Indians with white cloth for truce flags!)

A letter from Samuel Forry to a friend is interesting. Forry had been moved from Fort King to St. Augustine where he was awaiting orders. On October 19, he wrote as follows:

> . . . Coa-cuchee returned day before yesterday; and yesterday Gen. Hernandez went as far as Hewlitt's mills, carrying provisions for about 100 of Philip's people, who are approaching from different points. The Gen. met about 50 Indians, and brought to Fort Peyton 79 negroes. My friend, Joe Hicks, was there, and Powell [Osceola] and Coa-hadjo, they say, will be at Fort Peyton today. The Indians have

> not the least idea of emigrating. Tomoka John has no doubt held out false hopes to them, declaring that a portion of this territory will be assigned to them.

Herein lay the real reason for the peace overtures contemplated by Osceola and Coa Hadjo. "*Tomoka John has no doubt held out false hopes to them. . . .*" Forry went on:

> If these people once get into our power, they will be held as fast as the old Fort can make them. They come with a view of having a talk and a ball-play, and eating and drinking.
>
> Gen. Jesup and staff got here yesterday, doubtless concocting some direful plans to entrap the poor savage.

Which was also correct. Forry then went on to describe a dance held by General Hernandez on the night of the eighteenth. Coacoochee was present; Hernandez apparently could not restrain himself from the indecency of showing off his captives. And Coacoochee was definitely a captive, although he had not yet joined his father behind bars. That would happen shortly.

We can reconstruct the scene at the dance from Forry's fine account, and also from many old records of St. Augustine in this period. (Forry was enchanted by the ladies of St. Augustine; so were other officers who tasted the spiced cooking and heard the strange whispers in Spanish from mysterious courtyards. St. Augustine, in the times of Osceola and Forry, was Madrid with a frosting of Boston.)

If Forry liked the ladies of St. Augustine, the ladies literally swooned over Coacoochee. Like the mysterious Osceola, he was trim, youthful, menacing in imagination, astonishingly handsome, Byronic in almost every sense. Ladies were still reading Gordon Lord Byron, who had died in 1824, and were impressed by men of romantic appearance. Coacoochee was a suitable substitute for a Greek god.

Whale oil lamps or candles illuminated the scene of the dance. (Little or no "coal oil" or kerosene was used at the time.) In this dim illumination, the scented ladies waited to see their Indian. And there he was, costumed magnificently, eyes flashing, proud in posture, the perfect man. Did the dreaded Osceola look like this? Yes, officers from Fort King had said. Even better. The ladies fluttered their palmetto fans while Wildcat looked them over calmly. At one point, he was introduced to a man and woman.

"Are they married?" he asked. He could speak some English.

"Oh, yes. Just recently."

Coacoochee eyed the pretty girl, then shrugged. "I guess her husband enjoys her very much," he said bluntly. "But after she's had a few children she won't be worth the bother." [9]

Forry's usual brilliant reporting broke down at this point, so we do not know the social impact of the observation. But Forry does say that Coacoochee was the "lion of the night." He may even have danced; Indians could quickly follow movements and were naturally graceful. Coacoochee, who certainly drank the murderous rum punch of the period, would have enjoyed prancing with the frightened but happy ladies.

On the following day, Osceola and Coa Hadjo camped a mile from Fort Peyton and sent a messenger, John Cavallo (Cowaya) to General Hernandez asking him to meet for a conference at their camp. Hernandez consulted General Jesup, who wrote out a memorandum of questions to be asked Osceola:

> Ascertain the objects of the Indians in coming in at this time. Also their expectations. Are they prepared to deliver up the negroes taken from the citizens at once? Why have they not surrendered them already, as promised by Coa-Hajo at Fort King? Have the chiefs of the nation held a council in relation to the subjects of the talk at Fort King? What chiefs attended that council, and what was their determination? Have the chiefs sent a messenger with the decision of the council? Have the principal chiefs, Micanopy,

> Jumper, Cloud, and Alligator; sent a messenger, and if so, what is their message? Why have not those chiefs come in themselves? [10]

But that was not all. In his report to the President, made in July, 1838, Jesup stated directly: "I accordingly required General Hernandez to seize them, and take them to St. Augustine. . . ." [11] Jesup neglected to say exactly how this last order was delivered. The story is not a pretty one.

On the morning of October 21, General Hernandez set out from St. Augustine for Fort Peyton (commanded by Lieutenant Richard H. Peyton) and Osceola's encampment. At Fort Peyton he picked up some dragoons numbering about two hundred fifty men under the command of Major James A. Ashby. Hernandez apparently had already been told by General Jesup to seize the Indians; at least he had arranged a secret signal upon which Major Ashby was to close in.

A white flag of truce was flying above Osceola's camp. While Hernandez began to talk, the dragoons spread out casually until they had circled the Indians. Osceola apparently guessed what was coming; turning to Coa Hadjo, he said sadly, "I feel choked. You must speak for me." This has also been translated as, "You must talk. I am overcome." The white flag of truce still waved bravely almost above Osceola's head.

Earlier, according to a letter written later to a friend by General Jesup and published in the *Army and Navy Chronicle* for December 14, 1837, Jesup "without communicating my intention to anyone" followed Hernandez to Fort Peyton where, apparently from the woods, he sent in for Lieutenant Peyton to determine the number and position of the Indians. Peyton was ordered to go forward to find out whether the answers of the Indians to the memorandum questions were satisfactory. With Peyton on his way, Jesup then sent his aide to Hernandez with orders for the general to seize all of Osceola's party if the talk was not satisfactory.

Peyton returned with the Indians' answers. General Jesup, now inside the fort, ripped out an order which he sent back to Hernandez.[12] The order read:

> Let the chiefs and warriors know that we have been deceived by them long enough, and that we do not intend to be deceived again. Order the whole party directly to town. You have force sufficient to compel obedience, and they must move instantly.
>
> I have information of a recent murder by the Indians. They must be disarmed.
>
> They can talk in town, and send messengers out, if they please.[13]

About all that had happened during the parley was that the Indians said they had not come in to surrender but wanted peace. They had even brought in some runaway slaves—a major concession on the part of Osceola and the best indication that he truly wanted to discuss peace. (Supposedly he had said earlier that he did not believe the Seminoles could fight effectively for another year.)

The white flag of truce waved. Hernandez gave his signal. Ashby's dragoons closed in. No shots were fired. The Seminoles were armed, but apparently were too shocked to resist. The truce flag still waved. As Coe stated later, borrowing in part from artist George Catlin:

> We do not find a single instance recorded in the long war with the Seminoles of a failure on their part to respect that flag. Indeed, George Catlin, who spent forty years of his life studying Indian character and customs in every part of North and South America, says in this connection: "Among all Indian tribes that I have yet visited in their primitive as well as improved state, the white flag is used as a flag of truce, as it is in the civilized parts of the world, and held to be sacred and inviolable." [14]

The spectacle of General Jesup scuttling around in the woods outside Fort Peyton would be unthinkable except that his written order to Hernandez is dated Fort Peyton and there is an answering note, evidently written later, from Hernandez. The first few lines are significant; italics are the writers':

> Sir—For the purpose of carrying into effect your instructions, *conveyed to me verbally by your aid-de-camp*, Lieutenant Linnard, *after having left Fort Peyton*, that if the answers of the chiefs to my inquiries should not be satisfactory, they were to be made prisoners, I had given the necessary directions to Major Ashby to ensure their capture. . . .[15]

There were seventy-one warriors with Osceola and Coa Hadjo, six women, four Indian Negroes. Arranged in a column between lines of soldiers, the captives were marched to St. Augustine. Someone provided Osceola and Coa Hadjo with horses. Osceola looked ill, but he also seemed more a conqueror than a man who had just been seized by treachery. Motte said, ". . . though when captured evidently sad and care-worn, the fire of his flashing eyes was unsubdued."[16]

The prisoners were placed in Fort Marion, the famous Spanish prison, which will be described later. Osceola and Coa Hadjo immediately requested a meeting with Jesup, who wrote that he saw them in his quarters. They asked that a messenger be sent to their families, and that their wives and children be given a safe conduct to join them in prison. Jesup granted the request.

Word began to spread throughout the country that Osceola, the famous Seminole leader, had been seized while attending a conference under a flag of truce. The public reaction throughout the nation was one of outrage; Jesup had performed a dishonorable deed, staining the honor of his country.[17] Papers throughout the nation editorialized on the disgraceful means by which Osceola was captured. The English were shocked by the dishonorable performance of an American general; one English writer would later say, "Never was a more disgraceful piece of villainy perpetrated in a civilized land." This writer,

Andrew Welch, pointed out with considerable reason that the Americans had dealt with the Seminoles as a nation, by making treaties with them. They were not rebels. To seize a Seminole leader under a flag of truce was as much an act of infamy as it would be for an English general to seize an American general under similar circumstances.

Niles' Weekly Register for November 4, 1837, touched the heart of the matter. The paper predicted that Jesup's treachery would "produce more bloody and signal vengeance than has yet marked their ruthless doings." This, indeed, was the error that compounded Jesup's treachery. The capture of Osceola under a flag of truce not only disgusted countless Americans, but it doubtless prolonged the Seminole War by enraging the Indians and making them skeptical of any white treaty or peace overture.

Jesup spent much of the rest of his life trying to justify his action. Osceola, he said, had violated his past promises. The Seminole leader knew that Jesup would not discuss peace until the Indians had agreed once more to emigration and ". . . as the white flag had been allowed for no other purpose than to enable them to communicate and come in without danger of attack from our parties, it became my duty to secure them. . . ." [18]

When he really tried, General Jesup could produce even more asinine explanations for his rotten action. Many years later, according to Coe, he claimed that Osceola had come with the intention of capturing St. Augustine and releasing the prisoners! Yet, as Coe points out, Jesup had called Osceola an intelligent man.[19] Apparently, Jesup had the remarkable view that an "intelligent man" would undertake to attack a large town, occupied by soldiers, with a striking force of only seventy-two warriors, six women, and arms that added up to a total of fifty-two rifles. Jesup had not become senile when he made this remarkable observation; he must, then, have been scrambling desperately for just one more justification.

It would be easy for history to pat General Jesup on the head and excuse his treachery on the grounds that he did not believe the rules of civilized warfare, so-called, applied to Indians. But he had followed the rules before, up to the treachery involving Coacoochee (who, incidentally, quickly followed Osceola behind bars in Fort Marion).

It is useless to speculate on the causes of Jesup's shameful decision. The most likely explanation is that it was the result of frustration dating back to the Seminole abduction from Tampa Bay—an action managed by Osceola. Osceola had made a fool of Jesup and, quite possibly, had endangered his career. Jesup also had no love for Coa Hadjo; he suspected this chief had also made a fool of him. The step to a treacherous response was no great leap.

On the face of it, as Motte put it, the army "in one fell swoop" had secured Osceola, Coa Hadjo, some other war chiefs and eighty (actually seventy-one) Mikasuki warriors.[20] Already in captivity were Philip, Coacoochee, Euchee Billy, Holata Tustenuggee, and a number of others. Micanopy, Tiger Tail, Alligator, Arpeika, Jumper, and other important leaders were still free.

The building of Fort Marion (formerly Castle Marco), where Osceola was held, had been started in 1672 by the Spanish and was the oldest fort in the United States. It had been used before as a prison; Sprague noted that in 1821, a dungeon was found beneath the high turret with human bones and other indications of cruel imprisonment. Many thought this to be a "remnant of the Inquisition, and that the punishment was a lingering death." [21]

Osceola was not mistreated in Fort Marion; if anything, he was treated well. The prisoners had beds of straw covered with forage bags; probably they also had blankets. It does not appear that any were placed in solitary confinement. They could air themselves in the courtyard, and they were even permitted to hold a dance—probably a ritual affair. Forry wrote:

> A few nights ago, the Indians had a dance in the fort; the whoops and yells alarmed the city—the Mayor ran to Gen. Jesup and hoped that he would send for more troops, for Osceola would take the city before daylight. The Indians are perfectly secure, and do not dream of escape. Their large knives were taken from them the morning after imprisonment, and a barricade was erected to prevent a rush upon the passage leading to the door. Gen. Jesup, on leaving, gave a positive order that no man, except officers on duty, shall have any communication with the Indians.[22]

Osceola's suffering was that of a captive eagle. He knew he had been betrayed; he resented it fiercely, but his resentment was tinged with sorrow. In any great leader of tragic dimensions, there comes a time when he begins to regard his oppressor with pity. Later, when asked why he did not attempt to escape from Fort Marion, Osceola said, "I have done nothing to be ashamed of; it is for those to feel shame who entrapped me."

Historian Coe stepped into fairly deep water when he wrote:

> If the painter of the world-famous picture, "Christ before Pilate," should seek in American history a subject worthy of his brush, we would commend to him, "Osceola before General Jesup"—Osceola, the despised Seminole, a captive in chains—Jesup, in all the pomp and circumstance of an American Major-General; Osceola, who had "done nothing to be ashamed of," calmly confronting his captor, who cowers under the steady gaze of a brave and honorable man! [23]

But Osceola was no Christ and Jesup no Pilate; nor was Osceola in chains and Jesup cowering. Coe would have done better to quote Milton in *Samson Agonistes*:

> Ask for this great Deliverer now, and find him
> Eyeless in Gaza, at the mill with slaves,
> Himself in bonds under Philistian yoke.[24]

The analogy of Samson and Osceola is not unreasonable. Both fought for their people, both were victims of treachery. Both were sick during imprisonment; Samson's eyes had been put out, Osceola suffered gravely from a fever that was probably chronic malaria. Osceola was also beginning to crumble from another disease unknown then and now to most white men. He was so sickened by betrayal, so gnawed by injustice that he was slowly dying. He did not wish to die; there was no conscious "death wish," in the jargon of the modern psychologist. But the phenomenon of death as a result of despair has been common among American Indians.

While Osceola sat on his blanket in Fort Marion, a colored shawl thrown over his shoulders and his thoughts on the forests beyond St. Augustine, General Jesup put his fall campaign into motion. Sprague lists the arrangements in detail;[25] it is enough here to say that the command was spread all over Florida. The largest body, consisting of four columns, would operate east and west of St. Johns, moving toward the headwaters. As originally planned, another column was to go up the Caloosahatchee River toward Okeechobee. A Navy unit, under Lieutenant Levi N. Powell, a Navy officer, was to enter the Everglades from the Atlantic coast. Another newcomer, Colonel Zachary Taylor, was ordered to operate in the wild south central part of Florida roughly north of Lake Okeechobee, west of the Kissimmee, and east of the Gulf of Mexico. Taylor was a typical frontier officer who liked to fight and did well at it. He later fought with brilliance on the Rio Grande front, and became President of the United States in 1849.

Seminole leadership, in the view of most white officers, had fallen upon the unlikely and unlikable Arpeika (Sam Jones). Motte wrote:

> *Sam Jones* (*Apiaka*) is now the whole head and front of the Seminole war. He was represented by those who knew him as a great rascal; and assuming the attributes of a prophet, assisted by the fortuitous and frequent occurrence

> of our horses dying on the road, which he ascribed to his own spells and incantations, great confidence was reposed in his power of saving them by the hostile Indians, who at one time were said to have even deposed of the pacific and imbicile *Micanopy,* their hereditary chief, and elected him in his stead.[26]

Early in November, a delegation of Cherokees arrived in St. Augustine on a government-inspired mission aimed at persuading the Seminoles to agree to emigration and make peace. This group was under the instructions of a Cherokee half-breed, John Ross, who had written the Cherokee constitution and was a man of formidable intelligence and executive ability. General Jesup greeted the delegation coldly but agree to an interview with the prisoners in Fort Marion.

Jesup then permitted the Cherokees to go to Fort Mellon with Coa Hadjo. They arrived on November 26, as did General Jesup, and promptly went out to contact Micanopy. Part of the deal they offered was future negotiations of a treaty as well as amnesty for Osceola and other Seminole leaders.

Micanopy and a number of other chiefs were impressed. They came into Fort Mellon under a white flag on December 3, only a few days after the arrival there of Osceola's two wives and two of his children. (This earlier party, mostly members of the families of the prisoners, was promptly sent to St. Augustine.) With Micanopy were Yaholoochee (Cloud), Tuskegee, and nine or ten subchiefs.

The Cherokees went out again, this time to try their persuasive powers on Arpeika and also to bring in more families. Arpeika would have nothing to do with them; so they returned emptyhanded to Fort Mellon on December 14. There they found that some minor chiefs and several small bands of warriors had settled in the vicinity of the fort to await developments.

And now, to the amazement and horror of the Cherokees, General Jesup committed his next act of treachery. Although Micanopy had come in under a flag of truce, he and the other chiefs plus warriors near the fort were seized and shipped by steamer to St. Augustine. The total number of prisoners was seventy-eight.

The Cherokee mediators, feeling gravely dishonored, went to St. Augustine with the captives and were finally permitted by Jesup to talk to the prisoners, including those captured with Osceola. With the delegation was a Colonel J. H. Sherburne, who had accompanied the Cherokees to Florida. Jesup asked Sherburne to present the following proposition to the Seminoles in the presence of the Cherokee delegation:

Would the Seminoles accept for their exclusive use all of Florida south of Tampa Bay and bounded by the Gulf of Mexico and the Atlantic? Would they defend this area against foreign invasion, and would they return runaway Negroes who entered it? Would they go to Washington for treaty discussions if the government sanctioned the idea?

The offer was as amazing as it was unexpected; several writers have suggested that Jesup may have presented it because of remorse over his various acts of treachery. Actually, what had been suggested was about what the Seminoles had wanted all along: peace and a home in Florida. Except for old Philip, who now wisely mistrusted the word of anyone connected with the United States government, the chiefs agreed heartily to the proposition. Osceola stripped a white plume from his turban and told Sherburne, "Give this to our white father in token that Osceola will do as you have said." [27]

Nothing came of this proposition, of course, although it could have ended the Seminole War. Jesup may have been sincere in presenting the idea through Colonel Sherburne, although he had no clear authority to do so. If he was not sincere, the offer to the Seminoles, however qualified, was contemptible. No decent man would hold up false hopes to prisoners.

Just a few days after the Cherokees had arrived at Fort Mellon on their ill-fated mission, Coacoochee determined to escape from Fort Marion. He had discussed this with Osceola, but

Osceola was far too ill to do anything other than offer encouragement. He was also too proud to scramble up walls. And there was one other reason why Osceola made no attempt to escape, a reason overlooked by historians. At the time of Coacoochee's flight from Fort Marion, November 29, 1837, Osceola's wives and children had not yet arrived from Fort Mellon. Without much question, Osceola did not want his family held as hostages as a result of his escape. He said later he could have escaped but scorned to do so.

The standard account of Coacoochee's escape from the fort appears in Sprague's history and is presented as Coacoochee's own narrative.[28] The story is beautifully told, but the modern historian Kenneth W. Porter has analyzed it and put together a more reasonable version.

On the moonless night of November 29, about twenty prisoners were in a cell where there was a low platform beneath a ledge and a loophole. (If they were not all in the cell, they at least had access to it.) They had a number of knives and a rope made of forage bags that were used to cover the bed straw.

One of them—Kenneth Porter thinks it must have been John Cavallo, the Indian Negro—mounted the platform and boosted a companion up to the ledge. Probably one of the two iron bars in the loophole was rusted out or had secretly been filed loose before. The man on the ledge lowered his homemade rope out of the window until it touched ground in a muddy ditch about twenty feet below.

The other prisoners were boosted up on the ledge. One by one, they squeezed through the loophole, leaving skin behind, and lowered themselves to the ground. John Cavallo was either helped by someone else or came up to the ledge on the rope; in any event, he, too, escaped. Among the fugitives were two women (who must have been remarkably slim) as well as Philip's brother and two of his sons. Osceola was delighted to report the escape late on the morning of the following day, November 30.[29]

Jesup received news of this escape while he was at Fort Mellon with the Cherokee delegation. Some historians believe he was so infuriated by the flight of the prisoners that he seized Micanopy in retaliation. The guess is a worthy one; Jesup was certainly angered to the point of distraction. Finally, however, he calmed down in time for the happier news that on December 19 Jumper and some sixty-three warriors had surrendered. Jumper was tired of running and fighting.

On this same day, Colonel Zachary Taylor marched south toward Lake Okeechobee with a thousand men. There, on Christmas day, he met Alligator, Arpeika, Halleck-Tustenuggee, and Coacoochee, who had caught up with the war. The Seminole force was between three hundred eighty and four hundred eighty warriors.

It was unfortunate that Osceola could not have witnessed this battle, for many of his military ideas were put to excellent use. Sprague wrote:

> In front of the Indian line there was a deep morass of saw-grass and palmetto, almost impassable. In the rear was the lake, with a clear sandy beach, upon which a rapid retreat could be made if necessary. The grass in front in some places was cut down to invite the troops into the most impassable spot. Ten Indians were in trees enveloped in moss so as not to be discovered, which enabled them to oversee the advance on the command, and communicate the direction to those below. The trees were notched, behind which the most expert marksmen were posted, and in which they rested their rifles, and thus obtained a steady aim.[30]

The fight began at noon and ended at 3:00 P.M. when the Seminoles withdrew. Taylor later protested that his Missouri volunteers retreated after their commander was killed; if so they could hardly be blamed, for the Seminole fire was murderous. The Army later claimed a victory, but the reason for this claim defies explanation. The Seminole loss was 11 killed and 14 wounded, while the white men lost 27 killed and an incredible 111 wounded. Taylor, who shortly became a brevet brigadier general, could not have survived many victories of this sort.

It would be pleasant to know definitely that Osceola heard of this battle while he was still in Fort Marion. But just before Christmas day, he had learned that all the Seminole occupants of the St. Augustine fort were to be moved to Fort Moultrie at Charleston. General Jesup felt that Fort Marion was not a secure prison for important Seminoles; Coacoochee had shown its weaknesses.

Osceola was consoled by the presence of his wives and two of his children. But in the final days of 1837, two years after the start of the war, he was ushered to the S.S. *Poinsett* for the journey to Sullivan's Island in Charleston Harbor. With him were Micanopy, Philip, Coa Hadjo, Cloud, 116 warriors, and 82 women and children, including Osceola's own family.

His shawl drawn tightly around his shoulders and the fever sweat cold on his face, Osceola watched the shores of Florida disappear behind the sea. The breeze was off the land; he could smell, very faintly, the odor of earth and grass and trees. Morning light touched the gray turrets and battlements of Fort Marion, gulls wheeled above the ship. Behind him was the blue streak of the Gulf Stream.

Perhaps it was over now, perhaps the Seminoles were defeated, perhaps the dreams of freedom had blown away on the wind. But Osceola, turning toward the comfort of his wives and children, did not think so. Freedom had not gone away. It was just waiting for a while.

12

The Death of Osceola

Fort Moultrie, originally called Fort Sullivan for the island on which it was located, was built of palmetto logs during the American Revolution. On June 28, 1776, the fort had been attacked by a small British armada. Defended nobly by Colonel William Moultrie, it later was renamed for him. In 1811, a new brick fort was built on the site of the old log installation. At the time Osceola was imprisoned in Fort Moultrie, it was the most important harbor defense for Charleston, South Carolina.

The S.S. *Poinsett* arrived at Fort Moultrie on January 1, 1838, and the prisoners were promptly directed inside the enclosure. Osceola's quarters were sufficiently roomy to be shared by his wives and children; there is contemporary evidence that the room was heated and contained a pallet spread before a fire. Other furnishings are not described, but Osceola was permitted to keep his famous old knife and his war dress. He was also allowed the freedom of the fort.

Coe wrote that Osceola received many visitors:

> The fearless bravery and manly qualities of this chief, his unusual knowledge of scientific warfare, and, above all, his unswerving determination to defend to the last his chosen home, had spread his fame throughout the length and

> breadth of the country, and won for him respect and admiration even in the hearts of his bitterest enemies.[1]

Certainly there were numerous visitors and, as Coe suggests later, Osceola sometimes spoke of his betrayal with great indignation. He also wanted to continue the fight for a Seminole future in Florida. All of the prisoners, in fact, were grieved by the circumstances of their capture and their inability to carry on the battle for their land.

These men were warriors, not political figures except as circumstances had dictated, their women who had prepared the food, run the bullets, and tended the wounded, were the wives of warriors; and it was difficult for people of this background to adjust to prison life. That they did so gracefully is surprising.

News of the battle at Okeechobee must have reached Fort Moultrie early in January. Whenever it arrived, it certainly heartened the prisoners, particularly Philip, who was almost as ill as Osceola. But there were few battles of any significance during January, and news of the few engagements that did take place must have come in after the end of the month.

Despite visitors, there was not much for prisoners to do at Fort Moultrie. Many contemporary writers, however, have noted that on the evening of January 6, Osceola and the Seminole chiefs were "induced" (says Coe) to attend the Charleston Theater where they saw a play called *Honey-Moon* with a Miss Cooper in the role of Juliana.

A poet named James B. Ransom was present on this occasion to dignify it with some doggerel published a few days later in the Charleston *Courier*. He sets the scene—chandeliers blazing, every seat taken—and introduces Osceola and his "stern, unbending, stoic band." Then, unwittingly turning Osceola into a drama critic, he has this to say:

> The lovely glow of Juliana's face,
> Her smiles and blushes, and the tears she shed,

Her splendid attitudes and native grace,
Were to his war-lit fancy stale and dead.

Coe quoted more of this mercilessly [2] but neglected to point out the obvious indignity of displaying captured Seminoles in order to boost theater attendance for Miss Cooper's posturing. (One wonders what Osceola told Che-cho-ter about Miss Cooper and *Honey-Moon.*)

In the days that followed, Osceola had abundant time to review the events of the war before the treacherous hour of his capture. Had he been wrong to fight, to resist, to lead men to death or grave injury? Had the white man been right?

No, the white man had lied or deceived from the beginning. He had cheated the Indian and allowed him to starve. Then he had even robbed the Seminole of the bitter dignity of starvation; he had tried to force him at gunpoint from the land of his birth. Resistance had been the only choice left.

Perhaps the battle had not been lost. There had been the strange proposal made through Colonel Sherburne about the land south of Tampa Bay. Even the Indians knew little about these interminable wetlands with their wild hammocks and dark cypress swamps.

Osceola had heard that fish abounded in the waters of south Florida, that deer could be found on the hammocks, that wild turkeys flocked in the pinelands. But it was a strange country where trails followed water and the sky was endless as an old man's song. Even the trees were different; one tree was so poisonous that the sap could kill a man. Even so, the Seminoles could learn to live in this land and get along with the few Indians who already made it their home.

Osceola thought of these matters during the long days when he stared out over Sullivan's Island and watched the seabirds float above the stands of myrtle, live oak, and palmetto. Sometimes the sweat would break out, and he would have to lie beside the fire while his wives bathed his face. Sometimes he dreamed fiercely, living over old battles.

He was attended, during his periods of illness, by Dr. Frederick Weedon who, strangely enough, was the brother-in-law of the deceased General Wiley Thompson. Mrs. May McNeer Ward, a great-granddaughter of Dr. Weedon, has written that the doctor had become friendly with Osceola at Fort Marion where he was the attending physician, and had gone to Charleston at Osceola's request. Dr. Weedon, who realized that Osceola was seriously ill, told a famous visitor he expected the Seminole leader to die within a few weeks.

The visitor was George Catlin, the noted painter of American Indians, who had heard that the Seminole captives were at Fort Moultrie and hurried there to paint them. Catlin, who arrived on January 17, was put up comfortably in the officers' quarters where he entertained the Indians at night. He later wrote:

> . . . after painting all day at their portraits, I have had Osceola, Mickenopah, Cloud, Coeehajo, King Philip and others in my room until a late hour at night, where they have taken great pains to give me an account of the war and the mode in which they were captured, of which they complain bitterly. I am fully convinced from all I have seen, and learned from the lips of Osceola and from the chiefs who are around him, that he is a most extraordinary man, and one entitled to a better fate.

As an artist, Catlin was deeply intrigued by Osceola:

> In stature he is about at mediocrity, with an elastic and graceful movement; in his face he is good-looking, with rather an effeminate smile; but of so peculiar a character that the world may be ransacked over without finding another just like it. In his manners, and all his movements in company, he is polite and gentlemanly, though his conversation is entirely in his own tongue and his general appearance and actions, those of a full-blooded and wild Indian.

Catlin first painted Micanopy, then did two portraits of Osceola. One was the famous head and shoulders study, the other a full-length figure. Of the latter, he said:

> I painted him precisely in the costume in which he stood for his picture, even to a string and a trinket. He wore three ostrich feathers on his head and a turban made of a vari-colored cotton shawl, and his dress was chiefly of calicoes, with a handsome bead sash or belt around his waist, and his rifle in his hand.

(Could it have been Osceola's rifle? Perhaps. It may have been taken unloaded to Fort Moultrie.)

On the day Catlin finished his second painting, November 26, Osceola was seized with an attack of quinsy. (This is known as a peritonsillar abscess. There is severe pain and swelling in the throat accompanied by a temperature that frequently mounts to 105° F.)

Dr. Weedon later wrote this account:

> On the 26 of January . . . he was attacked in the night with a violent quinsy, of which I was informed very soon after, and hastened to his room. He was then laboring under considerable difficulty of deglutation and respiration, accompanied with pain and inflammation of the tonsils. To prevent suffocation it was necessary to support him in nearly an erect position. His pulse was full, quick and hard. Blood was instantly drawn and an emetic and blister prescribed.
>
> At this moment an Indian entered the room, who, as I afterward understood, was in high esteem as a Prophet and Doctor. From the moment of his entrance there was a refusal to take anything. Finding myself debarred from the administration of suitable remedies, and feeling the responsibility devolving upon me, I requested Prof. B. B. Strobel, to visit the patient with me. He attended and used his best exertions to prevail on the patient to submit to treatment, such as scarification, leeching, etc.—but he pertinaciously refused; not but what he would have been disposed to ac-

quiesce, had he not been overruled by the influence of his family.

B. B. Strobel, M.D., was professor of anatomy at the Medical School, College of South Carolina. He must have been called in on the evening of the twenty-seventh or twenty-eighth when George Catlin *and the officers of the post* stayed up much of the night to watch over Osceola. The vigil of Fort Moultrie's officers is worthy of note. The officers, along with anyone else who had encountered Osceola, had fallen under his spell.

Dr. Strobel entered Osceola's room at night. Che-cho-ter and the second wife, one on either side of Osceola, were bathing his neck with warm water in which herbs had been steeped. Their shadows, magnified by the candlelight, trembled and shifted on the wall. Osceola was lying on his blanket before the fire with his head in Che-cho-ter's lap.

Dr. Strobel wrote:

> I requested his permission, through the interpreter, to examine his throat, to which he assented. I discovered that the tonsils were so much enlarged as greatly to impede respiration, and that the mucuous membrane of the Pharynx was in a high state of inflammation. As there was some danger of suffocation unless the disease was arrested I proposed to scarify the tonsils. The patient referred us to his conjurer, who was sitting on the floor, covered up in his blanket, with all the air and dignity of a great man. He said, "No!" I next proposed to apply leeches to the throat and back of the ears—The conjurer said, "No!" I proposed lastly some medicine and a stimulating wash to be applied internally—which he also refused—saying that if the patient were not better in the morning he would give him up to us —I urged, entreated, and persuaded him to do somehing, for although I did not doubt his ability to cure, in the woods where he could have access to his roots and herbs—yet here he was placed under different circumstances and as he had no means within his reach, begged him to yield up the patient to us. All was in vain. . . .

George Catlin had to leave for New York on the morning of January 29. After Catlin had said good-bye, Osceola asked the interpreter to give a message to Dr. Weedon. He wished to have Weedon describe his final moments to the artist who had become his friend.

On the morning of the thirtieth, Osceola realized his life was over. Weedon recorded the end:

> About half an hour before he died, he seemed to be sensible that he was dying; and, although he could not speak, he signified by signs that he wished me to send for the chiefs and for the officers of the post, whom I called in. He made signs to his wives (of whom he had two, and also two fine little children) by his side, to go and bring his full dress which he wore in time of war; which having been brought in, he rose up in his bed, which was on the floor, and put on his shirt, his leggings and his moccasins, girded on his war belt, bullet-pouch and powder-horn, and laid his knife by the side of him on the floor.

Was there symbolism in Osceola's actions during his final moments? Perhaps he was only preparing for the battle with Death, but there may have been another meaning, a final gesture of defiance.

> He then called for his red paint and looking-glass, which latter was held before him, when he deliberately painted one-half of his face his neck and his throat with vermillion, a custom practiced when the irrevocable oath of war and destruction is taken. His knife he then placed in its sheath under his belt, and he carefully arranged his turban on his head and his three ostrich plumes that he was in the habit of wearing in it.
>
> Being thus prepared in full dress, he lay down a few moments to recover strength sufficiently, when he rose up as before, and with most benignant and pleasing smiles, extended his hand to me and to all the officers and chiefs that were around him, and shook hands with us all in dead silence, and with his wives and little children.

> He made a signal for them to lower him down upon his bed, which was done, and he then slowly drew from his war-belt his scalping-knife, which he firmly grasped in his right hand, laying it across the other on his breast, and in a moment smiled away his last breath without a struggle or groan.

Coe suggests that the officers and Seminole chiefs wept.

Osceola was given a military funeral on the following day. He was buried near the main entrance to Fort Moultrie. A marble slab at the gravesite, supplied by a Charleston resident, was inscribed:

OSCEOLA
PATRIOT AND WARRIOR
DIED AT FORT MOULTRIE
JANUARY 30TH, 1838

For reasons that are somewhat difficult to understand at a distance of 135 years, Dr. Weedon cut off Osceola's head before the burial. Although there have been some attempts to justify this bizarre act, none makes much sense. Mrs. May McNeer Ward, in a remarkable understatement, has said that Dr. Weedon was an unusual man. She notes that he "used to hang the head of Osceola on the bedstead where his three little boys slept, and leave it there all night as punishment for misbehavior."

The head was given to Dr. Weedon's son-in-law who, in 1843, sent it to Dr. Valentine Mott, a founder of New York University Medical School and the New York Academy of Medicine. It was lost in a fire in 1866.

Mark F. Boyd has summed up his account of Osceola with an anonymous letter that appeared in *Niles* for February 2, 1838:

> We shall not write his epitaph or his funeral oration, yet there is something in his character not unworthy of the re-

spect of the world. From a vagabond child he became the master spirit of a long and desperate war. He made himself —no man owed less to accident. Bold and decisive in action, deadly but consistent in hatred, dark in revenge, cool, subtle, and sagacious in council, he established gradually and surely a resistless ascendancy over his adoptive tribe, by the daring of his deeds, and the consistency of his hostility to the whites, and the profound craft of his policy. In council he spoke little—he made the other chiefs his instruments, and what they delivered in public, was the secret suggestion of the invisible master. Such was Osceola, who will long be remembered as the man that with the feeblest means produced the most terrible effects.

Coe's judgment is interesting:

The fame of Osceola was well earned; not for that inhuman cruelty such as characterized most of our Western tribes, but for true patriotism and determined effort, against the combined armies of a great and powerful nation, in one of the most remarkable struggles known to history. His fame will never die; centuries will come and go, but the name of Osceola will remain as long as the earth is peopled.[9]

One other epitaph should be added. Although he died in prison, Osceola was never conquered. He had never surrendered. His people were never conquered. They never surrendered as a nation; the United States government was unsucessful in its goal of removing all Seminoles from Florida. Osceola's death did not end the Second Seminole War. If anything, his spirit inspired the warriors who fought in later years. And in the sense that history has vindicated him, Osceola won his war.

EPILOGUE

Toward the end of February, 1838, the Seminoles at Fort Moultrie were sent in the brig *Homer* to New Orleans and thence eventually to Arkansas. Philip died while going up the Mississippi and was buried on the west shore near Baton Rouge. There is no further record of what happened to Osceola's wives and children.[1] Sprague referred to four children, so two may have remained in Florida, but it is next to impossible to trace Seminole lineage with accuracy.[2]

The Indians were furious about the seizure of Osceola and the other leaders. Most migrated to the southern part of the Florida peninsula where they accepted the leadership of Coacoochee and the amazing old Arpeika. Arpeika was perfectly willing to fight the United States government by himself, if necessary. The frail old medicine man managed to get a letter off to General Jesup in which he said that "he never made a treaty and never would; he and his people would fight it out forever." [3]

It becomes necessary to editorialize a little in this summary of Osceola's life, the later events in the Second Seminole War, and the emergence of the modern Seminole. Some of the Seminoles may have desired revenge for the seizure of Osceola and the others, but it is unlikely that all of the Indians kept on fighting merely as avengers. Seminoles were not inclined to deify leaders, and the influence of Osceola on his people had been far more complicated.

He had inspired them, particularly the young men, with a sense of tribal identity. Under his leadership, they had come to feel that they were a unified nation, not a conglomeration of weak bands or clans. He had given them a goal: defense of their tribal right to their homeland. In some respects, he had been chauvinistic and a demagogue, but the same thing might be said of various American Revolutionary leaders. Of the greatest importance, he had given back to the Indian man his manhood. Before Osceola worked his way up to leadership, the Seminole warrior and his chiefs had cringed before the power of the white man, accepting his annuities, begging for his food. Although he could never entirely wipe out this dependency, Osceola had reduced it. During his two years of leadership, he had shown that the Indian need not be dependent on white handouts. They were pleasant, but life could be sustained without them.

Most of all, he had demonstrated to the Indian warrior that he was the equal of the white man in battle. White soldiers and their leaders had no secret medicine; they made mistakes and could be defeated. Osceola's leadership had been marked by a notable series of victories that gave the Seminole warriors confidence in their fighting ability.

Not all of the Seminoles caught the fire of Osceola's spirit, of course. Many weakened under the privations of war or the heavy pressures of white military strength. This could not have been otherwise, for the Seminoles suffered greatly in the final years of the formal war. But enough fought on to provide clear evidence of the continuing strong influence of Osceola's ideas. This influence cannot easily be defined or catalogued neatly, but it has been evident down through the years in the persistent independence of the Florida Seminole.

Toward the end of January, 1838, General Jesup was personally engaged in a minor battle after which he ordered a small enclosure erected near Jupiter Inlet on Florida's east coast. This installation, one of the many log stockades built in Florida, was called Fort Jupiter and was notable mainly for events in February and March.

On February 7, the troops under General Jesup moved out from the fort about twenty miles to engage in battle near a cypress swamp. Jesup, however, was persuaded by General Eustis and Colonel David E. Twiggs to invite the chiefs to a peace conference instead. The officers felt terrain favored the Indians to such an extent that it would be best to let them remain in some part of Florida.[4]

Several of the Indians, arriving under a truce flag, responded with enthusiasm. Motte wrote that Halleck Hadjo made a moving speech in which he said:

> their wives and children were dying from the hardship of being chased about so much; that, being driven from land into the water, they must submit, and even emigrate if required; but earnestly prayed that we would let them remain in the country; they would thankfully receive the smallest piece of ground that might be given to them, no matter how bad, so that it was only in Florida, and big enough for them to spread their blankets upon.

Tuskegee, a more important chief, agreed. These chiefs also said they would lead the soldiers to Arpeika, who had moved his force of Mikasukis to some islands in Lake Okeechobee.

Jesup insisted that the Indians draw close to Fort Jupiter while he sent a letter to the War Department by his aide, Lieutenant Thomas B. Linnard. This remarkable document, addressed to the Secretary of War, J. R. Poinsett, and dated February 11, appears in Sprague's history and various of the military files. Jesup used a great many words to say the war was a failure, the Seminoles were not in the way of white expansion, and the government should consider permitting them to settle in south Florida. He added that if the government insisted on their unconditional surrender the decision should be confidential; the Indians would fly to the swamps if they learned that the removal policy would be continued.

While waiting for the government reply, some five hundred Seminoles camped about a mile from Fort Jupiter. Motte said the women were in particularly bad shape. At a council on February 24, an aged Seminole woman was permitted to break precedent by making a speech. Motte summarized her talk:

> [The warriors] were all her children; [she said] that she was tired of the war; that her warriors were slain; her village burnt; her little ones perishing by the roadside; that the great spirit frowned on his red children; that the star of her nation had set in blood. She desired that the hatchet should be buried forever, between her children and her white brethren.

This was what the whites wanted to hear. On March 1, the Seminoles surrended one hundred forty Negroes who belonged to Indians already sent west, and these unfortunates were escorted to Tampa for shipment. Finally, on the twentieth Lieutenant Linnard returned with a letter from Poinsett dated March 1. The Secretary of War had responded to Jesup's proposition with a sharp "No!" He concluded his letter with these remarkable words: "It is hoped, however, that you will be able to put it out of the power of these Indians to do any further mischief. They ought to be captured, or destroyed."

Jesup's overture may have been sincere, although some contemporary writers doubted it. The general's record for fair dealing was already badly stained. In any case, the eminent Secretary of War had given General Jesup his cue. On the night of March 20, he ordered Colonel Twiggs to surround the Seminole camp and seize every Indian. If one reads between the lines of Motte's narrative, it is clear that the Seminoles had an abundance of whiskey. Since liquor did not grow on trees, Jesup must have arranged for them to have it. They had a "grand frolic," says Motte, and when "the whole camp was buried in profound sleep, the order was given to close in on them. . . ." More than five hundred were captured.[5]

The episode has been related here in detail as evidence of the cynical attitude of the government and its representatives toward the Seminoles. The Secretary of War wanted them "destroyed." Jesup apparently felt no qualms about betraying them once again and getting them drunk enough so they could be captured easily. Scenes of this sort, repeated again and again during the remaining years of the Second Seminole War, typify one of the most contemptible periods in white treatment of the American Indian.

Colonel (now Brigadier General) Taylor captured Holatoochee and forty warriors during March. A few days later, Holatoochee and Abraham (who was now dealing with the whites) persuaded Alligator and John Cavallo to surrender north of Lake Okeechobee. Jesup wrote that three hundred sixty Indians and Negroes surrendered at this time, but the number appears to have been closer to a hundred. Whatever the case, Seminole resistance seemed to be crumbling.

Or was it? Lieutenant Colonel William S. Harney started looking for old Arpeika in late April. This search took place in the general area of what now is Greater Miami. The soldiers waded through mangrove swamps and cursed their way across knifelike coral until they encountered Arpeika, who peppered away at them before withdrawing. Motte, who was along on this expedition, collapsed on the following day, "my boots being cut into ribbons and my feet severely lacerated by the sharp rocks."[6] (Arpeika was by no means the only Seminole who was still fighting in the Osceola tradition.)

General Jesup was relieved (by his own request) at the end of April, 1838, to be replaced by Brigadier General Zachary Taylor. This was a continuation of the musical chairs game played by the War Department with its generals in Florida.

And of a total of nine top generals, only two are remembered today by most Americans—Scott and Taylor. Taylor's fame in Florida rests on one battle: the Okeechobee affair in December, 1837. Scott is remembered for what he did long after he had left Florida, and the record of mistakes in his ill-fated campaign.

General Taylor had the idea of dividing Florida into military districts each twenty miles square, with a small military post located at a convenient point in each district. He was unable, however, to get this plan under way, for in March, 1839, Major General Alexander Macomb, commanding general of the United States Army, was ordered by the Secretary of War to end the war in Florida. Macomb was not supposed to take over command from Taylor; his role was that of a peacemaker.

Macomb arrived at Fort King on April 27, 1839, and arranged for a council with the Indians on May 18. Present for this affair were Halleck-Tustenuggee, Tiger Tail, and a subchief called Chitto-Tustenugee representing (so it seems) Arpeika. (Arpeika would never have been bound by the decisions of a subchief.) Macomb, following Jesup's earlier proposal almost to the letter, offered the Seminoles peace and a home in south Florida where they were to remain "until further arrangements are made."

The Indians were under the impression that they would be allowed to live in south Florida on a permanent basis. Macomb saw to it that gifts and a good deal of whiskey were distributed, thus inspiring a St. Augustine editor (according to Coe) to publish this jingle:

The war is ended, past a doubt;
  Each breechless urchin's shouting frisky;
The General's had a battle—no,
  But bought a peace with knives and whiskey! [7]

In a letter of May 22, 1839, Macomb told the Secretary of War that he felt it unwise to say anything about Indian emigration. That could come up later, he suggested. In short, he calmed the Indians with misleading statements and then announced flatly that he had terminated the war with the Seminoles.[8]

Floridians roared with anger at Macomb's "peace," and the Seminoles either recognized the deception or felt that the few chiefs at the council had not represented the entire nation. In any event, on the night of July 23, 1839, Lieutenant Colonel William S. Harney and twenty-six men were attacked at a trading post on the Caloosahatchee River. Eighteen soldiers were captured or killed. This attack was conducted by Hospetarke and Chakaika (Chekika), neither of whom had been represented at the Fort King meeting. For that matter, Coacoochee was not represented, nor was a remarkable newcomer, Holata Mico or Billy Bowlegs. (He is not to be confused with the first Billy Bowlegs who may have been his uncle.) Billy Bowlegs, a brilliant man, was also involved in the raid on Harney, and in the later destiny of the Seminoles in Florida.

Arpeika did not consider himself bound by the Fort King council meeting; and an individual named Otulke Thlocko (The Prophet) shared Arpeika's strong objections to compromise. Macomb's peace was nearly worthless.

On May 5, 1840, Brigadier General Walker Keith Armistead took over command in Florida from General Taylor. (Macomb was back in Washington.) Armistead, not greatly liked by other officers, found that Coacoochee was operating in Osceola's old territory near Fort King and east toward St. Augustine. Sometime toward the end of May, Coacoochee attacked a touring Shakespearean company, killed three of the actors, and stole a huge collection of theatrical costumes. (Frank Slaughter attributed this raid to Chakaika in his pleasant 1951 novel, *Fort Everglades.*)

Until fall, the year 1840 was not particularly eventful. On November 10, Halleck-Tustenuggee and Tiger Tail attended a conference at Fort King. When General Armistead tried to bribe them with an offer of five thousand dollars each, they asked to think it over for a number of days. After being supplied with plenty to eat and drink, they simply disappeared with their warriors.

In a grimmer vein, Lieutenant Colonel William Harney set out from Fort Dallas (now within modern Miami) early in December to pay a call on Chakaika, who had slain his men back in July. Presumably, he took his force up the Miami River in sixteen canoes and penetrated the Everglades where Chakaika was overtaken and killed with a number of warriors. Harney ordered several of the prisoners hanged.

By early January, there had been no real change in the Florida war. The Indians were deep in the wilderness where white expeditions could not get at them. The war was not over by any means; Seminole leaders even refused to hear messengers from the whites.[9]

One friendly messenger named Micco was effective in March, however. He was sent out to get Coacoochee into Fort Cummings for a conference. This stockade, built in January, 1839, was not far from modern Cypress Gardens. Coacoochee's pretty twelve-year-old daughter was being held there as a hostage; the child had been captured earlier near Fort Mellon.

Few amusing things happened in a war as bitter as the Second Seminole War, but certain of the events of March 5, 1841, were funny in a bizarre way. At noon, the arrival of Coacoochee was announced. When he drew near, the officers at Fort Cummings gulped and choked. As noted earlier, Coacoochee was a strikingly handsome man who enjoyed elaborate dress. For this occasion, he had outdone himself.

Coacoochee, son of Philip, friend of Osceola, relentless leader of Seminole warriors, was costumed as Hamlet. Next to him was a warrior in the theatrical dress of Horatio. Richard III, garbed in ermine and royal purple, strode majestically a few paces to the rear. Others among the top Seminoles in Coacoochee's band wore parts of the Shakespearean costumes stolen back in May.

No one laughed. For as Coacoochee greeted the officers, his daughter raced from a tent where she was being held until a time in the ceremonies when she would be returned as a surprise to her father. The girl had been saving powder and musketballs she had managed to collect during her captivity. When she offered Coacoochee the gift, he burst into tears. Later he said he would try to bring in his warriors promptly, but this was not done.

On May 31, 1841, in a further game of musical chairs, Armistead was relieved, to be replaced by Colonel William Jenkins Worth. John T. Sprague, the historian, was his aide-de-camp and later his son-in-law. Coacoochee, meanwhile, had been playing his cards a little too close to his vest. Repeatedly, he had promised to deliver his people for emigration; but at last, on June 4, Major Thomas Childs at Fort Pierce seized him and sent him to Tampa where Lieutenant William Gates promptly shipped him to New Orleans.

Colonel Worth, who wanted to use Coacoochee to persuade warriors to surrender, was infuriated by this development. The disbursing agent, L. G. Capers, was hurried off to New Orleans to bring Coacoochee back. Colonel Worth met the prisoner in Tampa Harbor early in July.

Coacoochee and the warriors who had been brought back with him were in foot irons and handcuffs. Colonel Worth said Coacoochee should select five warriors to go as emissaries to the chief's friends and relatives and have them come in. If they refused, Coacoochee and "these warriors now seated before us shall be hung to the yards of this vessel. . . ." [10] Worth apparently believed in the primitive justice of his predecessor.

Coacoochee replied with a touching speech during which he said, in part:

> [The white man] said he was my friend; he abused our women and children, and told us to go from the land. Still he gave me his hand in friendship; we took it; whilst taking it, he had a snake in the other; his tongue was forked; he lied, and stung us. I asked but for a small piece of these lands, enough to plant and to live upon, far south, a spot

> where I could place the ashes of my kindred, a spot only sufficient upon which I could lay my wife and child. This was not granted me. . . . You say I *must* end the war! Look at these irons! Can I go to my warriors? Coacoochee chained! No; do not ask me to see them. I never wish to tread upon my land unless I am free. If I can go to them *unchained*, they will follow me in; but I fear they will not obey me when I talk to them in irons. They will say my heart is weak, I am afraid. Could I go free, they will surrender and emigrate.[11]

Coacoochee was told this could not be done; messengers would have to represent him. A curious incident had taken place while he was making his speech. A government ship, moored nearby, opened fire with her batteries at 12:00 noon. The roar was repeated again and again.

"What's that for?" Coacoochee asked.

No one among the white officers replied. Coacoochee asked again. Still there was an embarrassed silence. *The date happened to be July 4, 1841, and the guns were firing in celebration of American independence.*

Coacoochee's messengers went out, and by early August, all but a few of his people had come in. On October 12, 1841, Coacoochee with more than two hundred of his band was shipped to New Orleans and the west. As we will see later, his spirit was far from broken and he had an unusual, dramatic future ahead of him.

Two days after the departure of Coacoochee, Alligator and a small party arrived at Fort Brooke with the aim of inducing some relatives to go west with them. The old chief was successful in persuading Tiger Tail and his brother to surrender with almost two hundred men, women, and children. From this point on, into the early months of 1842, the Seminole War began to sputter to an end, at least by white standards. A number of minor chiefs and several major figures either surrendered or were captured. At last, on August 14, 1842, Colonel Worth announced pontifically that hostilities with the Indians in Florida had ceased.

But Billy Bowlegs had not given up; he remained in the depths of the Everglades along with Alligator, old Arpeika, a number of subchiefs, and approximately three hundred men, women, and children. From this core of independent men and women grew the present Seminole population of Florida.

The situation of the Seminoles in Indian Territory west of the Mississippi was not favorable, for they were settled with the Creeks and resented it bitterly. As one curious development, in 1850 Coacoochee and John Cavallo set out for Mexico where they established a successful colony of Seminoles and Seminole Negroes. Coacoochee died of smallpox in 1856; John Cavallo supposedly died in 1882 after a career as an Army scout.

In 1868, while trouble with the Creeks was still going on, the Seminole Nation was established with a capital at Wewoka, Oklahoma. The nation had a magnificent record of orderly progress, but the Seminoles suffered along with other tribes during the Oklahoma land grab period. Holdings simply melted away into the hands of speculators; little remains today of the original Seminole lands in Oklahoma.

In Florida, following the formal end of the Seminole War, matters were almost equally confused. Billy Bowlegs, subject of a rather silly sketch in *Harper's Weekly* for June 12, 1858, kept his people deep in the Everglades and decreed at one time that any Seminole who had contact with a white man would be executed. Sprague commented on the ease of life in the wilderness:

> The Indians were now secure in their hiding places, enjoying the cool shades of the dense hammocks, luxuriating in an abundant harvest of green corn, melons, pumpkins, squashes, beans, peas, sweet potatoes, and almost every other vegetable. . . . Desirous of being undisturbed, they molest no one, postponing their excursions and outrages until after harvest.[12]

The Everglades in particular also offered abundant hunting and fishing.

In 1849, there was an outburst of hatred against the Florida Seminoles because of the murder of a white man. The government tried to bribe them into moving with a fat offer of $215,000, but Bowlegs would have nothing to do with it. A year later, another offer was turned down.

In 1858, the Secretary of the Interior made a remarkable statement in which he virtually admitted the Seminoles had won the war. He said that the Seminoles had completely "baffled the energetic efforts of our Army to effect their subjugation and removal." The ghost of Osceola must have smiled.

At the urging of Seminole agents from Indian Territory, Bowlegs finally capitulated. On March 27, 1858, he accepted these inducements: $6,500 for himself, $1,000 each for every subchief, $500 for each warrior, and $100 for each woman and child. Of the 164 who agreed to move west on these terms, 121 were women and children. Fully 200 refused to emigrate and remained hidden in the Everglades. One was Arpeika, now senile at a hundred and eight but still bound firmly to his native soil.

There was a touching scene when the emigrating party left Fort Myers on Florida's lower west coast. Warriors wept as they stepped to the deck of the steamer *Grey Cloud*. Someone quoted by Coe wrote:

> Patience, heroism, and fidelity, such as the world may admire, have been exhibited to us, inculcating a lesson not to be lost upon us now that our national councils are torn by intestine [?] strife. The Seminoles as a nation [in Florida] have been destroyed, but what an array of glory, faith, horrors, and anguish does this retrospect present! Conquered, they leave us proud and defiant.[13]

Coe knew better. A page later in his history, he asked:

> How shall we fitly characterize the little band of perhaps a hundred—the remnant of a remnant—whose intense love of

> home, and determination to remain in their native land, showed them worthy descendants of the immortal Osceola. We might call them the flower of the nation, with patriotism and fidelity the most deep-rooted of all! [14]

It is not easy to condense the life of the Seminole in Florida between 1860 and 1960. The problem is one of geography and recent settlement; south Florida emerged from wilderness only after 1900 or even later and thus was unknown territory for many years. Miami, with three or four houses in 1895, was almost engulfed on the west by the Everglades, a region as large as Connecticut and known only to Seminoles, plume hunters, a few traders, and an occasional criminal reckless enough to hide there.

The Tamiami Trail, crossing the Everglades from Miami to Naples and thence north to Tampa, was started in 1915 but not completed until 1927 after years of desperate effort and a monumental investment of thirteen million dollars. Florida and the nation knew little about Florida Seminoles of the middle and late nineteenth century until the Reverend Clay MacCauley did his brilliant ethnological studies in the 1880s. And only scholars read studies produced by the Bureau of American Ethnology.

Thus, in the period between the Civil War and 1900, the Florida Seminoles were nearly invisible. They lived almost exclusively in the wilderness of the Everglades, the *Pa-hay-okee* ("Grassy Waters") south of Lake Okeechobee, and emerged only to trade at the few coastal trading posts. Men and women still alive in Miami remember their infrequent trips down the Miami River.

These brief trading periods were about the only contact the Seminoles cared to have with whites. An Indian man or woman in 1880 was not far removed from the horrors of the Seminole War; whites were to be avoided as treacherous and probably murderous as well. The Seminoles who had remained in the

Everglades—about four hundred by 1900, although the census was certainly inaccurate in counting a people who did not wish to be counted—still believed firmly that the United States might at any time ship them out of Florida or even arrest and imprison the men. *Remember,* they told their children, *what happened to Osceola.*

While they mistrusted and even feared the white man, they also rejected him and his culture as utterly foreign. They rarely spoke to the white man and would never have had the bad manners to be insulting, but they might have summed up their feelings in these words: "To us, you are a liar and a thief. We neither need you nor want anything whatsoever to do with you. Leave us alone."

Seminoles within the Everglades traveled mainly in dugouts and lived on hammocks or islands in palmetto-thatched *chickees,* a type of housing still common today. Supposedly, the *chickee* was first used during the Seminole War as a temporary shelter. *Chickees* are open-sided and, if used for sleeping, have a raised platform. They are surprisingly durable structures.

Until the 1920s, the economy of the Seminoles was based largely on hunting, fishing, and minor agriculture. Gradually, with the passage of years, the nation in Florida divided into two groups: the Mikasukis, or Miccosukees (both spellings are acceptable), and the Cow Creek Seminoles, or Muskogees. A large number of the latter live today on the Brighton reservation northwest of Lake Okeechobee, where cattle raising is the main occupation. The language is Muskogee.

Mikasukis live on the Big Cypress reservation, which has been expanded during recent years to include a large tract in western Broward County. Cattle raising and general agriculture are carried on here. The Mikasuki language is Hitchiti. A small reservation in Hollywood, Florida, is headquarters for the Seminole Tribe of Florida, Inc.

A change in Seminole economy began to take place in 1927 with the completion of the Tamiami Trail and the use of the automobile. Many Mikasuki families settled along the Tamiami Canal flanking the Trail, and later along various other roads penetrating south Florida. According to the records of the late Deaconess Harriet Bedell, who ministered to the Trail Indians from a Protestant Episcopal mission in Everglades City, there were about seventy Mikasuki families in Dade and Collier counties during the 1930s and thereafter.[15]

These families built tiny villages, sold souvenirs to tourists, maintained small gardens, and also fished and hunted. The men performed agricultural work during the growing season. Of all Seminoles, these perhaps have been the most independent. As recently as 1955, the Trail Mikasuki Seminole would trade with the white man, sell him bright dresses and jackets made by the women, work in the white man's fields, or serve as a guide in the Everglades; but he would have nothing to do with white efforts to give him economic assistance or place him on a reservation.

These Seminoles, considerably influenced by Ingram (Ingraham) Billy, a medicine man, were anachronistic to such an extent that as late as the mid-1930s men would refuse to enter a white man's building in a group. (*Remember what happened to Osceola!*) When government representatives wished to consult with these Mikasukis at a council to be held in the Everglades City movie house, the Indians refused. The council was held outdoors on a lawn.

A glance through Deaconess Bedell's *Indian Families* record book may explain this attitude on the part of the Mikasuki Trail Indians. Although lineage may not be a factor, the names are those of the Second Seminole War—"Osceola," "Tiger Tail," "Jumper."

There have been changes, however, in recent years. Independent as ever, the Trail Seminoles split off from the larger Seminole tribe to establish the Miccosukee Tribe. The Bureau of Indian Affairs granted them a five-hundred-foot-wide strip of land for five miles along the Tamiami Trail (U.S. 41), the land to be available to them for fifty years. Some four hundred Mikasukis now live along this strip where they operate a restaurant, have a school, sell bait and souvenirs, run airboats, and drive to scores of "white" jobs. Many, however, still come home to *chickees.*

Some are adamant about following the old customs. Bobby Clay, thirty-nine, refused in 1972 to permit his children to attend the white man's school. Challenged in a court case, he won on the ground that he and his family were entitled to religious freedom. Clay, who wants to bring his children up in the Mikasuki tradition, was quoted as saying, "Our god is almost the same as the one in the white man's Bible, but we never wrote down our beliefs. We must keep them in our heads and pass them on to our children." Most modern Seminoles would agree with this, although they avoid going to extremes.

The Seminoles have never signed a formal peace treaty with the United States, but they have recognized themselves as citizens of the United States and Florida through various acts of incorporation. And, as noted in the opening pages of this book, the U.S. Court of Claims ruled in 1964 that the Seminole Indians of Florida and Oklahoma were entitled to compensation for the land taken from them by the Treaty of Moultrie Creek.

On May 13, 1970, the Indian Claims Commission offered the Seminoles $12,347,500, or 52 cents per acre for part of the land and 35 cents per acre for the rest. The Seminoles appealed, pointing out through their attorneys, Roy Struble and Paul Niebell, that land sold for between $1.00 and $1.25 per acre at the time. In February, 1972, the Indian Claims Commission was ordered to make a new evaluation.

At about the same time, however, the Creek Nation east of the Mississippi also filed a claim to portions of Florida. When this book was being written, settlement had been stalled until the Creek question was decided. It is of more than parenthetical interest to note that the Creek claim is based primarily on the old notion that the Seminoles were always part of the Creek Confederacy.

The Seminoles today have almost the same population that existed in Osceola's time: about fourteen hundred in Florida and approximately thirty-five hundred in Oklahoma, although the Oklahoma Seminoles prefer to list seven thousand persons with at least one-quarter Seminole blood. (They would like to have the eventual land payment made on a head-count basis.)

Despite much of the recent modernization in Seminole life, the memory of Osceola is remarkably strong. The writers of this account talked at length with Joe Dan Osceola, a remarkable Seminole who most recently has been service unit director of the Indian Health Service located in Hollywood, Florida. He is a past president of the Seminole Tribe of Florida, Inc., and the United Southeastern Tribes, Inc., a member of the Florida Commission on Indian Affairs, and a member of the National Congress of the American Indian. Osceola was told by his uncle, Billy Osceola, that he is a lineal descendant of the Seminole leader.

"Osceola was one man who represents an unconquered people," Joe Dan Osceola says. "He himself was unconquered because he stood up for what he believed in. The moment he fought for his country, of course, he was branded as a savage.

"What we had was tremendous determination to fight for the things we believed in—in our freedom, in our land. For the Seminoles, Osceola is like a George Washington or a Lincoln. That's what Osceola means to the people of my tribe, not only the old people but also the young. We are proud that the original Osceola was a member of our tribe.

"We know he didn't give up, so this is what I say to my children: 'You can't give up, no matter what you're doing. If you're playing ball or working or doing something constructive, you must not give up. You're a Seminole and you come from the heritage of Osceola.' That's what we tell all our children, and they take pride in being American Indians.

"There's one thing I'd like everybody to know. When the United States armies were fighting the American Indian, the Army leaders were educated men who were trained as soldiers accustomed to traditional tactics. When they met the Seminoles, it was the first time they had ever encountered hit-and-run tactics—guerrilla war tactics—and this is what they were not trained to do: fight that kind of war. That helped the Seminoles. The Seminole leaders, of course, never had any educational background, yet they held their own. That's one thing I wish the public would realize."

Joe Dan Osceola has a number of important goals for the Seminoles in Florida. If and when the land claim is paid, he would like to see part of the money used for higher education. He also wants a medical center for the older people who are out on the reservations. He wants recreation centers for the young people.

"That's why you don't see any Jim Thorpes today. We have almost no American Indians in football, baseball, and basketball because the recreational setup on the reservations is bad.

"If we ever get the money from the Claims Commission, the hell with buying Cadillacs. That isn't our priority. If we buy cars, it's because we need transportation. The nearest town to our reservation in the Big Cypress is forty-five miles away. Obviously, the people can't walk there, but they don't need fancy cars.

"Our people must also have a better knowledge of English. You can speak ten different languages, but it means nothing in the United States if you don't speak English. I would say this is the greatest weakness in the structure of our political and tribal group. We want the best teachers available to teach English to our children, but we also want them to keep their own language.

"Just think! Only a few years ago, we Indians were punished in boarding school for speaking our own language! We'd be standing in a corner all day if we got caught.

"Some Indians may have a problem living in two worlds, but I value and believe in both of the cultures. I want to take the best of each culture. Others may want to retain the Indian identity and leave the Western culture out. That's up to the individual. But I like good sports, good theater, good food; and that's what the white man's civilization brings me. I appreciate this because I'm part of it. I'm an American citizen.

"At the same time, I can go to the Green Corn Dance, which is my Seminole ritual. I appreciate this, and I hope my children will do the same. Oh, yes, they know how badly Indians have been treated, and also what they contributed to present civilization. I hope they won't react in a radical fashion when they grow up. And I hope they will always stand up for their rights and beliefs the way Osceola did."

These are the reflections of a modern Seminole leader who thinks in terms of the survival of his people in a world dominated by white culture and economy. Most Indian leaders would agree with Joe Dan Osceola. To survive, to compete, the Indian of today must use everything that truly benefits white civilization—education, modern medicine, progress in science, the determination to compete.

Buffalo Tiger, chairman of the Miccosukee tribe, also recognizes this need for the Indian to adjust to the white world and particularly the white economy. He may not like it; not all Indians, and certainly not all Seminoles, are enchanted by a culture that has eroded the wilderness. But Buffalo Tiger and the Tamiami Trail Mikasukis need only glance at the sky when a jet screams overhead in order to realize that the world has changed.

The nostalgia is present, of course. More than any other American Indian, the Seminole is close to the past. Because of his isolation until relatively recent years, he was able almost to duplicate the life of his ancestors. A Seminole man of today need be only forty years of age to remember a youth spent in hunting and fishing; even today, many Seminole children are closer to the outdoors than they are to the schoolroom.

Nostalgia is particularly strong among the older nonreservation Seminoles to whom the Green Corn Dance is still a sacred and important event. Many of these old people speak no English and exist almost as Seminoles did before the Civil War.

For Seminoles who live away from the cities, as most do, the nostalgia can be powerful. When dawn spreads across the eastern sky, a man sees the birds hovering to fish along the quiet canal. The *anhinga* dries its wing in a nearby tree, children stir in the *chickee,* the smell of wood ash is heavy on the damp morning air. The highway, dead and empty, probes like an arrow toward the horizon. A rooster shrieks proudly at the sky.

In these moments, it is hard indeed for the Seminole man to remember the job at the gas station. The white man's world slips away on the morning breeze, and the old days draw close. This is the true dilemma of Osceola's people. Instincts developed over thousands of years must somehow be sublimated to a world of jet planes, gas stations, time clocks, school buses, television sets, supermarkets, and the values established by a modern white society.

The adjustment is not an easy one. But the thoughtful Seminole of today knows his people must make the adjustment if they are to remain unconquered. Today's battlefield is the world of industry, business, and modern agriculture; the ammunition is education and developed skills; and the battles are won by those who are best supplied. The Seminoles have the vitality to compete in the modern world. Certainly they have the intelligence. And they can always stand strong in the knowledge that their heritage is a proud one.

BIBLIOGRAPHICAL NOTES

Introduction

1. Alvin M. Josephy, *The Patriot Chiefs* (New York, 1961), p. 178.
2. Charles H. Coe, *Red Patriots* (Cincinnati, 1898), p. 14.
3. James Pierce, in *American Journal of Science and Arts,* IX (June, 1825), 119–136.
4. Coe, *Red Patriots,* p. 15.
5. Summarized decision before the Indian Claims Commission, combined dockets Nos. 73 and 151, May 8, 1964.
6. M. M. Cohen, *Notices of Florida and the Campaigns* (Charleston and New York, 1836), p. 31.
7. Coe, *Red Patriots,* pp. 64 ff.
8. R. S. Cotterill, *The Southern Indians* (Norman, Oklahoma, 1954), p. 11.
9. Treaty of Amity . . . Between the United States and His Catholic Majesty, February 22, 1819, *American State Papers: Foreign Relations,* IV, 623–625. Also *American Historical Documents,* Harvard Classics (New York, 1938), p. 271.
10. Theodore Roosevelt, *Life of Thomas H. Benton* (Boston and New York, 1886), p. 187.
11. William and Ellen Hartley, *A Woman Set Apart* (New York, 1963), pp. 207 ff; *The Reader's Digest,* February, 1965, p. 204. (Also oral, Harriet M. Bedell.)

1

1. M. M. Cohen, *Notices of Florida and the Campaigns* (Charleston and New York, 1836), p. 62 n.

2. E. R. Ott, in *Florida Historical Quarterly [FHQ]*, XLVI (July, 1967), 29 ff.
3. John Bemrose, *Reminiscences of the Seminole War,* edited by John K. Mahon (Gainesville, Florida, 1966), p. 20.
4. R. W. Patrick, *Aristocrat in Uniform* (Gainesville, Florida, 1963), pp. 76–81.
5. John K. Mahon, *History of the Second Seminole War* (Gainesville, Florida, 1967), p. 87.
6. *Ibid*., p. 95.
7. For the meeting of April 22–23, 1835, see Mahon, *Second Seminole War,* pp. 95 ff; Patrick, *Aristocrat in Uniform,* pp. 77 ff; John T. Sprague, *The Florida War* (New York, 1848), p. 84; E. C. McReynolds, *The Seminoles* (Norman, Oklahoma, 1957), p. 145; C. H. Coe, *Red Patriots* (Cincinnati, 1898), p. 50; Mark F. Boyd, *FHQ,* XXX (July, 1951), 51; Boyd, *FHQ,* XXXIII (January–April, 1955), 272; Minutes of Council of April 22–23, 1835. Doc. 152: 37–41.
8. Cohen, *Notices of Florida,* p. 239.
9. Patrick, *Aristocrat in Uniform,* p. 77; House Document 271, pp. 188–91 (paraphrased).
10. Sprague, *Florida War,* p. 101.
11. Cohen, *Notices of Florida,* p. 62 n.
12. *Ibid*., p. 234.
13. *Ibid*., p. 235.
14. *Ibid*., pp. 237, 239.
15. Jacob R. Motte, *Journey into Wilderness,* edited by James F. Sunderman (Gainesville, Florida, 1953), pp. 140–141.
16. Ex. Doc. 638, 1st Session, 24th Congress. Also Coe, *Red Patriots,* p. 51.
17. Cohen, *Notices of Florida,* p. 55.
18. Sprague, *Florida War,* p. 85.
19. Mahon, *Second Seminole War,* p. 96.
20. Cohen, *Notices of Florida,* p. 51.
21. *Ibid.* There is controversy about the time and gesture. For detailed discussion, see Boyd, *FHQ,* XXXIII (January–April, 1955), 273.

2

1. Mark F. Boyd, *FHQ,* XXXIII (January–April, 1955) p. 255; M. M. Cohen, *Notices of Florida and the Campaigns* (Charleston and New York, 1836), p. 234.
2. Boyd, *FHQ,* XXXIII, (January–April, 1955), 250 ff; C. H. Coe, *Red Patriots* (Cincinnati, 1898), p. 27.
3. Coe, *Red Patriots,* p. 28.
4. C. H. Coe, *FHQ,* XVII (April, 1939), p. 307.

5. Cohen, *Notices of Florida*, p. 234.
6. T. S. Woodward, *Woodward's Reminiscences* (Montgomery, Alabama, 1859), p. 9.
7. Cohen, *Notices of Florida*, p. 238.
8. John K. Mahon, *History of the Second Seminole War* (Gainesville, Florida, 1967), p. 10.
9. *Ibid.*, p. 91.
10. Sprague places the separation in 1808, but moves Polly to Florida. This seems unlikely. Boyd believes the separation was in 1814. This mystery will never be solved, but the writers lean toward Sprague's date and feel there is circumstantial evidence to place Osceola in Alabama until the end of the Creek War.
11. Clay MacCauley, *The Seminole Indians of Florida* (Washington, 1887), pp. 505–506.
12. Mahon, *Second Seminole War*, p. 10; Mark F. Boyd, "Florida Aflame," *FHQ*, XXX (July, 1951), 7 (summarized).
13. Andrew Welch, *Osceola Nikkanochee* (London, 1814), pp. 119 ff (paraphrased).
14. Mahon, *Second Seminole War*, p. 15.
15. Louis Capron, *Bulletin 151, Anthropological Paper No. 35*. Smithsonian Institution, Bureau of American Ethnology (Washington, 1953), pp. 182–183.
16. Mahon, *Second Seminole War*, p. 10.
17. B. McKenzie and R. Fish, *Indian School Journal*, XVII (October, 1916), 79–81.
18. MacCauley, *Seminole Indians*, p. 506.
19. James Parton, *Life of Andrew Jackson* (New York, 1861), Vols. I and II.
20. For the Creek War, see: Parton, *Andrew Jackson*, Vol. I; R. S. Cotterill, *The Southern Indians* (Norman, Oklahoma, 1954), pp. 176 ff; E. C. McReynolds, *The Seminoles* (Norman, Oklahoma, 1957), pp. 52 ff.
21. Woodward, *Reminiscences*, p. 44.
22. Capron, *Bulletin 151*, pp. 172 ff.
23. William and Ellen Hartley, conversation with William (Buffalo) Tiger, Mikasuki leader, 1964; others.
24. *Ibid.*
25. DuVal to Calhoun, Apr. 11, 1824, in *American State Papers, Indian Affairs*, II, 616–617; Coe, *Red Patriots*, p. 25.
26. Joshua R. Giddings, *The Exiles of Florida* (Columbus, Ohio, 1858), p. 39.
27. *Ibid.*, p. 46.
28. R. W. Patrick, *Aristocrat in Uniform* (Gainesville, Florida, 1963), p. 33.
29. Parton, *Andrew Jackson*, II, 430 n.

30. *Ibid.*, II, 428.
31. *Ibid.*, II, 430.
32. Giddings, *Exiles*, p. 48.
33. Parton, *Andrew Jackson*, II, 459–460; Woodward, *Reminiscences*, p. 44.
34. Parton, *Andrew Jackson*, II, 460.
35. *Territorial Papers of the United States*, Vol. XXII, *Florida. 1821–1824*, 463–465.

3

1. Comte de Castelnau, "Essay on Middle Florida," *FHQ*, XXVI (January, 1948), 249; also contemporary drawings.
2. *FHQ*, XIII (October, 1934), 91.
3. *Territorial Papers of the United States*, Vol. XXII, *Florida. 1821–1824*, p. 465.
4. Charles H. Coe, *Red Patriots* (Cincinnati, 1898), p. 22.
5. John T. Sprague, *The Florida War* (New York, 1848), p. 5.
6. Coe, *Red Patriots*, pp. 34 ff.
7. Clay MacCauley, *The Seminole Indians of Florida* (Washington, 1887), pp. 481–482.
8. *Ibid.*
9. Castelnau, "Essay on Middle Florida," p. 249.
10. O. O. Howard, *My Life and Experiences Among Our Hostile Indians* (Hartford, 1907), pp. 89 ff.
11. MacCauley, *Seminole Indians*, p. 491.
12. K. H. Grismer, *Tampa* (Saint Petersburg, 1950), p. 53.
13. Coe, *Red Patriots*, p. 29.
14. *Territorial Papers*, XXII, 294.
15. *Ibid.*, p. 503.
16. *Ibid.*, p. 504.
17. *Ibid.*, pp. 533–534.
18. Mark F. Boyd, *FHQ*, XXXIII (January–April, 1955), 251.
19. Louis Capron, *Bulletin 151, Anthropological Paper No. 35*, Smithsonian Institution, Bureau of American Ethnology (Washington, 1953), p. 163.
20. *Ibid.*, pp. 159–207.
21. Gadsden to Calhoun, June 11, 1823, in *American State Papers, Indian Affairs*, II, 433–434.
22. Gadsden to Calhoun, June 11, 1823, in *Territorial Papers*, XXII, 696.
23. "A Diary of Joshua Nichols Glenn: St. Augustine in 1823," *FHQ*, XXIV (October, 1945), 148–149.
24. *American State Papers, Indian Affairs*, II, 437–438.
25. John K. Mahon, "The Treaty of Moultrie Creek, 1823," *FHQ*, XL (April, 1962), 367.

26. Sprague, *Florida War,* p. 23.
27. Mahon, "Treaty of Moultrie Creek," p. 370.
28. *Ibid.,* p. 368.
29. Sprague, *Florida War,* p. 23.
30. Joshua R. Giddings, *The Exiles of Florida* (Columbus, Ohio, 1858), p. 72.
31. R. W. Patrick, *Aristocrat in Uniform* (Gainesville, Florida, 1963), p. 68.
32. Gadsden to Calhoun, Sept. 29, 1823, *Territorial Papers,* XXII, 752.
33. Mahon, "Treaty of Moultrie Creek," p. 369.
34. Sprague, *Florida War,* p. 24.
35. Gadsden to Calhoun, June 11, 1823, *Territorial Papers,* XXII, 696.
36. Gadsden to Calhoun, Sept. 29, 1823, *Territorial Papers,* XXII, 696.

4

1. Thomas L. McKenney and James Hall, *The Indian Tribes of North America* (Edinburgh, 1933–1934), II, 368.
2. *Ibid.*
3. M. M. Cohen, *Notices of Florida and the Campaigns* (Charleston and New York, 1836), p. 235.
4. Clay MacCauley, *The Seminole Indians of Florida* (Washington, 1887), p. 482.
5. Brooke to Brown, Apr. 6, 1824, *Territorial Papers,* Vol. XXII, *Florida 1821–1824,* p. 918.
6. DuVal to Calhoun, July 29, 1824, *Territorial Papers,* Vol. XXIII, *Florida 1824–1828,* p. 22.
7. Mark F. Boyd, "*The Seminole War: Its Background and Onset,*" *FHQ,* XXX (July, 1951), 34.
8. Walton to McKenney, Oct. 6, 1825, *Territorial Papers,* XXIII, 335.
9. Brooke to Gibson, Dec. 20, 1825, *American State Papers, Indian Affairs,* II, 655.
10. DuVal to McKenney, Feb. 22, 1826, *Territorial Papers,* XXIII, 445.
11. Woodburne Potter, *The War in Florida* (Baltimore, 1836), pp. 9–11; Cohen, *Notices of Florida,* p. 234; Mark F. Boyd, *FHQ,* XXXIII (January–April, 1955), 261; McKenney and Hall, *Indian Tribes,* p. 372.
12. Barbour to Florida Indians, May 10, 1826, *Territorial Papers,* XXIII, 539; Florida Indians' Reply, May 17, 1826, *ibid.,* 548.
13. G. A. McCall, *Letters* (Philadelphia, 1868), pp. 153–160.
14. Potter, *War in Florida,* p. 17.

15. *Ibid.*, p. 16.
16. Cohen, *Notices of Florida,* p. 237.
17. John T. Sprague, *The Florida War* (New York, 1848), p. 101.
18. MacCauley, *Seminole Indians,* p. 496.
19. Sprague, *Florida War,* p. 37.
20. *Ibid.*, pp. 37–38.
21. Cohen, *Notices of Florida,* p. 236.
22. Sprague, *Florida War,* p. 72.
23. Cohen, *Notices of Florida,* p. 235.
24. Potter, *War in Florida,* pp. 9–10.
25. W. A. Croffut, *Fifty Years in Camp and Field: Diary of Maj. Gen. Ethan Allen Hitchcock* (New York, 1909), pp. 78–80.
26. Eaton to Cass, *American State Papers, Military Affairs,* VI, 492.

5

1. Thomas L. McKenney and James Hall, *The Indian Tribes of North America* (Edinburgh, 1933–1934), II, 373.
2. Charles H. Coe, *Red Patriots* (Cincinnati, 1898), p. 45.
3. John K. Mahon, "*Two Seminole Treaties,*" *FHQ,* XLI (July, 1962), 18.
4. Thompson to Cass, Dec. 2, 1833, *Territorial Papers,* Vol. XXIV, *Florida 1828–1834,* pp. 916–918.
5. Graham to Gadsden, Nov. 22, 1833, *American State Papers, Military Affairs,* VI, 508.
6. John T. Sprague, *The Florida War* (New York, 1848), p. 90.
7. Woodburne Potter, *The War in Florida* (Baltimore, 1836), pp. 50–66; Sprague, *Florida War,* pp. 79–80; M. M. Cohen, *Notices of Florida and the Campaigns* (Charleston and New York, 1836), pp. 57–63; Coe, *Red Patriots,* pp. 47–49; John K. Mahon, *History of the Second Seminole War* (Gainesville, Florida, 1967), pp. 89–92; Mark F. Boyd, "Asi Yaholo or Osceola," *FHQ,* XXXIII (January–April, 1955), 268–270; *American State Papers, Military Affairs,* VII, 64.
8. Thompson to Herring, Oct. 28, 1834, *Territorial Papers,* Vol. XXV, *Florida 1834–1839,* pp. 58–63.

6

1. Thompson to Herring, Oct. 28, 1834, *Territorial Papers,* Vol. XXV, *Florida 1834–1839,* pp. 60–61.
2. John T. Sprague, *The Florida War* (New York, 1848), p. 81.
3. M. M. Cohen, *Notices of Florida and the Campaigns* (Charleston and New York, 1836), p. 237.
4. Joshua R. Giddings, *The Exiles of Florida* (Columbus, Ohio, 1858), pp. 98–99.

5. Kenneth W. Porter, "The Episode of Osceola's Wife. Fact or Fiction?," *FHQ*, XXVI (July, 1947), 92 ff.
6. Sprague, *Florida War*, p. 101.
7. John T. Bemrose, *Reminiscences of the Seminole War*, edited by John K. Mahon (Gainesville, Florida, 1966), p. 42.
8. *Ibid.*, p. 21.
9. Cohen, *Notices of Florida*, p. 237.
10. *Ibid.*
11. Bemrose, *Reminiscences*, p. 17.
12. *Ibid.*, pp. 18–20.
13. Sprague, *Florida War*, p. 86.
14. *Ibid.*
15. *Ibid.*, p. 101.
16. Cohen, *Notices of Florida*, p. 237.
17. *Niles' Weekly Register*, May 2, 1835, p. 147.
18. Woodburne Potter, *The War in Florida* (Baltimore, 1836), p. 86.
19. Sprague, *Florida War*, p. 86.
20. Giddings, *Exiles*, p. 98.
21. Porter, "Osceola's Wife."
22. Thomas L. McKenney and James Hall, *The Indian Tribes of North America* (Edinburgh, 1933–1934), II, 376.
23. *Ibid.*, p. 377.
24. Charles H. Coe, *Red Patriots* (Cincinnati, 1898), p. 52.
25. Jackson to the House of Representatives, *American State Papers, Military Affairs*, VI, 437.
26. Potter, *War in Florida*, pp. 96–97, McKenney and Hall, *Indian Tribes*, II, 380–381.
27. Fanning to Clinch, Nov. 27, 1835, *Territorial Papers*, XXV, 200–201.
28. Fanning to Clinch, Nov. 28, 1835, *Territorial Papers*, XXV, 203–204.
29. Coe, *Red Patriots*, p. 56.
30. Cohen, *Notices of Florida*, p. 78.
31. Harris to Gibson, Dec. 30, 1835, *American State Papers, Military Affairs*, VI, 561; Sprague, *Florida War*, pp. 88–89; Potter, *War in Florida*, pp. 109–111; Cohen, *Notices of Florida*, pp. 68–69; Coe, *Red Patriots*, p. 57; *Niles' Weekly Register*, Jan. 30, 1836, p. 368.
32. Sprague, *Florida War*, p. 90.

7

1. Numerous sources for entire episode, including: Frank Laumer, *Massacre!* (Gainesville, Florida, 1968); *American State Papers*, Vol. VI; John Bemrose, *Reminiscences of the Seminole War*, edited by John K. Mahon (Gainesville, Florida, 1966), pp. 62–69;

Mark F. Boyd, "Florida Aflame," *FHQ*, XXX (July, 1951), 84–109; *Niles' Weekly Register*, Apr. 2, 1836, p. 87; John T. Sprague, *The Florida War* (New York, 1848), pp. 90–91; A. H. Roberts, "The Dade Massacre," *FHQ*, V (January, 1927), 123–138; Woodburne Potter, *The War in Florida* (Baltimore, 1836), pp. 102–109; Charles H. Coe, *Red Patriots* (Cincinnati, 1898), pp. 59–64; M. M. Cohen, *Notices of Florida and the Campaigns* (Charleston and New York, 1836), pp. 69–78.

2. Boyd, "Florida Aflame," p. 73.
3. Episode, Coe, *op. cit.*, 65; Sprague, *op. cit.*, 92; Cohen, *op. cit.*, 82.
4. Bemrose, *Reminiscences*, p. 60.
5. Gadsden to Jackson, Jan. 14, 1836, *Territorial Papers*, XXV, 224–226.
6. Coe, *Red Patriots*, pp. 67–68.
7. Sprague, *Florida War*, p. 94.
8. *Niles' Weekly Register*, Feb. 6, 1836, p. 395.
9. Coe, *Red Patriots*, p. 68.
10. *Niles' Weekly Register*, Feb. 6, 1846, p. 395.

8

1. John Bemrose, *Reminiscences of the Second Seminole War*, edited by John K. Mahon (Gainesville, Florida, 1966), p. 60.
2. *Ibid.*, p. 78.
3. John K. Mahon, *History of the Second Seminole War* (Gainesville, Florida, 1967), p. 119.
4. Based on John T. Sprague, *The Florida War* (New York, 1848), p. 113.
5. M. M. Cohen, *Notices of Florida and the Campaigns* (Charleston and New York, 1836), p. 104.
6. Numerous sources for entire episode, including: Woodburne Potter, *The War in Florida* (Baltimore, 1836), pp. 145–166; Cohen, *Notices of Florida*, pp. 96–105; *Niles' Weekly Register*, March–April, 1836; Sprague, *Florida War*, pp. 107–113; Bemrose, *Reminiscences*, pp. 73–80; R. W. Patrick, *Aristocrat in Uniform* (Gainesville, Florida, 1963), pp. 119–125.

9

1. John Bemrose, *Reminiscences of the Second Seminole War*, edited by John K. Mahon (Gainesville, Florida, 1966), p. 88.
2. M. M. Cohen, *Notes of Florida and the Campaigns* (Charleston and New York, 1836), pp. 226–227.
3. Bemrose, *Reminiscences*, p. 89.

4. Cohen, *Notes of Florida*, pp. 198–200; Tom Knotts, "History of the Blockhouse on the Withlacoochee," *FHQ*, XLIX (January, 1971), 245–254.
5. Cohen, *Notes of Florida*, pp. 196–198.
6. *Ibid.*, pp. 194–195.
7. *Ibid.*, pp. 221–231.
8. John T. Sprague, *The Florida War* (New York, 1848), p. 166.
9. For Call's campaign see: Sprague, *Florida War*, pp. 158–166; Herbert J. Doherty, *Richard Keith Call* (Gainesville, Florida, 1961), pp. 99–106; *Territorial Papers*, Vol. XXV, *Florida 1834–1839*, pp. 335–336, 339–358; John K. Mahon, *History of the Second Seminole War* (Gainesville, Florida, 1967), pp. 178–189.

10

1. *Territorial Papers*, Vol. XXV, *Florida 1834–1839*, pp. 341–342.
2. Samuel Forry, "Letters of Samuel Forry . . . 1837," *FHQ*, VI (January, 1928), 135.
3. Based on John T. Sprague, *The Florida War* (New York, 1848), p. 167; *American State Papers, Military Affairs*, VII, 825–826; Mark F. Boyd, *FHQ*, XXXIII (January–April, 1955), 289.
4. Sprague, *Florida War*, p. 173.
5. Jacob R. Motte, *Journey Into Wilderness . . . 1836–1838*, edited by James F. Sunderman (Gainesville, Florida, 1953), pp. 100–102; Sprague, *Florida War*, pp. 168–170.
6. Jesup to Poinsett, *Territorial Papers*, XXV, 380–381.
7. Jesup to Poinsett, *ibid.*, p. 386.
8. Jesup to Poinsett, *ibid.*, p. 390.
9. *FHQ*, VI (January, 1928), 134.
10. *Ibid.*
11. *Ibid.*, p. 135.
12. Charles H. Coe, *Red Patriots* (Cincinnati, 1898), p. 78.
13. *FHQ*, VI (January, 1928), p. 134.
14. Boyd, *FHQ*, XXXIII (January–April, 1955), 293–294; Sprague, *Florida War*, p. 180.
15. Coe, *Red Patriots*, p. 79.

11

1. Samuel Forry, "Letters of Samuel Forry . . . 1837," *FHQ*, VI (January, 1928), 142.
2. *Ibid.*, p. 146.
3. Forry, "Letters," *FHQ*, VI (April, 1928), 206–208.
4. John T. Sprague, *The Florida War* (New York, 1848), pp. 185–186.
5. Phelps to Helen Phelps, *FHQ*, VI (October, 1927), 82.

6. Jacob R. Motte, *Journey Into Wilderness . . . 1836–1838*, edited by James F. Sunderman (Gainesville, Florida, 1953), pp. 116-134.
7. Forry, "Letters," *FHQ*, VI (April, 1928), 219.
8. Motte, *Journey*, pp. 135–136.
9. Forry, "Letters," *FHQ*, VII (July, 1928), 88.
10. Sprague, *Florida War*, p. 217.
11. *Ibid.*, p. 188.
12. Charles H. Coe, *Red Patriots* (Cincinnati, 1898), pp. 85–86.
13. Sprague, *Florida War*, p. 218.
14. Coe, *Red Patriots*, p. 87.
15. Sprague, *Florida War*, p. 218.
16. Motte, *Journey*, p. 141.
17. Coe, *Red Patriots*, p. 88.
18. Sprague, *Florida War*, p. 188.
19. Coe, *Red Patriots*, p. 91.
20. Motte, *Journey*, p. 139.
21. Sprague, *Florida War*, p. 337.
22. Forry, "Letters," *FHQ*, VII (July, 1928), 95.
23. Coe, *Red Patriots*, p. 91.
24. John Milton, *Samson Agonistes*, li.40.
25. Sprague, *Florida War*, pp. 188–191.
26. Motte, *Journey*, p. 143.
27. Coe, *Red Patriots*, pp. 93–101; Sprague, *Florida War*, pp. 191–192; Mark F. Boyd, *FHQ*, XXXIII (January–April, 1955), 300–302.
28. Sprague, *Florida War*, pp. 325–327.
29. Kenneth W. Porter, "Seminole Flight from Fort Marion," *FHQ*, XXII (January, 1944), 112–133.
30. Sprague, *Florida War*, pp. 213–214.

12

1. Charles H. Coe, *Red Patriots* (Cincinnati, 1898), p. 103.
2. *Ibid.*, p. 104.
3. Numerous sources for entire episode, including: *Ibid.*, pp. 102–118; Mark F. Boyd, "Asi-Yaholo or Osceola," *FHQ*, XXXIII (January–April, 1955), 303–305; George Catlin, *North American Indians* (Edinburgh, 1926), pp. 247–251; May McNeer Ward, "The Disappearance of the Head of Osceola," *FHQ*, XXXIII (January–April, 1955), 193–201.

Epilogue

1. Charles H. Coe, *Red Patriots* (Cincinnati, 1898), p. 119; John T. Sprague, *The Florida War* (New York, 1848), p. 324.

2. The authors have a rare compilation made by the late Deaconess Harriet Bedell of almost a hundred Mikasuki Seminole families, as studied in the twentieth century. Many Osceolas are listed, but the depth is usually two generations only. Modern Seminoles are handicapped in tracing lineage clearly because of the absence of written tribal history, and because of reticence among nineteenth-century Seminoles to talk about the war period.
3. Coe, *Red Patriots*, p. 120n.
4. Sprague, *Florida War*, p. 193.
5. Numerous sources for entire episode, including: Jacob R. Motte, *Journey Into Wilderness . . . 1836–1838*, edited by James F. Sunderman (Gainesville, Florida, 1953), pp. 204–218; Sprague, *Florida War*, pp. 199–202; Coe, *Red Patriots*, pp. 129–138; AG files.
6. Motte, *Journey*, pp. 235–236.
7. Coe, *Red Patriots*, p. 145.
8. Sprague, *Florida War*, pp. 228–232; Coe, *Red Patriots*, pp. 142–149.
9. Sprague, *Florida War*, p. 247.
10. *Ibid.*, p. 288.
11. *Ibid.*
12. *Ibid.*, p. 270.
13. Coe, *Red Patriots*, p. 221.
14. *Ibid.*, p. 222.
15. Harriet Bedell, *Indian Families, 1935–1959*. (Notes. Manuscript, files William and Ellen Hartley.)

Index